THE CLAY SANSKRIT LIBRARY

FOUNDED BY JOHN & JENNIFER CLAY

GENERAL EDITOR

Sheldon Pollock

EDITED BY

Isabelle Onians

www.claysanskritlibrary.com

www.nyupress.org

Artwork by Robert Beer.
Typeset in Adobe Garamond Pro at 10.25 : 12.3+pt.
XML-development by Stuart Brown.
Editorial input from Csaba Dezső, Oliver Fallon,
Ridi Faruque, Anne Freeland, Chris Gibbons & Tomoyuki Kono.
Printed and bound in Great Britain by
T.J. International, Cornwall, on acid-free paper.

MĀLAVIKĀ AND AGNIMITRA

by KĀLIDĀSA

TRANSLATED BY

Dániel Balogh

&

Eszter Somogyi

NEW YORK UNIVERSITY PRESS

JJC FOUNDATION

2009

First Edition 2009

The Clay Sanskrit Library is co-published by
New York University Press
and the JJC Foundation.

Further information about this volume
and the rest of the Clay Sanskrit Library
is available at the end of this book
and on the following websites:
www.claysanskritlibrary.com
www.nyupress.org

ISBN-13: 978-0-8147-8702-1 (cloth : alk. paper)
ISBN-10: 0-8147-8702-9 (cloth : alk. paper)

Library of Congress Cataloging-in-Publication Data
Kālidāsa.
[Mālavikāgnimitra. English & Sanskrit]
Malavika and Agnimitra / by Kalidasa ;
translated by Dániel Balogh &
Eszter Somogyi. -- 1st ed.
p. cm. -- (The Clay Sanskrit library)
Sanskrit texts with parallel English translations on facing pages.
Includes bibliographical references.
ISBN-13: 978-0-8147-8702-1 (cl : alk. paper)
ISBN-10: 0-8147-8702-9 (cl : alk. paper)
1. Kings and rulers--India--Drama.
2. India--Social life and customs--To 1200--Drama.
3. Sanskrit drama--Translations into English.
I. Balogh, Dániel. II. Somogyi, Eszter. III. Title.
PK3796.M3B36 2009
891'.22--dc22
2009021931

CONTENTS

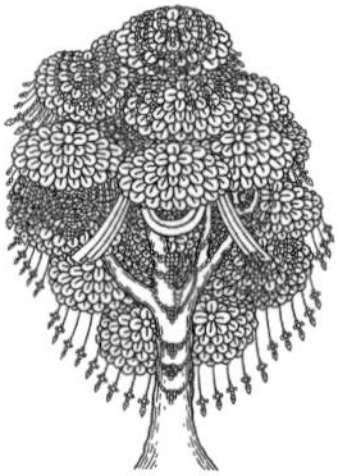

CSL CONVENTIONS

Sanskrit Alphabetical Order

Vowels:	*a ā i ī u ū ṛ ṝ ḷ ḹ e ai o au ṃ ḥ*
Gutturals:	*k kh g gh ṅ*
Palatals:	*c ch j jh ñ*
Retroflex:	*ṭ ṭh ḍ ḍh ṇ*
Dentals:	*t th d dh n*
Labials:	*p ph b bh m*
Semivowels:	*y r l v*
Spirants:	*ś ṣ s h*

Guide to Sanskrit Pronunciation

a	b*u*t
ā, â	f*a*ther
i	s*i*t
ī, î	f*ee*
u	p*u*t
ū, û	b*oo*
ṛ	vocalic *r*, American p*ur*dy or English p*re*tty
ṝ	lengthened *ṛ*
ḷ	vocalic *l*, ab*le*
e, ê, ē	m*a*de, esp. in Welsh pronunciation
ai	b*i*te
o, ô, ō	r*o*pe, esp. Welsh pronunciation; Italian s*o*lo
au	s*ou*nd
ṃ	*anusvāra* nasalizes the preceding vowel
ḥ	*visarga*, a voiceless aspiration (resembling the English *h*), or like Scottish lo*ch*, or an aspiration with a faint echoing of the last element of the preceding vowel so that *taiḥ* is pronounced *taih*^{i}
k	lu*ck*
kh	blo*ckh*ead
g	*g*o
gh	bi*gh*ead
ṅ	a*n*ger
c	*ch*ill
ch	mat*chh*ead
j	*j*og
jh	aspirated *j*, he*dgeh*og
ñ	ca*ny*on
ṭ	retroflex *t*, *t*ry (with the tip of tongue turned up to touch the hard palate)
ṭh	same as the preceding but aspirated
ḍ	retroflex *d* (with the tip

	of tongue turned up to touch the hard palate)
ḍh	same as the preceding but aspirated
ṇ	retroflex *n* (with the tip of tongue turned up to touch the hard palate)
t	French *t*out
th	ten*t h*ook
d	*d*inner
dh	guil*dh*all
n	*n*ow
p	*p*ill
ph	u*ph*eaval
b	*b*efore
bh	a*bh*orrent
m	*m*ind
y	*y*es
r	trilled, resembling the Italian pronunciation of *r*
l	*l*inger
v	*w*ord
ś	*sh*ore
ṣ	retroflex *sh* (with the tip of the tongue turned up to touch the hard palate)
s	hi*ss*
h	*h*ood

CSL Punctuation of English

The acute accent on Sanskrit words when they occur outside of the Sanskrit text itself, marks stress, e.g., Ramáyana. It is not part of traditional Sanskrit orthography, transliteration, or transcription, but we supply it here to guide readers in the pronunciation of these unfamiliar words. Since no Sanskrit word is accented on the last syllable it is not necessary to accent disyllables, e.g., Rama.

The second CSL innovation designed to assist the reader in the pronunciation of lengthy unfamiliar words is to insert an unobtrusive middle dot between semantic word breaks in compound names (provided the word break does not fall on a vowel resulting from the fusion of two vowels), e.g., Maha·bhárata, but Ramáyana (not Rama·áyana). Our dot echoes the punctuating middle dot (·) found in the oldest surviving samples of written Indic, the Ashokan inscriptions of the third century BCE.

The deep layering of Sanskrit narrative has also dictated that we use quotation marks only to announce the beginning and end of every direct speech, and not at the beginning of every paragraph.

CSL Punctuation of Sanskrit

The Sanskrit text is also punctuated, in accordance with the punctuation of the English translation. In mid-verse, the punctuation will not alter the sandhi or the scansion. Proper names are capitalized. Most Sanskrit meters have four "feet" (*pāda*); where possible we print the common *śloka* meter on two lines. In the Sanskrit text, we use French *Guillemets* (e.g., *«kva saṃcicīrṣuḥ?»*) instead of English quotation marks (e.g., "Where are you off to?") to avoid confusion with the apostrophes used for vowel elision in sandhi.

SANDHI

Sanskrit presents the learner with a challenge: *sandhi* (euphonic combination). Sandhi means that when two words are joined in connected speech or writing (which in Sanskrit reflects speech), the last letter (or even letters) of the first word often changes; compare the way we pronounce "the" in "the beginning" and "the end."

In Sanskrit the first letter of the second word may also change; and if both the last letter of the first word and the first letter of the second are vowels, they may fuse. This has a parallel in English: a nasal consonant is inserted between two vowels that would otherwise coalesce: "a pear" and "an apple." Sanskrit vowel fusion may produce ambiguity.

The charts on the following pages give the full sandhi system.

Fortunately it is not necessary to know these changes in order to start reading Sanskrit. All that is important to know is the form of the second word without sandhi (pre-sandhi), so that it can be recognized or looked up in a dictionary. Therefore we are printing Sanskrit with a system of punctuation that will indicate, unambiguously, the original form of the second word, i.e., the form without sandhi. Such sandhi mostly concerns the fusion of two vowels.

In Sanskrit, vowels may be short or long and are written differently accordingly. We follow the general convention that a vowel with no mark above it is short. Other books mark a long vowel either with a bar called a macron (*ā*) or with a circumflex (*â*). Our system uses the

VOWEL SANDHI

Final vowels:

a	ā	i	ī	u	ū	ṛ	e	ai	o	au	*Initial vowels:*
' â	" â	y a	y a	v a	v a	r a	e '	ā a	o '	āv a	a
' ā	" ā	y ā	y ā	v ā	v ā	r ā	a ā	ā ā	a ā	āv ā	ā
' ê	" ê	' î	" î	v i	v i	r i	a i	ā i	a i	āv i	i
' ē	" ē	' ī	" ī	v ī	v ī	r ī	a ī	ā ī	a ī	āv ī	ī
' ô	" ô	y u	y u	' û	" û	r u	a u	ā u	a u	āv u	u
' ō	" ō	y ū	y ū	' ū	" ū	r ū	a ū	ā ū	a ū	āv ū	ū
a' r	a" r	y ṛ	y ṛ	v ṛ	v ṛ	' ṛ̂	a ṛ	ā ṛ	a ṛ	āv ṛ	ṛ
' âi	" âi	y e	y e	v e	v e	r e	a e	ā e	a e	āv e	e
' āi	" āi	y ai	y ai	v ai	v ai	r ai	a ai	ā ai	a ai	āv ai	ai
' âu	" âu	y o	y o	v o	v o	r o	a o	ā o	a o	āv o	o
' āu	" āu	y au	y au	v au	v au	r au	a au	ā au	a au	āv au	au

CONSONANT SANDHI

				Permitted finals:			*(Except āḥ/aḥ)*			
k	ṭ	t	p	ṅ	n	m	ḥ/r	āḥ	aḥ	*Initial letters:*
k	ṭ	t	p	ṅ	n	ṃ	ḥ	āḥ	aḥ	k/kh
g	ḍ	d	b	ṅ	n	ṃ	r	ā	o	g/gh
k	ṭ	c	p	ṅ	ṃś	ṃ	ś	āś	aś	c/ch
g	ḍ	j	b	ṅ	ñ	ṃ	r	ā	o	j/jh
k	ṭ	ṭ	p	ṅ	ṃṣ	ṃ	ṣ	āṣ	aṣ	ṭ/ṭh
g	ḍ	ḍ	b	ṅ	ṇ	ṃ	r	ā	o	ḍ/ḍh
k	ṭ	t	p	ṅ	ṃs	ṃ	s	ās	as	t/th
g	ḍ	d	b	ṅ	n	ṃ	r	ā	o	d/dh
k	ṭ	t	p	ṅ	n	ṃ	ḥ	āḥ	aḥ	p/ph
g	ḍ	d	b	ṅ	n	ṃ	r	ā	o	b/bh
ṅ	ṇ	n	m	ṅ	n	ṃ	r	ā	o	*nasals* (n/m)
g	ḍ	d	b	ṅ	n	ṃ	r	ā	o	y/v
g	ḍ	d	b	ṅ	n	ṃ	*zero*[1]	ā	o	r
g	ḍ	l	b	ṅ	l̃[2]	ṃ	r	ā	o	l
k	ṭ	c ch	p	ṅ	ñ ś/ch	ṃ	ḥ	āḥ	aḥ	ś
k	ṭ	t	p	ṅ	n	ṃ	ḥ	āḥ	aḥ	ṣ/s
gg h	ḍḍ h	dd h	bb h	ṅ	n	ṃ	r	ā	o	h
g	ḍ	d	b	ṅ/ṅṅ[3]	n/nn[3]	m	r	ā	a[4]	*vowels*
k	ṭ	t	p	ṅ	n	m	ḥ	āḥ	aḥ	*zero*

[1]ḥ or r disappears, and if a/i/u precedes, this lengthens to ā/ī/ū. [2]e.g. tān+lokān=tāl̃ lokān.
[3]The doubling occurs if the preceding vowel is short. [4]Except: aḥ+a=o '.

macron, except that for initial vowels in sandhi we use a circumflex to indicate that originally the vowel was short, or the shorter of two possibilities (*e* rather than *ai*, *o* rather than *au*).

When we print initial	before sandhi that vowel was
â,	*a*
î or *ê*,	*i*
û or *ô*,	*u*
âi,	*e*
âu,	*o*
ā,	*ā*
ī,	*ī*
ū,	*ū*
ē,	*ī*
ō,	*ū*
ai,	*ai*
āu,	*au*
', before sandhi there was a vowel *a*	

When a final short vowel (*a*, *i*, or *u*) has merged into a following vowel, we print ' at the end of the word, and when a final long vowel (*ā*, *ī*, or *ū*) has merged into a following vowel we print " at the end of the word. The vast majority of these cases will concern a final *a* or *ā*. See, for instance, the following examples:

What before sandhi was	is represented as
atra asti	*atr' âsti*
atra āste	*atr' āste*
kanyā asti	*kany" âsti*
kanyā āste	*kany" āste*
atra iti	*atr' êti*
kanyā iti	*kany" êti*
kanyā īpsitā	*kany" ēpsitā*

Finally, three other points concerning the initial letter of the second word:

(1) A word that before sandhi begins with *ṛ* (vowel), after sandhi begins with *r* followed by a consonant: *yatha" rtu* represents pre-sandhi *yathā ṛtu*.

(2) When before sandhi the previous word ends in *t* and the following word begins with *ś*, after sandhi the last letter of the previous word is *c*

and the following word begins with *ch*: *syāc chāstravit* represents pre-sandhi *syāt śāstravit*.

(3) Where a word begins with *h* and the previous word ends with a double consonant, this is our simplified spelling to show the pre-sandhi form: *tad hasati* is commonly written as *tad dhasati*, but we write *tadd hasati* so that the original initial letter is obvious.

COMPOUNDS

We also punctuate the division of compounds (*samāsa*), simply by inserting a thin vertical line between words. There are words where the decision whether to regard them as compounds is arbitrary. Our principle has been to try to guide readers to the correct dictionary entries.

Exemplar of CSL Style

Where the Devanagari script reads:

कुम्भस्थली रक्षतु वो विकीर्णसिन्धूररेणुर्द्विरदाननस्य ।
प्रशान्तये विघ्नतमश्छटानां निष्ठ्यूतबालातपपल्लवेव ॥

Others would print:

kumbhasthalī rakṣatu vo vikīrṇasindūrareṇur dviradānanasya /
praśāntaye vighnatamaśchaṭānāṃ niṣṭhyūtabālātapapallaveva //

We print:

kumbha|sthalī rakṣatu vo vikīrṇa|sindūra|reṇur dvirad'|ānanasya
praśāntaye vighna|tamaś|chaṭānāṃ niṣṭhyūta|bāl'|ātapa|pallav" êva.

And in English:

May Ganésha's domed forehead protect you! Streaked with vermilion dust, it seems to be emitting the spreading rays of the rising sun to pacify the teeming darkness of obstructions.

("Nava·sáhasanka and the Serpent Princess" I.3)

Wordplay

Classical Sanskrit literature can abound in puns (*śleṣa*). Such paronomasia, or wordplay, is raised to a high art; rarely is it a *cliché*. Multiple meanings merge (*śliṣyanti*) into a single word or phrase. Most common are pairs of meanings, but as many as ten separate meanings are attested. To mark the parallel senses in the English, as well as the punning original in the Sanskrit, we use a *slanted* font (different from *italic*) and a triple colon (⁝) to separate the alternatives. E.g.

> yuktaṃ Kādambarīṃ śrutvā kavayo maunam āśritāḥ
> *Bāṇa|dhvanāv* an|adhyāyo bhavat' îti smṛtir yataḥ.
>
> It is right that poets should fall silent upon hearing the Kadámbari, for the sacred law rules that recitation must be suspended when *the sound of an arrow ⁝ the poetry of Bana* is heard.
>
> (Soméshvara·deva's "Moonlight of Glory" I.15)

Drama

Classical Sanskrit literature is in fact itself bilingual, notably in drama. There women and characters of low rank speak one of several Prakrit dialects, an "unrefined" *(prākṛta)* vernacular as opposed to the "refined" *(saṃskṛta)* language. Editors commonly provide such speeches with a Sanskrit paraphrase, their "shadow" *(chāyā)*. We mark Prakrit speeches with ⌜opening and closing⌟ corner brackets, and supply the Sanskrit *chāyā* in endnotes. Some stage directions are original to the author but we follow the custom that sometimes editors supplement these; we print them in italics (and within brackets, in mid-text)

INTRODUCTION

"Málavika and Agni·mitra" (*Mālavikāgnimitra*) is sometimes considered to be the least significant of the three dramas of Kali·dasa, the poet laureate of Indian antiquity who probably lived in the fifth century CE. Yet the play's lively and playful plot more than makes up for its lack of deities, heroic prowess or pathos. The machinations of King Agni·mitra's jester to help him add a dancing girl to his harem in spite of the subtle intrigues of the two jealous queens carry the gallant hero through hope and despair to the happy ending. This is often thought to be the first of Kali·dasa's dramas, or indeed of all his oeuvre,[1] though of course any chronology of his writings can be based on conjecture alone. Apart from a perceived "immaturity,"[2] the introductory scene of "Málavika and Agni·mitra" is often cited to substantiate such claims. The play humbly describes itself as "the work of a contemporary poet" (1.7) as opposed to the time-honored works of the great predecessors—but in fact the introductory scenes of his two other dramas use very similar terms.[3]

Warder (1990: 129) actually calls "Málavika and Agni·mitra" Kali·dasa's best play. Tieken (2001) opines that it is a late work, possibly Kali·dasa's last, and feels that its novelty consists in a divergence from the poet's previous works, and perhaps from the entire dramatic tradition prevalent in his time. While Kali·dasa's other epic and dramatic works are populated by divine and semi-divine beings and have a curse as the crux of their plots, "Málavika and Agni·mitra" is a work based on historical events, featuring thoroughly mortal human characters. The only trace of the supernatural in it is the lucky coincidence thanks to which Málavika ends up married to Agni·mitra after her travails. This realistic vein was perhaps the core of the play's modernity.

Agni·mitra and his Times

To find background to the setting and characters of the play we must go back to the second century BCE, some six hundred years before the likely time of Kali·dasa. At the beginning of that century, the remnants of the illustrious Maurya dynasty dominated northern India. After the death of Ashóka the Great in 232 BCE, his house began to decline. Few and sometimes conflicting data are available about his successors, and it is possible—though far from certain—that two or three of his descendants ruled in parallel over patches of the former empire. Around 185 BCE the Maurya ruler Brihad·ratha was slain by his general Pushya·mitra, who replaced him on the throne. In "Málavika and Agni·mitra" the usurper appears as Agni·mitra's father, General Pushpa·mitra. Henceforth we'll use the name Pushya·mitra to refer to the historical person, and Pushpa·mitra for the character in the drama.

Genealogical lists—set in the form of prophecies purported to predate the rulers—found in the *purāṇas* (early compendia of Hindu myths and legends, largely compiled in the fourth to sixth centuries CE but containing plenty of earlier material) tell us that after 137 years of Maurya rule the Shungas came to the fore. The term "Shunga period" is commonly used by historians to refer to the time from about 185 BCE to 73 BCE, but the existence of an actual dynasty of this name is not well supported by evidence. A "commander" by the name of Pushya·mitra is referred to as a "performer of two horse sacrifices" in the Ayódhya inscription of Dhana·deva.[4] The historicity of Agni·mitra as well as of Su·jyeshtha and Vasu·mitra is confirmed by some coins bearing their names. Yet the picture that the coins of the age paint seems to indicate the existence of several localized ruling houses (many of them with names ending in *mitra*) rather than a single supreme dynasty of Shungas.[5] The origin and the meaning of "Shunga" itself are uncertain; the commonly accepted meaning is the banyan tree,[6] and it may have been the name of a priestly clan.[7]

The lists of the *purāṇas*[8] call the founder of the dynasty, Pushya·mitra, a general (*senānī*, *senāpati*) and say he killed Brihad·ratha, the last of the Maurya rulers. They relate that he was followed on the throne by his son Agni·mitra, who was succeeded by Su·jyeshtha and then by Vasu·mitra. These latter names also appear in the variant forms Vasu·jyeshtha and Su·mitra. Entering the realm of speculation, (Va)su·jyeshtha may have been a brother or other close relative of Agni·mitra who ruled by seniority (*jyeṣṭha* in his name means "elder") before Agni·mitra's son Vasu·mitra, or an elder brother of Vasu·mitra. Only the latter is mentioned in "Málavika and Agni·mitra."

An interesting feature of these genealogies is that though they are quite consistent in giving the number of years each Shunga king reigned, the sum of these comes to six or eight years longer than the total term of Shunga rule, on which the *purāṇas* are again unequivocal.[9] This ties in well with the notion that Pushya·mitra and Agni·mitra might have ruled simultaneously for some time, as depicted in "Málavika and Agni·mitra." In the play Agni·mitra is clearly called king (*rājan*) of Vídisha, yet Pushpa·mitra is just as clearly alive and well—though consistently called general (*senāpati*), and never king. There is a possibility that for a number of years Pushya·mitra ruled from the former Maurya capital of Pátali·putra in the northeast, and assigned his son—as a sort of viceroy—to control the southwest, with his seat in Vídisha.[10]

It is probably on the basis of such accounts that "The Deeds of Harsha" (*Harṣacarita*) of Bana—a loosely biographical romance about king Harsha written in the seventh century, certainly after Kali·dasa's time—makes a passing reference to Pushya·mitra.[11] The context is advice given to Harsha to be careful whom he trusts, justified by a long list of people killed by ones they trusted—including Brihad·ratha by Pushya·mitra. A detail not found elsewhere is that the coup took place under the pretext of a review of the troops. The *Avantisundarī*—written by Dandin probably in the late seventh century—also makes a cursory reference to Pushya·mitra, describing him as a general of brahmin origin and a Shunga.[12]

A couple of sentences[13] in the *Mahābhāṣya* of Patáñjali—the "great commentary" to the grammar of Pánini—utilized to illustrate the use of tenses in Sanskrit has elicited conjectures to the effect that Patáñjali lived under Pushya·mitra and that at their time Greek forces were invading the North Indian heartland. The reference to a clash with "Greeks" in "Málavika and Agni·mitra" along the banks of a river named Sindhu seems to corroborate this, but Bhan-

DARE (2006) justly warns against building circular arguments that rely on "internal support" in the available textual evidence whilst the interpretation of a vague text reference had been guided in the first place by assumptions about another vague reference. In this particular case, he points out, there are no rivers named Sindhu near either of the towns said in Patáñjali's work to have been besieged by Greeks. Though either or both towns might have been wrongly identified, and the name Sindhu might refer to a river other than the Indus (such as the river now called Kali Sindh, not very far to the west of the town of Vídisha) or just mean "a river" in general, the resemblance of the two references is certainly too loose to be counted as corroboration of evidence. Attempts have been made to identify the "Greeks" of the play as an army of Demetrius—who established an Indo-Greek kingdom in the northwest of the subcontinent, possibly taking advantage of the political vacuum created there by Pushya·mitra's deposition of the Mauryas—or of Menander, a somewhat later Graeco-Bactrian ruler who led conquests deep into the territory of India.[14]

Another citation often understood to refer to Pushya·mitra's person comes from the "Lineage of Hari" (*Harivaṃśa*), an appendix to the "Maha·bhárata" where—again in the form of prophecy—it is said that a certain "victorious" general (*senānī*), a brahmin of the Káshyapa clan (*gotra*), will reinstate the horse sacrifice in the *kali/yuga*, the current age of strife,[15] and in the play Kali·dasa's Pushpa·mitra is in the midst of carrying out just a sacrifice. The qualification "victorious"[16] may well be intended as a politically correct reference to Pushya·mitra's dethroning of the Mauryas. It is also a widely accepted notion that Pushya·mitra belonged to a brahmin family, though he is normally held to belong to the Bharadvája *gotra*.[17] To complicate the family name problem further, in our play Agni·mitra once refers to himself as a Báimbika—a patronymic meaning "a descendent of Bimba" (or "a descendent of Bímbaka"). A form of this appellation, Báimbaki, is known from early sources[18] as a priestly clan name, and this may be taken as corroboration that the Shungas were brahmins by origin. The Báimbakis are said to belong to the Káshyapa *gotra*, to which the *Harivaṃśa* assigns Pushya·mitra. Two inscriptions of King Dama·mitra Báimbika are known from the area slightly to the north of Vídisha (BHANDARE 2006), hinting that Báimbika may have been the family name of one of the several lines of "Mitra" kings in the region at the time.

We have a detailed account of Pushya·mitra's alleged persecution of Buddhists in the "Heavenly Exploits" (*Divyāvadāna*),[19] a collection of Buddhist narratives about the religiously significant deeds of historical or quasi-historical persons. Interestingly, this book claims that Pushya·mitra belonged to the Maurya dynasty. While it is possible to surmise that the general of the Mauryas was related to the royal family, it is unlikely that he would have been sixth in a direct line of descent from Ashóka, as the *Divyāvadāna* claims. The story relates that he once asked his ministers how he could ensure that his name lived on forever. They suggested that he follow the example of Ashóka, whose glory would abide as long as the Buddha's teaching. The king asked if they could recommend some other means, and, acting on the proposition of his (Hindu) house priest, he proceeded to destroy the heritage of the Buddha. This may tie in well with his brahminhood and his revival of Hindu rites such as the horse sacrifice, but such atrocities are not recorded elsewhere about Pushya·mitra, and archaeological evidence indicates that Buddhist communities and monuments flourished in Shunga times.

It is possible that Pushya·mitra's successors did not continue with his anti-Buddhist policy, and indeed it has been proposed (TAWNEY 1875) that a difference in their attitudes toward Buddhism might have caused a conflict between Pushya·mitra and Agni·mitra, to which the letter in Act v of our play (5.154; see also note to 5.154 ad loc) possibly alludes. The presence of Káushiki—a renunciate woman who is likely to be a Buddhist—as a respected figure in Agni·mitra's court indicates that the Agni·mitra envisioned by Kali·dasa was friendly to Buddhism, though we must keep in mind that in Kali·dasa's times Buddhists were probably not viewed as dangerous heretics, but as just another sect in search of liberation from worldly bondage.

Fact and fiction are always hard to separate when dealing with ancient history. Much of what we think we know about Pushya·mitra and Agni·mitra is actually based on Kali·dasa's play,[20] while much of the rest relies on sources Kali·dasa too may have used. Whether he had access to any chronicles, accounts or even legends that are now lost (or waiting to be rediscovered) is anyone's guess, but it is important to keep in mind that "Málavika and Agni·mitra" is a work of fiction: a playful play designed to entertain its audience. Given Kali·dasa's freehanded treatment of the quasi-historical material he used in his other two plays,[21] we must exercise caution in relying on him as a source of history. Details that are not corroborated by studier sources—such as the names and number of Agni·mitra's queens, the existence of a half-caste brother of Queen Dhárini (employed as an army commander by Agni·mitra in the drama), and the existence and name of the young Princess Vasu·lakshmi—may have been figments of the poet's imagination, or may have been supplied in analogy with the politics and circumstances of his own age.

Kali·dasa and his Times

Tradition connects Kali·dasa to King Vikramáditya, but this epithet—meaning "sun of valor"—has been used by multiple kings. The most famous of them is the legendary ruler of Újjayini who lived in the first century BCE (and whose victory over the Saka people in 56 BCE became the starting point of the Víkrama calendar that remains in use in India to the present day). Attempts to prove that Kali·dasa lived and worked in his court are unpersuasive, and seem to be motivated largely by a feeling that hoary antiquity is required to enhance a poet's merit.[22] Two other Vikramádityas, both of the Gupta dynasty, are much more likely to have been Kali·dasa's patron(s): Chandra·gupta II (376–415) and his grandson Skanda·gupta (455–467).[23]

The period of their reign (and of Kumára·gupta between them) is often referred to as a Golden Age, when sciences and arts flourished thanks to the peace and relative prosperity of the Gupta heartland. The political developments of this age present some striking parallels with the background of "Málavika and Agni·mitra."[24] HANS BAKKER has produced an excellent article on the subject, the salient points of which we will paraphrase here.[25] See the map (p. xliv) for assistance in locating the areas and towns referred to.

In the early fifth century most of northern India was controlled by the Gupta dynasty. After the death of Chandra·gupta II, Kumára·gupta won the succession struggle against his elder brother, the heir apparent Govínda·gupta. While Kumára·gupta reigned as emperor (mainly from the ancient capital at Pátali·putra), the important southwestern frontier area of Vídisha was controlled by his appointed heir Ghatótkacha·gupta, the third—probably much younger—son of Chandra·gupta. The region of Málava had been ruled by Naga clans (whose emblem was presumably the snake, *nāga*), with whom Chandra·gupta forged an alliance by marrying a princess of theirs, Kubéra·naga. The other major power of the age was the Vakátaka dynasty, ruling a large territory south of the river Nármada. The two branches of this house governed from the cities of Vatsa·gulma and Nandi·várdhana, with the river Várada as their boundary.

A period of peaceful Gupta–Vakátaka relations (which may well have been the time Kali·dasa was active) brought general prosperity after the marriage of Prabhávati·gupta—daughter of Chandra·gupta and Kubéra·naga—to the Vakátaka prince (and subsequently king) Rudra·sena II (395–405) of the Nandi·várdhana branch, and especially after the premature death of Rudra·sena that resulted in Prabhávati ruling as regent over the Vakátaka kingdom, remaining on good terms with her younger brothers Kumára and Ghatótkacha. Their relations were further cemented by the marriage of Prabhávati's daughter (possibly named Atibhávati) to Ghatótkacha.

Not an exact likeness of the conditions pictured in "Málavika and Agni·mitra," but many of the details, though shifted and slightly warped, are too similar to be accidental. Agni·mitra rules from Vídisha in his father's lifetime as does Ghatótkacha·gupta in his elder brother's, and marries Málavika of Vidárbha as Ghatótkacha weds Atibhávati, also from Vidárbha and with ancestry in Málava. The senior queen Dhárini with her snake-ring resembles Ghatótkacha's mother-in-law (and aunt) Prabhávati who is proud of her "snake" (Naga) ancestry and bears the family name Dhárana. The Vidárbhan brothers Yajña·sena and Mádhava·sena recall the Vakátaka rulers of Vidárbha, whose names usually end in *sena*. The Vakátakas rule a kingdom divided in two by the Várada river, like the brothers in the play after Agni·mitra defeats the rebellious Yajña·sena, and they may have taken different sides in the Gupta succession struggles—just as Yajña·sena seems in the play to be a supporter of the former Maurya regime while Mádhava·sena is quick to ally himself with Agni·mitra.

Behind the Scenes

Though Sanskrit drama is not known for its depth of characterization and the plot of "Málavika and Agni·mitra" is fairly simple despite its twists and turns, there is quite a lot going on behind the scenes. One thing leads to another—but precisely how, Kali·dasa does not say. In this section we will outline our understanding of the motives of the key characters and the events that may have occurred between the acts. If you are reading the play for the first time and don't want to spoil the suspense, we advise you to skip this part of the introduction and return to it once you have finished with the story.

Agni·mitra is no epic hero who rides his chariot to battle demons: though the political thread in the background of the play shows he is rather successful as a statesman, the predominant "flavor" (*rasa*, q.v. note to 1.42) of the play is that of love (*śṛṅgāra*), not heroism (*vīrya*). The king's foremost trait is *dākṣiṇya*, "courtesy," as he himself proclaims in 4.181 [14]. He controls himself and does his best to respect the feelings of all three women in his life, thus effectively tying his own hands.

His eldest queen, Dhárini—true to her name, which means "earth" and comes from a root meaning "to bear"—is the epitome of the Indian wife patiently submitting to the will and whims of her husband. Secure in her position as first queen and mother of the heir apparent, she is still concerned enough with proprieties to have second thoughts about letting her husband wed a lowly nautch girl. Indeed, though she seems to relent gradually and to be on the verge of accepting the marriage, her ultimate approval is only granted when Málavika is confirmed to be of noble birth. Dhárini is also a shrewd woman proud of her intellect, quick to see through the guiles of both Káushiki and Gáutama, and equally quick to bristle at their attempts to lead her by the nose.

Irávati is a more ambiguous character, in many respects Dhárini's antithesis. Presumably she is young, beautiful and sensuous—and she is definitely a woman of temper. Her marriage to Agni·mitra had probably been brought about by passion rather than politics, and she is not ready to relinquish her position as the king's favorite without a fight. Throughout the play it is her status as the king's lover—rather than spouse—that she worries about. When Dhárini's sprained foot prevents her from kicking the *aśoka* tree (see 3.47), Irávati should logically have been assigned the task. Yet it is not this transgression of protocol that she resents, but the king's courtship of Málavika. Nor is she a gracious loser—though at the end of the play Dhárini attempts to conciliate her and asks for her consent, she gives it only grudgingly and because she has no choice, and does not join the jubilation.

The heroine, Málavika, is a simple creature: a young and beautiful girl who accepts her servitude in Agni·mitra's court and the king's ardent love for her with equal good nature. What Kali·dasa does not reveal is when and why she begins to return his affections. Her feelings are not mentioned in the first act; all we know at this time is that the king has seen a picture of her and is interested in seeing her in the flesh. One might believe that she falls in love with him when they first meet face to face; but we learn from a later chance remark of hers (4.135) that at that time she had been so anxious she couldn't even get a good look at Agni·mitra. Yet early in the third act—definitely no more than a few days later—she is revealed to be pining for him. Commentators insinuate that Málavika is in love already before the second act (compare note to 1.16 on the *chalita* dance as a veiled expression of the performer's own feelings). Without having met him, the only way we can conceive of this is that Málavika had been told before the play's events by her brother Mádhava·sena that she would be given in marriage to Agni·mitra—and, like the dutiful girl she is, proceeded consciously to fall in love with her unknown intended.

One thing that baffles us about her is her name, which means "woman of Málava"—a strange thing to call a princess born and raised in Vidárbha. The heroines of "The Lady of the Jewel Necklace" (*Ratnāvalī*) and "The Lady Who Shows Her Love" (*Priyadarśikā*)—two later plays whose plots are similar to that of "Málavika and Agni·mitra"—receive their servant names (Ságarika, "woman of the ocean" and Arányika, "woman of the jungle") after the circumstances in which they had been found. Málavika had lost her company on the way from her homeland to Agni·mitra's palace, and had been found or rescued by Vira·sena somewhere on the Marches (see 5.103). The region of Málava overlaps with the country of Vídisha, so with some stretch it might be possible to argue that she was found in Málava even though this land is largely to the west and north of Vídisha, while Málavika's native country is to the south and east. But this is repudiated by a clear statement in the fifth act (5.86) that her name had been Málavika before coming to Agni·mitra's court. Kali·dasa may have nodded, ignoring the chronology of cause and effect, or simply chosen a soft-sounding name without intending to express a message by its meaning; alternatively he may have named his heroine in allusion to his own period (see p. xxiii).

The *vidūṣaka*—"jester" in our translation—is a stock figure in Sanskrit drama. No English term covers his role exactly; we prefer to avoid the translation "clown" because his basic nature is different from that of a clown in the Shakespearean sense, despite having many traits in common. The *vidūṣaka* is a grotesque parody of a brahmin, always thinking of his belly, lazy and dull or pretending to be dull (but never mad or pretending to be mad), and providing comic relief by his odd and inconsiderate remarks (which, however, hardly ever have a tragic overtone, nor contain epiphanic insights). The character of Gáutama in "Málavika and Agni·mitra" is not quite your run-of-the-mill *vidūṣaka*: rather than being a mere participant observer of events, he takes a most active hand in shaping them to suit the interests of his patron the king. He derides himself and pretends to be humble and dense, but his cunning earns him the epithet "Minister of Amorous Affairs" (4.236). He invents scheme after devious scheme to permit the king to see, speak with and marry Málavika.

The mendicant woman Káushiki is a cultured lady adept in several sciences: she offers learned comments on dancing (2.40 [8]) and curing snakebite (4.63 [4]), and she is also proficient in elegant dressing (5.27). She speaks Sanskrit, despite the fact that women in drama—even queens—normally use Prakrit, as all other female characters in "Málavika and Agni·mitra" do. Her noble birth is a well-guarded secret, yet she is respected by all, including Queen Dhárini. Her Sanskrit appellation *parivrājikā* simply means "itinerant woman," referring to one who has entered the fourth of the traditional stages of life, that of homelessness and complete renunciation. This would be equally possible in the Hindu, Buddhist or Jain religion (though orthodox Hinduism does not quite endorse women becoming ascetics).

She refers to her retirement from the affairs of the world as "donning the russets" (5.122), and russet (*kāṣāya*) robes are associated with Buddhism. This tilts the balance in favor of the assumption that she is a Buddhist, though she is never expressly described as such.

Buddhist nuns also have a reputation in Indian literature as reliable go-betweens who help young lovers. Káushiki definitely wants Agni·mitra to notice and subsequently marry Málavika, but assured by a prophecy (5.132) that this is bound to happen, she is in no particular hurry. As an intimate companion of Dhárini, she may have had insight into—and perhaps influence on—the education of Málavika as a dancer. We are of the opinion that at the beginning of the play she does not know she has an ally in Gáutama, but is quick to catch on when she sees the argument of the two dance teachers egged on by the jester. Whether Gáutama is as quick to realize that Káushiki is his "crony" (*pīṭhamardikā*, see note to 1.119) rather than the queen's, and whether they actively collaborate later on, is left in darkness. The circumstances of Dhárini's opportune accident (3.47) are certainly suspicious. It is more than likely that the jester actually pushed the queen off the swing, and it could have been the mendicant woman who then subtly steered her toward the idea of sending Málavika to kick the tree.

One of the minor characters deserves some extra attention too: Irávati's cheeky handmaiden Nípunika—"Miss Shrewd." When in Act III she leads Irávati to meet the king at the swing gazebo, she acts the part of the innocent bystander surprised to find Agni·mitra dallying with

Málavika. But her innocuous questions and remarks gradually nudge an otherwise rather disinterested Irávati to the place where she can see for herself, and to the conclusion that Agni·mitra is purposely scorning her. Had Nípunika made a direct accusation, she might have been ignored or silenced, but now Irávati has no choice but to react to the situation to which Nípunika has guided her. When Irávati asks her how she knows the king is already at the swing, she replies that Gáutama, eager for spring gifts, had told her (3.104). But Gáutama has not left the stage since he persuaded the king to go to the swing—so if Nípunika heard anything from him, it must have been earlier, when he was only intending to take the king there. We speculate that Gáutama had known of Málavika's mission with the tree, and was going to treat the king to a "chance" meeting with his lover. If so, he may well have alluded to this plan when Nípunika weakened him with a plate of sweets, giving her an opportunity to interfere.

Text and Translation

The work of possibly the most famous of all Sanskrit authors, "Málavika and Agni·mitra" has been translated into English repeatedly. Before creating yet another rendition, we consulted three of the most renowned translations: the pioneering work of CHARLES HENRY TAWNEY from 1875, the translation in the classical student edition by MORESHWAR RAMCHANDRA KALE (as revised in 1960), and EDWIN GEROW's modern translation published in 1984. TAWNEY says his version, based on the editions of PANDIT and TARKAVACHASPATI, is intended for "persons beginning the study of Sanskrit literature" and for "Englishmen who have chosen an Indian career, as throwing a flood of light upon ... Hindú society." His work probably accomplished these objectives brilliantly in the late nineteenth century, but for the modern reader we feel his translation is slightly too literal and somewhat on the archaic side. The same—to a greater degree—may be said of KALE's translation, which has been infinitely helpful to generations of young Sanskritists, but sacrifices ease of diction for the sake of lexical and syntactical accuracy. The translation of GEROW, based primarily on SASTRI's edition (1929),[26] is described by its author as a literal translation. While we find it an excellent and enjoyable read in itself, we feel that it avails of the translator's license rather freely. We have endeavored to create a translation—in keeping with the goal of the Clay Sanskrit Library—that is both literal enough to be read side by side with the Sanskrit text and to facilitate its direct understanding, and liberal enough to be enjoyable in English.

No proper critical edition of "Málavika and Agni·mitra" is available as yet, though several editions have been based on a collation of multiple sources and include a critical apparatus of varying precision. The general consensus of editors seems to be that there are no distinct recensions of the play, but our perception is that variations in the text—some of them fairly large-scale—follow a pattern, and this points to the existence of at least two regional versions if not distinct recensions. Mapping these is a task for the future that presupposes the creation of a comprehensive critical edition.

Before embarking on the translation, we examined some samples from several editions of the play to see what variants each prefers. On the basis of this scrutiny we selected the Sahitya Akademi edition of K.A. SUBRAMANIA IYER (1978) as our principal source. We agree with Gerow[27] that this edition does not rise to the level of a true critical edition, and we must emphasize that it contains an inordinate number of misprints. Nevertheless, it does carry a critical apparatus that refers to some earlier editions as well as to manuscripts from distinct areas of India, and—more importantly to us—we feel that its choice of readings is well considered and convincing.

We frequently consulted three other editions for variant readings, and often adopted some of their text where we felt it may have been more original—or, in some unacademic sense, better. One of these was M.R. KALE's student edition, possibly the most widely circulated edition of the play. KALE's choice of readings and his emendations sometimes seem arbitrary, and his limited apparatus does not reveal the origin of the variants shown. However, we benefited greatly from his ultraliteral translation and from his copious notes: even where we disagree with him, the amount of explanation he gives has helped us formulate our own ideas. Another is the Srirangam edition by V.T. RANGASWAMY AIYANGAR, published in 1908. This is an edition that bears the marks of careful consideration, resulting in a text that reads well and is internally consistent. It also includes a rudimentary critical apparatus that shows variant readings without providing their sources. In our initial comparison of editions this book came barely behind IYER's edition, and the only reason it was not chosen as our principal text is that some of its readings seem to have been chosen too arbitrarily for our taste. The third edition we used in creating our text is that of C. Sankara Rama Sastri, published in Madras in 1929. This too is an early work based on a collation of several sources, though again, witnesses for the variant readings are not given. A number of other early editions—which we looked up for the more dubious or problematic passages but have not adopted readings from—are listed in the Bibliography under Editions and translations.

A further edition that should be mentioned here even though we have not used it is that of Rewāprasāda Dwivedī, published in 1986 by the Banaras Hindu University as part of a *Kālidāsa granthāvalī*, an edition of the complete works of Kali·dasa. This edition is apparently based on careful research and comes with a detailed critical apparatus, despite the rather small number of sources (manuscripts and editions) collated. The choice of preferred readings in this edition is so unlike the other editions we consulted that comparison with it would have turned this work of ours into an unwieldy volume consisting largely of text-critical notes.

The detailed fourteenth-century commentary of Kāṭayavema—as printed in Kale's edition—has often helped us with the text and provides many interesting citations relevant to parts of the play. Aiyangar's edition also contains selections from Kāṭayavema (in a slightly different version than Kale's), as well as another commentary by Nīlakaṇṭha, composed in the eighteenth century. We have frequently referred to both of these commentaries, and, where possible, we have noted their readings among our variants. We have occasionally referred to the detailed modern commentary called the *Sārārthadīpikā* by Sahṛdayatilaka Rama Pisharody,[28] published in SASTRI's edition.

We have noted the variant readings available in our editions at every locus where we have deviated from the text of IYER's edition (apart from the minor changes described below), as well as in a number of places where we opted to retain IYER's reading but feel that the variants are noteworthy. When recording the alternative readings provided as variants in the editions we referred to, we have not retained the information (if any) they give about the sources of those variants. The edition of AIYANGAR provides no Prakrit variants (giving instead variant readings for the *chāyā*, the Sanskrit translation of a Prakrit passage), so when reproducing Prakrit alternative readings from this edition, we have taken the liberty of retranslating those to Prakrit as best we could.

In IYER's text we have corrected obvious misprints[29] and typographical errors without recording these as variants. We have also standardized the spelling of Prakrit passages to some extent[30] without recording this as our emendation, and changed IYER's *chāyā* wherever it diverged from his Prakrit text, so that the *chāyā* in this volume mirrors the Prakrit as accurately as possible. Furthermore, we have standardized the use of *sandhi* in stage directions.[31]

Acknowledgements

We dedicate this book to our teachers Csaba Töttössy, who taught us to dissect Sanskrit and understand the parts, and Ferenc Ruzsa, who taught us to put it together again and see the whole. Our sincere thanks go to the CSL editors Isabelle Onians and Sheldon Pollock for their support and their untiring efforts without which this volume would not have come into being. We are grateful to Csaba Dezső for his help with the text, to Anne Freeland for her patient and sensitive assistance in polishing our translation, and to Oliver Fallon for his careful attention to both text and translation.

Abbreviations

Kā	Kāṭayavema
Nī	Nīlakaṇṭha
NŚ	*Nāṭyaśāstra*
MW	"A Sanskrit-English Dictionary" by MONIER-WILLIAMS (1899)
VSA	The "Practical Sanskrit-English Dictionary" of APTE (1957–59)

Notes

1 WARDER (1990: 126): "Kālidāsa's most admired work is the *Meghasandeśa*, followed in popularity by the *Kumārasambhava* ..., *Abhijñānaśākuntala*, *Raghuvaṃśa*, *Vikramorvaśīya* and *Mālavikāgnimitra* ... It might be a reasonable conjecture that this is the reverse of the order in which the *kāvya*s were written, the poet's art gradually maturing..."

2 E.g. KEITH (1992: 147): "The great merits of the poet are far less clearly exhibited here than in his other plays;" see also WARDER in the previous note.

3 The *Abhijñānaśākuntala* calls itself "a new play" twice over (*kālidāsagrathitavastunā navena nāṭakenopasthātavyam* and *apuruvaṃ ṇāḍaaṃ*), and the *Vikramorvaśīya* professes to be "a play that has never been performed" (*apūrvaṃ nāṭakam*).

4 The commissioner of the inscription describes himself as "the sixth of Pushya·mitra"—perhaps sixth in descent from him, though not necessarily in a direct line.

5 For example the coins of Su·jyeshtha and Vasu·mitra are typologically so distinct that they may have belonged to separate dynasties. Coins bearing the name of Agni·mitra (possibly two distinct Agni·mitras) do not hail from Vídisha (where most coins issued by rulers who can be matched to the list of Shunga kings in the *purāṇa*s seem to originate) but from further north and east. See BHANDARE (2006) for a detailed discussion.

6 See also Introduction, note 16.

7 Pánini (*Aṣṭādhyāyī* 4.1.117: *vikarṇaśuṅgacchagalād vatsabharadvājātriṣu*) connects the Shungas with the brahmin family of the Bharadvájas; teachers with names implying descent from a person called Shunga appear in the *Bṛhadāraṇyaka Upaniṣad* and the *Vaṃśa Brāhmaṇa*; the Shungas are known as teachers in the *Āśvalāyana Śrautasūtra*. See RAYCHAUDHURI (1923: 197) for details.

8 See, for example, the *Brahmāṇḍapurāṇa* (2.74.149ff.): *ity ete nava mauryā vai bhokṣyanti ca vasuṃdharām / saptatriṃśacchataṃ pūrṇaṃ tebhyaḥ śuṅgo gamiṣyati / puṣyamitras tu senānīr uddhṛtya sa bṛhadratham / kārayiṣyati vai rājyaṃ ṣaṭtriṃśati samā nṛpaḥ / agnimitraḥ sutaś cāṣṭau bhaviṣyati samā nṛpaḥ / bhavitā cāpi sujyeṣṭhaḥ sapta varṣāṇi vai tataḥ / vasumitras tato bhāvyo daśa varṣāṇi pārthivaḥ...*; or *Viṣṇupurāṇa* (4.24.31ff.): *tasyānu bṛhadrathanāmā bhavitā. evam ete mauryā daśa bhūpatayo bhaviṣyanti abdaśataṃ saptatriṃśaduttaram. teṣām ante pṛthivīṃ daśa śuṅgā bhokṣyanti. puṣyamitraḥ senāpatiḥ svāminaṃ hatvā rājyaṃ kariṣyati. tasyātmajo 'gnimitraḥ. tasmāt sujyeṣṭhas tato vasumitras...* According to BHANDARE (2006) the *Matsya*, *Vāyu* and *Bhaviṣya purāṇa*s also contain relevant information.

9 Following LASSEN, as quoted by TAWNEY (1875: x–xi).

10 BHANDARE (2006) says the *purāṇa*s name the city of Vídisha as the capital of the Shungas.

11 In *ucchvāsa* 6: *prajñādurbalaṃ ca baladarśanavyapadeśadarśitāśeṣasainyaḥ senānīr anāryo mauryaṃ bṛhadrathaṃ pipeṣa puṣyamitraḥ svāminam.* Incidentally, a few lines earlier in the same chapter Su·mitra, son of Agni·mitra, is said to have met his end because of his excessive fondness of dancing. A certain Mitra·deva purportedly joined a troop of dancers or actors and cut off the head of the unwary Su·mitra (*atidayitalāsyasya ca śailūṣamadhyam adhyāsya mūrdhānam asilatayā mṛṇālam ivālunād agnimitrātmajasya sumitrasya mitradevaḥ*). Though this is moving far from history into the realm of capricious conjecture, it is quite easy to imagine the adolescent Su·mitra (Vasu·mitra in our play) returning home after his first martial achievement to find his father married to a ravishing danseuse barely older than the prince, and soon becoming an ardent dance aficionado himself.

12 *Avantisundarī* (p. 184): *puṣyamitro nāma śuṅgas tasyaiva senāpatir brāhmaṇāyano.*

13 The sentences are *iha puṣyamitraṃ yājayāmaḥ*, "we are performing a sacrifice here for Pushya·mitra" (3.2.123.1), and the pair *aruṇad yavanaḥ sāketam*, "the Greek has besieged Sakéta," and *aruṇad yavano madhyamikām*, "the Greek has besieged Mádhyamika" (3.2.111.2). See CARDONA (1997: 263ff.) for a summary of the debate about using these sentences for dating Patáñjali.

14 See e.g. RAYCHAUDHURI (1923: 204ff.) for a discussion.

15 *Harivaṃśa* 115.40: *audbhido bhavitā kaś cit senānīḥ kāśyapo dvijaḥ / aśvamedhaṃ kaliyuge punaḥ pratyāhariṣyati.*

16 The literal meaning (MW s. v.) of *audbhida* is "springing forth," and an established secondary meaning is "forcing one's way towards an aim, victorious." The word, and especially its variant *audbhijja*, also has connotations of the vegetable kingdom (the prefixed verb *ud√bhid* refers to the growth of plant shoots). A highly conjectural alternative interpretation would be that it is an allusion to the name Shunga in this *Harivaṃśa* passage, as *śuṅga* (possibly related to *śṛṅga*, "horn") might mean a shoot or leaf-bud of the banyan tree rather than the tree in general.

17 See Introduction, note 7.

18 See GHOSH (1937) for a discussion.

19 Story 29, *Aśokāvadāna* (*Divyāvadāna*: p. 433ff.). The *Divyāvadāna* was composed rather late (probably in the eighth century CE), but many of its stories, including this one, may well have originated far earlier, possibly around the beginning of the Common Era.

20 RAYCHAUDHURI (1923: 198), for example, sketches a complete scenario according to which during the reign of Brihad·ratha there were two factions in the Maurya empire, one headed by the king's minister and the other by his general. The minister's partisan Yajña·sena was appointed governor of Vidárbha, while the general's son Agni·mitra got the viceroyalty of Vídisha. When Pushya·mitra accomplished his coup, he imprisoned the minister (see 1.64 [7] and note to 1.64); simultaneously, Yajña·sena declared his independence in Vidárbha—and the stage is hereby set for "Málavika and Agni·mitra."

21 The plot of the *Abhijñānaśākuntala* is based on a story from the *Mahābhārata* also found in the *purāṇas*; the core of the *Vikramorvaśīya* is recorded as early as the *Ṛgveda* (10.95) and elaborated by numerous subsequent texts, including the *Śatapatha Brāhmaṇa* and the *Mahābhārata*. Admittedly the heroes of these stories are closer to the mythical end of the reality continuum, but we cannot be sure if Kali·dasa (or his audience) imagined Agni·mitra and his contemporaries as belonging to a much more recent or much more tangible past than the figures of the epics and legends. Dushyánta in the *Abhijñānaśākuntala* and Puru·ravas in the *Vikramorvaśīya* are both believed to have been ancestors of ruling houses.

22 Another view held by some authors—beginning with the commentator Kátaya·vema—is that Kali·dasa's king was none other then Agni·mitra. The main argument for this is the mention of the king by name in the actors' benediction at the very end of the play (5.208 [20]).

23 See e.g. Warder (1990: 122–23) for a summary of the arguments for assigning Kali·dasa to the Gupta period, or Keith (1992: 143–47) and Mirashi & Navlekar (1969: 1–35) for an overview of the various proposed dates of Kali·dasa and the arguments for and against them.

24 As noted by Warder (1990: 129): "... the presentation of the new Gupta–Vākāṭaka politics of marriage alliances and vassal kingdoms ... in the guise of ancient history."

25 Refer to Bakker (2006) for details.

26 The other editions Gerow consulted for his translation are one published in 1950 in Bombay by N.R. Acharya, and another by F. Bollensen, published in Leipzig in 1879. He dismisses Iyer's edition as "less reliable than its predecessors and ... not truly critical."

27 In Stoler Miller (1999: 368).

28 The author of the commentary is named Sahṛdayatilaka Rāmaṣāraka on the Sanskrit title page of the volume.

29 Apart from the frequent substitution of similar-looking Devanagari letters (such as *ṭa* for *ṭha* or *ma* for *bha*), our chief rule of thumb was to classify a reading as an "obvious misprint" if it is unintelligible, is not attested in any of our other sources and Iyer himself provides no variant information about it.

30 We have changed Prakrit final *m* to *anusvāra* throughout, used the conjuncts *ṇh* and *mh* consistently instead of *hṇ* and *hm*, and shortened long vowels wherever they are followed by double or conjunct consonants.

31 We have consistently applied vowel *sandhi* in the stage directions except where we feel that a hiatus is called for, but we have retained the apparently universally attested final *e* of *sarve* and *ubhe* followed by *i* or *u*. We have used *m* instead of final *anusvāra* at the end of all stage directions including those not ending in a *daṇḍa*.

Bibliography

EDITIONS AND TRANSLATIONS OF "MÁLAVIKA AND AGNI·MITRA"

AIYANGAR, V.T.R. (ed.) 1908. *Mālavikāgnimitram (nīlakaṇṭhakāṭaya-vemavyākhyādvayena samupetam)*. Śrīraṅgam: Śrī Vāṇīvilāsa Mudrālaya.

DWIVEDĪ, R.P. (ed.) 1986. *Kālidāsa-granthāvalī (sa-rūpāntara-pāṭhāntara-saṃṣodhitamūlā)*. Varanasi: Banaras Hindu University.

GEROW, E. (tr.) *Mālavikā and Agnimitra*. In: STOLER MILLER 1999.

IYER, K.A.S. (ed.) 1978. *The Mālavikāgnimitra of Kālidāsa*. Delhi: Sahitya Akademi.

KALE, M.R. (ed. and tr.) 1999. *Kālidāsa's Mālavikāgnimitram*. Delhi: Motilal Banarsidass. (First revised edition: Bombay, 1960.)

PANDIT, S.P. (ed.) 1869. *The Mâlavikâgnimitra, a Sanskrit Play by Kâlidâsa*. Bombay: Government Central Book Depot. Bombay Sanskrit Series, no. VI.

SASTRI, C.S.R. (ed.) 1929. *Mālavikāgnimitra of Kālidāsa with the Commentary Sārārthadīpikā by Sahṛdayatilaka Rama Pisharody*. Madras: Sri Balamanorama Series, no. 12.

SASTRI, R. and SASTRI, K. (eds.) 1900. *Malavikagnimitra of Kalidasa with Bhavabodhini commentary*. Trivandrum.

TARKAVACHASPATI, T. (ed.) 1870. *Malavikagnimitra: a drama by Kalidasa*. Calcutta: Kavyaprakasha Press.

TAWNEY, C.H. (tr.) 1875. *The Málavikágnimitra: a Sanskrit Play by Kálidása*. Calcutta: Thacker, Spink & Co.

SANSKRIT TEXTS

Abhijñānaśākuntala of KĀLIDĀSA in: VASUDEVA, S. (tr.) 2006. *The Recognition of Shakúntala*. New York: New York University Press & JJC Foundation.

Amarakośa or the *Nāmaliṅgānuśāsana* of AMARASIṂHA in: RAMANATHAN, A.A. (ed.) 1971. *Amarakośa*. Madras: Adyar Library and Research Centre.

Arthaśāstra of KAUṬILYA in: KANGLE, R.P. (ed. and tr.) 1969. *The Kauṭilīya Arthaśāstra* (Part I: Sanskrit text; Part II: translation). Delhi: Motilal Banarsidass.

Aṣṭādhyāyī of PĀṆINI in: BÖHTLINGK, O. 1839. (ed.) *Pânini's acht Bücher grammatischer Regeln* (vol. I) Bonn: H.B. König.

Avantisundarī of DAṆḌIN in: SASTRI, K.S.M. & PILLAI, P.K.N. (eds.) 1954. *Avantisundarī of Ācārya Dandin*, Trivandrum: Trivandrum Sanskrit Series, no. 172.

Divyāvadāna in: COWELL, E.B. & NEIL, R.A. (eds.) 1886. *The Divyâvadâna, A Collection of Early Buddhist Legends*. Cambridge: Cambridge University Press.

Harivaṃśa in: VAIDYA, P.L. et. al. (ed.) 1969. *The Harivaṃśa: Being the khila or supplement of the Mahābhārata*. Vol. 1. Poona: Bhandarkar Oriental Research Institute.

Harṣacarita of BĀṆA in: KANE, P.V. (ed.) 1986. *The Harshacarita of Bāṇabhaṭṭa*. Delhi: Motilal Banarsidass.

Kāmasūtra of VĀTSYĀYANA in: DONIGER, W. and KAKAR, S. (tr.) 2003. *Kamasutra: A New, Complete English Translation of the Sanskrit Text*. Oxford: Oxford University Press.

Mahābhārata in: SUKTHANKAR, V.S. et al. (eds.) 1933–66. *The Mahabharata for the First Time Critically Edited*. (19 vols.) Poona: Bhandarkar Oriental Institute.

Mahābhāṣya of PATAÑJALI in: KIELHORN, F. (ed.) 1883. *Patanjali's Vyâkaraṇa-Mahâbhâshya*. Vol. 2. Bombay: Government Central Book Depôt.

Manusmṛti in: OLIVELLE, P. (ed. and tr.) 2005. *Manu's Code of Law*. Oxford: Oxford University Press.

Meghadūta of KĀLIDĀSA in: MALLINSON, J. (tr.) 2006. *Messenger Poems*. New York: New York University Press & JJC Foundation.

Pañcatantra of VIṢṆUŚARMAN in: KALE, M.R. (ed.) 1986. *Pañcatantra of Viṣṇuśarman*. Delhi: Motilal Banarsidass.

Priyadarśikā and *Ratnāvalī* of HARṢA in: DONIGER, W. (tr.) 2006. *"The Lady of the Jewel Necklace" and "The Lady who Shows Her Love."* New York University Press & JJC Foundation.

Rāmāyaṇa of Vālmīki. *Bālakāṇḍa* in: Goldman, R.P. (tr.) 2005. *Ramáyana I: Boyhood*. New York: New York University Press & JJC Foundation.

Nāṭyaśāstra of Bharata in: Nagar, R.S. (ed.) 1983. *Nāṭyaśāstra of Bharatamuni with the commentary Abhinavabhāratī*. (4 vols.) Delhi: Parimal Publications (Parimal Sanskrit Series, no. 4).

Vikramorvaśīya of Kālidāsa in: Rao, V.N. and Shulman, D. (tr.) 2009. *How Úrvashi Was Won*. New York: New York University Press & JJC Foundation.

OTHER WORKS

Ali, S. 2002 (13th edition). *The Book of Indian Birds*. Oxford: Oxford University Press.

Apte, V.S. 1957–59 (revised and enlarged edition). *The Practical Sanskrit-English Dictionary* (3 vols.) Poona: Prasad Prakashan.

Bakker, H. 2006. "A Theatre of Broken Dreams: Vidiśā in the Days of Gupta Hegemony." In: Brandtner, M. and Panda, S.K. (eds.) *Interrogating History: Essays for Hermann Kulke*. pp. 165–87. New Delhi: Manohar.

Banerji, S.C. 1968. *Kālidāsa-kośa*. The Chowkhamba Sanskrit Studies, vol. LXI. Varanasi: Chokhamba Sanskrit Series Office.

Bhandare, S. 2006. "Numismatics and History: The Maurya-Gupta Interlude in the Gangetic Plain." In: Olivelle, P. (ed.) *Between the Empires. Society in India 300* BCE *to 400* CE. pp. 67–109. Oxford: Oxford University Press.

Bhat, G.K. 1975. *Bharata-Nāṭya-Mañjarī. Bharata: On the Theory and Practice of Drama*. Poona: Bhandarkar Oriental Research Institute.

Boesche, R. 2003. "Kautilya's Arthaśāstra on War and Diplomacy in Ancient India." *Journal of Military History* 67 (1): 9–37. Available at http://muse.jhu.edu/journals/journal_of_military_history/v067/67.1boesche.html

Cardona, G. 1997. *Pāṇini: A survey of research*. Delhi: Motilal Banarsidass.

Ghosh, J. C. 1937. "The Dynastic-Name of the Kings of the Puṣyamitra Family." *Journal of the Bihar and Orissa Research Society*, 23: 353–64.

Gitomer, D. "The Theater in Kālidāsa's Art." In: Stoler Miller 1999.

Ingalls, D.H.H. 1976. "Kalidasa and the Attitudes of the Golden Age." *Journal of the American Oriental Society* 96 (1): 15–26.

Keith, A.B. 1992. *The Sanskrit Drama in its Origin, Development, Theory & Practice*. Delhi: Motilal Banarsidass. Original edition: Clarendon Press, Oxford 1924.

Marasinghe, E.W. 1989. *The Sanskrit Theatre and Stagecraft*. Delhi: Sri Satguru Publications (Sri Garib Dass Oriental Series, no. 78).

Mehta, T. 1995. *Sanskrit Play Production in Ancient India*. Delhi: Motilal Banarsidass.

Mirashi, V.V. & Navlekar, N.R. 1969. *Kālidāsa: Date, Life and Works*. Bombay: Popular Prakashan.

Monier-Williams, M. 1899. *A Sanskrit-English Dictionary*. Original edition published by Oxford University Press; reprints by Motilal Banarsidass.

Nairne, A.K. 1894. *The Flowering Plants of Western India*. London: W.H. Allen & Co. (Numerous reprints and editions.)

Raghavan, V. 1978. *Bhoja's Sṛṅgāra Prakāśa*. Madras: Punarvasu. (Third revised enlarged edition.)

Raychaudhuri, H. 1923. *Political History of Ancient India*. Calcutta: University of Calcutta.

Stoler Miller, B. (ed.) 1999. *The Plays of Kālidāsa: Theater of Memory*. Delhi: Motilal Banarsidass. Original edition by Columbia University Press, 1984.

Tarlekar, G.H. 1991. *Studies in the Nāṭyaśāstra: With Special Reference to the Sanskrit Drama in Performance*. Delhi: Motilal Banarsidass.

Tieken, H. 2001. "The Place of the Mālavikāgnimitra within Kālidāsa's Oeuvre." *Indo-Iranian Journal* 44: 149–66.

Upadhyaya, B.S. 1947. *India in Kalidasa*. Allahabad: Kitabistan.

Warder, A.K. 1990 (2nd revised edition). *Indian Kavya Literature*, vol. iii. *The Early Medieval Period*. Delhi: Motilal Banarsidass.

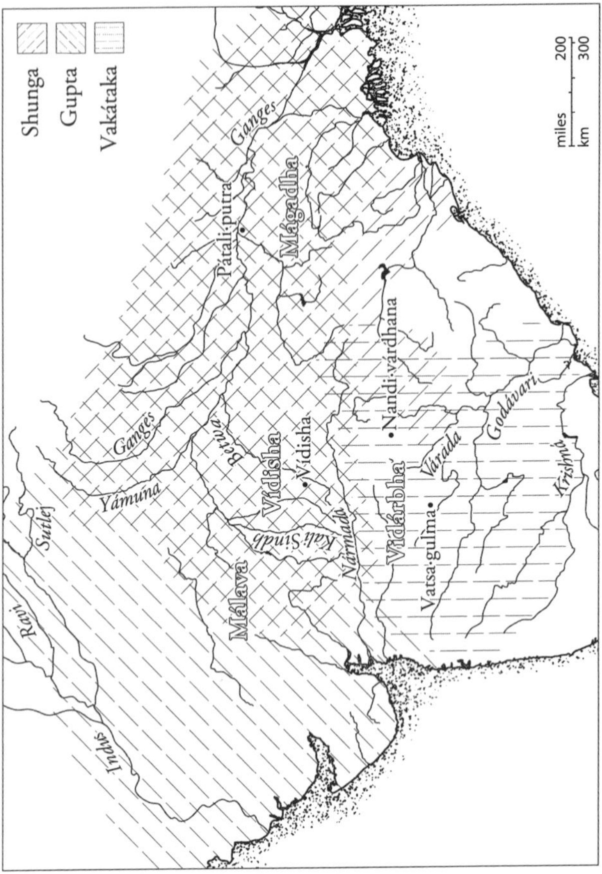

Map showing the Shunga empire, and territories under Gupta and Vakátaka dominion in Kali·dasa's time. See p. xxiii for a discussion.

Cast of Characters

This is a spoiler-free description of the characters appearing in the play. See the Glossary of Names and Terms (pp. 285ff.) for more details and for persons not listed here.

Assistant *(pāripārśvikaḥ)*	An actor, assistant to the director, appearing in the introductory scene.
Attendants *(parijanaḥ)*	Queen Dhárini's and King Agni·mitra's retinue.
Bakulávalika *(Bakulāvalikā, ceṭī)*	Queen Dhárini's maid and Málavika's friend.
Chamberlain *(kañcukī)*	A high-ranking servant at the court of King Agni·mitra, an elderly gentleman in charge of the palace and the harem. His name is Maudgálya.
Two court bards *(vaitālikau)*	Panegyrists of King Agni·mitra.
Director *(sūtradhāraḥ)*	The head of the troupe of actors, appearing in the introductory scene.
Gana·dasa *(Gaṇadāsaḥ)*	A teacher of dance and acting patronized by Queen Dhárini, in rivalry with Hara·datta.
Hara·datta *(Haradattaḥ)*	A teacher of dance and acting patronized by King Agni·mitra, in rivalry with Gana·dasa.
Irávati *(Irāvatī)*	King Agni·mitra's junior queen, subordinate to Queen Dhárini. She is young, beautiful and jealous of her position.
Jaya·sena *(Jayasenā, pratīhārī)*	A female official of the harem subordinate to the chamberlain. She runs errands, announces visitors and ceremoniously leads royalty around the palace.
Jester *(vidūṣakaḥ)*	The personal companion and friend of King Agni·mitra. A comical figure, but not exactly

	a jester in the Western sense: he is a brahmin by birth but performs no priestly function and speaks Prakrit. Timid and gluttonous, he has a ready wit, which he employs in the service of the king's amorous affairs. His name is Gáutama.
Jyótsnika *(Jyotsnikā)* *(prathamā)*	One of a pair of slave girls skilled in music, sent as a present to King Agni·mitra from the country of Vidárbha.
Káumudika *(Kaumudikā)*	One of the maids in the palace.
Káushiki *(Kauśikī)* *(parivrājikā)*	A mendicant woman staying in the palace palace, respected by Queen Dhárini and sympathizing with Málavika and King Agni·mitra.
King *(rājā)*	agni·mitra, the king of Vídisha and hero of the play. Past his prime, he is apparently quite effective as a ruler, but not quite lord of his own home. His chief wife is Queen Dhárini and his second wife is Irávati. He is presently on the lookout for a young and pretty new woman, and when he sets eye on Málavika, the plot of the play begins. However, he must proceed with extreme care so as to spare the feelings of his two queens.
Madhu·kárika *(Madhukarikā, udyāna/pālikā)*	A serving woman in charge of the palace gardens.
Málavika *(Mālavikā)*	A maid in Queen Dhárini's retinue, recently sent to the palace by the commander of a borderland fort. She studies dance under Gana·dasa and is hopelessly in love with King Agni·mitra. Her cause is fostered by her friend Bakulávalika and by the mendicant woman Káushiki.
Minister *(amātyaḥ)*	Minister or chief secretary of King Agni·mitra. His name is Váhatava.

Nágarika *(Nāgarikā)* *(ceṭī)*	A maid in the service of Queen Dhárini.
Nípunika *(Nipuṇikā)*	Irávati's maid and companion, a shrewd and meddlesome young woman.
Queen *(devī)*	Dhárini, King Agni·mitra's first wife and mother of the adolescent heir apparent. A proud and practical woman no longer in the bloom of her youth, her chief interest is in preserving proprieties and maintaining harmony in the palace.
Rájanika *(Rajanikā)* *(dvitīyā)*	One of a pair of slave girls skilled in music, sent as a present to King Agni·mitra from the country of Vidárbha.
Samáhitika *(Samāhitikā)* *(paricārikā)*	A maid serving Káushiki.
Sárasaka *(Sārasakaḥ)*	A hunchback footman in the service of Queen Dhárini.

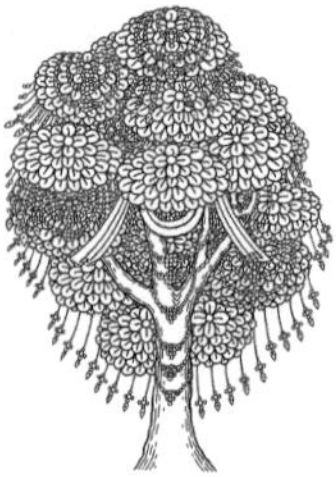

MÁLAVIKA AND AGNI·MITRA

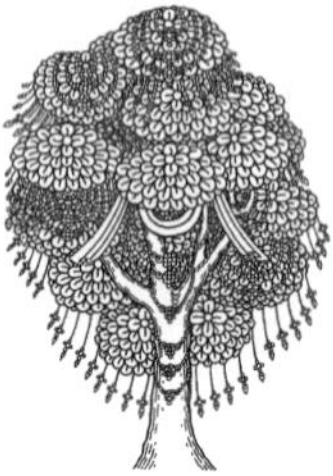

INTRODUCTORY SCENE

1.1 EK'|ĀIŚVARYE STHITO 'pi praṇata|bahu|phale
yaḥ svayaṃ kṛtti|vāsāḥ;
kāntā|saṃmiśra|deho 'py a|viṣaya|manasāṃ
yaḥ parastād yatīnām;
aṣṭābhir yasya kṛtsnaṃ jagad api tanubhir
bibhrato n' âbhimānaḥ:
san|mārg'|ālokanāya vyapanayatu sa vas
tāmasīṃ vṛttim Īśaḥ. [1]

(nāndy|ante)

SŪTRADHĀRAḤ *(nepathy'|âbhimukham avalokya)*: māriṣa, itas tāvat!

(praviśya)

1.5 PĀRIPĀRŚVIKAḤ: bhāva, ayam asmi.

SŪTRADHĀRAḤ: abhihito 'smi pariṣadā, «Kālidāsa|grathita|vastu Mālavik"|Âgnimitraṃ nāma nāṭakam asmin vasant'|ôtsave prayoktavyam» iti. tad ārabhyatāṃ saṃgītakam!

PĀRIPĀRŚVIKAḤ: mā tāvat! prathita|yaśasāṃ Bhāsa|Saumilla|Kaviputr'|ādīnāṃ prabandhān atikramya vartamāna|kaveḥ Kālidāsasya kriyāyāṃ kathaṃ bahu|mānaḥ?

SŪTRADHĀRAḤ: ayi, viveka|viśrāntam abhihitam! paśya:

purāṇam ity eva na sādhu sarvaṃ,
na c' âpi kāvyaṃ navam ity a|vadyam.
santaḥ parīkṣy' ânyatarad bhajante—
mūḍhaḥ para|pratyaya|neya|buddhiḥ. [2]

EVER THE SOLE sovereign heaping rewards on the 1.1
humble—yet wearing but a raw hide;*
body merged with his beloved*
—yet surpassing withdrawn-minded ascetics;
supporting no less than the entire world with his
eight bodies*—yet without conceit:
may this Lord* dispel the darkness of your ways
so you may behold the path of the virtuous.

At the end of the benediction enter the DIRECTOR.*

DIRECTOR *(looking toward the back-stage*)*: Over here, mate!

Enter the ASSISTANT.

ASSISTANT: Here I am, sir. 1.5

DIRECTOR: Our audience has told me to stage the play "Málavika and Agni·mitra," whose plot was woven by Kali·dasa, for this present spring festival. So bring on the song and dance!

ASSISTANT: Hang on! How come they have such high regard for the work of this contemporary poet,* this Kali·dasa, and spurn the oeuvres of widely-famed Bhasa,* Saumílla,* Kavi·putra,* et cetera?

DIRECTOR: Hah! You make noises but your good sense is asleep! Consider:

All that is old does not glitter,
nor does novelty make a play detestable.
Gentlemen assay both, then pick one—
the thoughts of dimwits go with the herd.

1.10 PĀRIPĀRŚVIKAḤ: ārya|miśrāḥ pramāṇam.

SŪTRADHĀRAḤ: tena hi tvaratāṃ bhavān!

śirasā prathama|gṛhītām
  ājñām icchāmi pariṣadaḥ kartum,
devyā iva Dhāriṇyāḥ
  sevā|dakṣaḥ parijano 'yam. [3]

iti niṣkrāntau.

prastāvanā.

ASSISTANT: Their lordships know best. 1.10

DIRECTOR: Then hurry up, good man!

I've humbly accepted the audience's bidding.
So now I'm eager to fulfill it,
as these nimbly serving maids
wish to carry out Queen Dhárini's orders.

Exeunt.

End of the introductory scene.

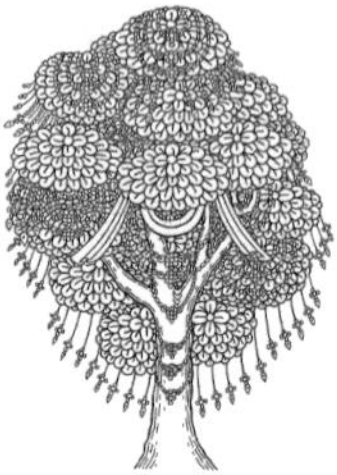

PRELUDE TO ACT ONE

1.15 *tataḥ praviśati* CEṬĪ.

CEṬĪ: ⌜āṇatta mhi devīe Dhāriṇīe «a|ira|ppaütt'|ôvadesaṃ chaliaṃ ṇāma ṇaṭṭaaṃ antareṇa kīrisī Mālavia?» tti ṇaṭṭ'|āariaṃ ajja|Gaṇadāsaṃ pucchiduṃ. tā jāva saṃgīda|sālaṃ gacchamhi.⌟

iti parikrāmati.

tataḥ praviśaty ābharaṇa|hastā DVITĪYĀ CEṬĪ.

PRATHAMĀ *(*DVITĪYĀṂ *dṛṣṭvā)*: ⌜halā Komudie, kudo de iaṃ dhīradā, jaṃ samīveṇa vi adikkamantī ido diṭṭhiṃ ṇa desi?⌟

1.20 DVITĪYĀ: ⌜amho, Baülāvaliā! sahi, idaṃ devīe sippi|saāsādo āṇīdaṃ ṇāga|muddā|saṇāhaṃ aṅgulīaaṃ siṇiddhaṃ ṇijjhāantī tuha uvālambhe paḍida mhi.⌟

BAKULĀVALIKĀ *(vilokya)*: ⌜ṭhāṇe khu sajjadi diṭṭhī! imiṇā aṅgulīaeṇa ubbhiṇṇa|kiraṇa|kesareṇa kusumido via de agga|hattho paḍibhādi.⌟

KAUMUDIKĀ: ⌜halā, kahiṃ patthidā si?⌟

BAKULĀVALIKĀ: ⌜devīe† vaaṇeṇa ṇaṭṭ|āariaṃ ajja|Gaṇadāsaṃ pucchiduṃ, «uvadesa|ggahaṇe kīrisī Mālavia?» tti.⌟

KAUMUDIKĀ: ⌜sahi, īriseṇa vāvāreṇa a|saṃṇihidā vi diṭṭhā kila sā bhaṭṭiṇā.⌟

1.25 BAKULĀVALIKĀ: ⌜āṃ. so jaṇo devīe passa|gado citte diṭṭho.⌟

Enter the maid BAKULÁVALIKA. 1.15

BAKULÁVALIKA: Her Majesty Dhárini has commanded me to ask Mister Gana·dasa the dance teacher about Málavika's progress in the *chálita* dance,* which he's recently started teaching her. So I'm off to the concert hall.

She walks about.

Enter another maid, KÁUMUDIKA, *carrying a piece of jewelry.*

BAKULÁVALIKA *(seeing* KÁUMUDIKA*)*: Káumudika dear, what makes you so preoccupied that you don't even look my way when you trot right past?

KÁUMUDIKA: Why, it's Bakulávalika! Friend, the reason I 1.20
deserve your rebuke is that I was admiring this ring of the queen's with a snake seal,* which I'm just bringing from the goldsmith.

BAKULÁVALIKA *(studying the ring)*: No wonder it attracts your eyes! The rays bursting from this ring make your hand look like a flower with so many filaments.

KÁUMUDIKA: Where were you going, my dear?

BAKULÁVALIKA: The queen said to ask Mister Gana·dasa the dance teacher about Málavika's progress in learning.

KÁUMUDIKA: My friend, I hear the lord's caught a glimpse of her, though she's been kept so busy dancing all the time.

BAKULÁVALIKA: Indeed. He saw her attending on the queen 1.25
—in a picture.

KAUMUDIKĀ: ⌜kahaṃ via?⌟

BAKULĀVALIKĀ: ⌜suṇāhi. citta|sālaṃ gadā devī paccagga|vaṇṇa|rāaṃ citta|lehaṃ āariassa oloantī ciṭṭhadi. tassiṃ antare bhaṭṭā uvaṭṭhido.⌟

KAUMUDIKĀ: ⌜tado tado?⌟

BAKULĀVALIKĀ: ⌜uvaār'|âṇ|andaraṃ ekk'|āsaṇ|ovaviṭṭheṇa bhaṭṭiṇā citta|gadāe devīe pariaṇa|majjha|gadaṃ āsaṇṇa|dāriaṃ pekkhia devī pucchidā—⌟

1.30 KAUMUDIKĀ: ⌜kiṃ ti?⌟

BAKULĀVALIKĀ: ⌜«*a/puvvā* iaṃ dāriā tuha āsaṇṇā ālihidā kiṃ|ṇāma|hea?» tti⌟

KAUMUDIKĀ: ⌜ṇaṃ ākidi|visese āaro padaṃ karodi. tado tado?⌟

BAKULĀVALIKĀ: ⌜tado avahīria|vaaṇo bhaṭṭā saṅkido deviṃ puṇo vi aṇubandhiduṃ paütto. jāva devī ṇa kahedi, dāva kumārīe Vasulacchīe ācakkhidaṃ: «āutta, esā Mālavia» tti.⌟

KAUMUDIKĀ: ⌜sarisaṃ khu bāla|bhāvassa! tado varaṃ kahehi.⌟

1.35 BAKULĀVALIKĀ: ⌜kiṃ aṇṇaṃ? sampadaṃ Mālaviā sa|visesaṃ bhaṭṭiṇo daṃsaṇa|pahādo rakkhīadi.⌟

KAUMUDIKĀ: ⌜halā, aṇuciṭṭha attaṇo ṇioaṃ. ahaṃ vi edaṃ aṅgulīaaṃ devīe uvaṇaïssaṃ.⌟

KÁUMUDIKA: How's that?

BAKULÁVALIKA: Listen. Here's the queen standing in the picture gallery, looking at this picture that's still vibrant with fresh paint. Meanwhile, here comes the king.

KÁUMUDIKA: Then what?

BAKULÁVALIKA: As soon as he's got over the courtesies and sat down sharing a seat with her, the king spots this girl among all the servants attending the queen in the picture, and asks—

KÁUMUDIKA: Asks what? 1.30

BAKULÁVALIKA: "What's the name of this *new⁝gorgeous* lass painted next to you?"

KÁUMUDIKA: Outstanding looks just draw attention, don't they? Then what?

BAKULÁVALIKA: Then the queen ignores what the king says, and he gets suspicious and starts nagging her again. The queen says nothing, but Princess Vasu·lakshmi blurts out, "Papa,* it's Málavika."

KÁUMUDIKA: Just what a child would do! So tell me, what next?

BAKULÁVALIKA: What else? They're now making a special 1.35
effort to keep Málavika out of the king's sight.

KÁUMUDIKA: You go on with your duty, my dear. And I'd better go and take this ring to the queen.

iti niṣkrāntā.

BAKULĀVALIKĀ *(parikramy', âvalokya)*: ⌜eso ṇaṭṭ|āario ajja|Gaṇadāso saṃgīda|sālādo ṇikkamadi. jāva se attāṇaṃ daṃsemi.⌟

iti parikrāmati.

1.40 *(praviśya)*

GAṆADĀSAḤ: kāmaṃ khalu sarvasy' âpi kula|vidyā bahu matā. na punar asmākaṃ nāṭyaṃ prati mithyā|gauravam. kutaḥ?

devānām idam āmananti munayaḥ
kāntaṃ kratuṃ cākṣuṣaṃ.
Rudreṇ' êdam Umā|kṛta|vyatikare
sv'|âṅge vibhaktaṃ dvidhā.
traiguṇy'|ôdbhavam atra loka|caritaṃ
nānā|rasaṃ dṛśyate.
nāṭyaṃ bhinna|rucer janasya bahudh" âpy
ekaṃ samārādhanam. [4]

BAKULĀVALIKĀ *(upetya)*: ⌜ajja, vandāmi.⌟

GAṆADĀSAḤ: bhadre, ciraṃ jīva.

1.45 BAKULĀVALIKĀ: ⌜ajja, devī pucchadi: «avi uvadesa|ggahaṇe ṇ' âdikilisedi vo sissā Mālavia?» tti.⌟

GAṆADĀSAḤ: bhadre, vijñāpyatāṃ devī: «parama|nipuṇā medhāvinī ca» iti. kiṃ bahunā?

Exit KÁUMUDIKA.

BAKULÁVALIKA *(walking about, looking)*: Here's Mister Gana·dasa the dance teacher, just coming out of the concert hall. I'll just let him notice me.

She walks about.

Enter GANA·DASA. 1.40

GANA·DASA: All right, everyone thinks highly of his family trade. But my respect for dance is not in vain. Why?

> Sages declare it to be the gods' favorite
> visual sacrifice.
> Rudra divided it into two parts* in his own body
> that is mingled with Uma.*
> It encompasses the various sentiments* of the ways
> of people, motivated by the three qualities.*
> Though the appetites of people are manifold,
> dance is their one common satisfaction.

BAKULÁVALIKA *(approaching him)*: Greetings, mister.

GANA·DASA: Long may you live, good girl.

BAKULÁVALIKA: Mister, Her Majesty enquires if your pupil 1.45
Málavika is not too troublesome to teach.

GANA·DASA: Inform Her Majesty that she is most adroit and intelligent. What else to say?

yad yat prayoga|viṣaye
  bhāvikam upadiśyate mayā tasyai,
tat tad viśeṣa|karaṇāt
  pratyupadiśat' îva me bālā. [5]

BAKULĀVALIKĀ *(ātma|gatam)*: ⌜adikkamantiṃ via Irāvadiṃ pekkhāmi.⌟ *(prakāśam)* ⌜kid'|atthā dāṇiṃ vo sissā, jassiṃ guru|aṇo evvaṃ tussadi.⌟

GAṆADĀSAḤ: bhadre, tad|vidhānām a|su|labhatvāt pṛcchāmi: kuto devyās tat pātram ānītam?

BAKULĀVALIKĀ: ⌜atthi devīe vaṇṇ'|âvaro bhādā Vīraseṇo ṇāma. so bhaṭṭiṇā Ṇammadā|tīre anta|vāla|dugge ṭhāvido. teṇa «sipp'|âhiāre joggā iaṃ dāria» tti bhaïṇīe uvāaṇaṃ pesidā.⌟

GAṆADĀSAḤ *(sva|gatam)*: ākṛti|vinaya†|pratyayād enām an|ūna|vastukāṃ saṃbhāvayāmi. *(prakāśam)* bhadre, may" âpi yaśasvinā bhavitavyam. yataḥ:

pātra|viśeṣe nyastaṃ
  guṇ'|ântaraṃ vrajati śilpam ādhātuḥ,
jalam iva samudra|śuktau
  muktāphalatāṃ payodasya. [6]

BAKULĀVALIKĀ: ⌜aha kahiṃ vo sissā?⌟

GAṆADĀSAḤ: idānīm eva pañc'|âṅg'|âbhinayam upadiśya mayā «viśramyatām» ity abhihitā dīrghik"|âvalokana|gavākṣa|gatā pravātam āsevamānā tiṣṭhati.

Whatever emotional expression
I teach the girl to perform,
she teaches it to me in turn, as it were,
by doing it so excellently.

BAKULÁVALIKA *(to herself)*: I guess she surpasses Irávati.* *(aloud)* If her teacher is so satisfied with her, then your pupil has achieved all she can.

GANA·DASA: I only ask because a girl like that is a rare find: where did Her Majesty get such good material?

BAKULÁVALIKA: Her Majesty has a baseborn brother* called Vira·sena. His Majesty had placed him in command of a borderland fort on the bank of the Nármada.* He sent Málavika as a present to his sister, saying "this girl is fit for an education in the arts."

GANA·DASA *(to himself)*: Her comeliness and decorum lead me to believe she is of no inferior stock. *(aloud)* I too shall become famous. Look:

When planted in the right receptacle,
the art of a preceptor attains greater virtue,
just as the water of a cloud becomes a pearl
when dropped in an oyster* of the seas.

BAKULÁVALIKA: Where is your pupil now?

GANA·DASA: I've just finished a class in the art of fivefold acting,* and told her to rest a while. She's now enjoying the breeze at the window overlooking the pond.

1.55 BAKULĀVALIKĀ: ⌜teṇa hi aṇujāṇādu maṃ ajjo. jāva se ajjassa paritosa|ṇivedaṇeṇa ussāhaṃ vaḍḍhemi.⌟

GAṆADĀSAḤ: dṛśyatāṃ sakhī. aham api labdha|kṣaṇaḥ sva|gṛhaṃ gacchāmi.

iti niṣkrāntau.

miśra/viṣkambhakaḥ.

BAKULÁVALIKA: Then if you'll give me leave, mister, I'll just go and cheer her by telling her how satisfied you are. 1.55

GANA·DASA: Do go and see your friend. As for me, I'll go to my quarters now that I've got a moment to myself.

Exeunt.

End of the prelude.

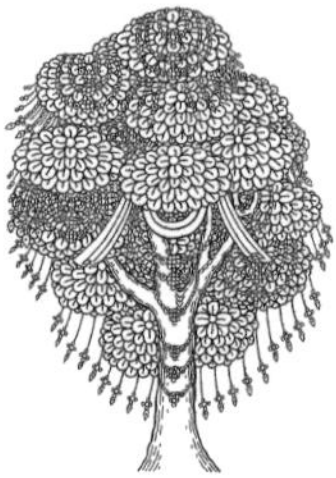

ACT ONE

*tataḥ praviśaty ek'|ânta|stha|*PARIJANO MANTRIṆĀ *lekha|hasten' ânvāsyamāno* RĀJĀ.

1.60 RĀJĀ *(anuvācita|lekham* AMĀTYAM *avalokya)*: Vāhatava,† kiṃ pratipadyate Vaidarbhaḥ?

AMĀTYAḤ: deva, ātma|vināśam.

RĀJĀ: nideśam idānīṃ śrotum icchāmi!

AMĀTYAḤ: idam idānīm anena pratilikhitam: «pūjyen' âham ādiṣṭaḥ, ‹pitṛvya|putro bhavataḥ, kumāro Mādhavasenaḥ, pratiśruta|saṃbandho mam' ôpāntikam upasarpann antarā tvadīyen' ânta|pālen' âvaskandya gṛhītaḥ. sa tvayā mad|apekṣayā sa|kalatra|sodaryo moktavyaḥ› iti. tan na vo na viditaṃ† yat tuly'|âbhijaneṣu bhūmi|hareṣu† rājñāṃ pravṛttir īdṛk.† ato 'tra madhya|sthaḥ pūjyo bhavitum arhati. sodaryā punar asya grahaṇa|viplave vinaṣṭā. tad|anveṣaṇāya prayatiṣye. atha avaśyam eva Mādhavaseno mayā pūjyena mocayitavyaḥ, śrūyatāṃ abhisaṃdhiḥ.

Maurya|sacivaṃ vimuñcati
  yadi pūjyaḥ saṃyataṃ mama śyālam,
moktā Mādhavasenaṃ
  tato 'ham api bandhanāt sadyaḥ.» [7]

1.65 RĀJĀ *(sa|roṣam)*: kathaṃ? kārya|vinimayena mayi vyavaharaty an|ātmajñaḥ? Vāhatava, prakṛty|amitraḥ pratikūla|kārī ca me Vaidarbhaḥ. tad yātavya|pakṣe sthitasya pūrva|saṅkalpita|samunmūlanāya Vīrasena|pramukhaṃ daṇḍa|cakram ājñāpaya.

Enter the KING, *attended by a* MINISTER *with a letter in hand, with his* RETINUE *standing apart.*

KING *(looking at the* MINISTER, *who has finished reading the letter)*: Váhatava,* what does the Vaidárbha* propose? 1.60

MINISTER: His own destruction, sire.

KING: It's his message I want to hear!

MINISTER: Here is his present reply: "Your worship has instructed me, 'Your grace's paternal cousin, Prince Mádhava·sena, who had promised to ally himself with me, was set upon and captured by your border force while on his way to me. Out of respect to me, you must release him along with his spouse and sister.' But surely you are aware that this is how kings behave toward rivals in inheritance who are of equal birth. Therefore your worship should please to remain neutral in this matter. As for his sister, she was lost in the confusion of the capture. I shall make an effort to locate her. Now if your worship insists on me setting Mádhava·sena free, kindly hear my terms.

> If your worship releases my confined brother-in-law
> the Maurya minister,*
> then I too shall immediately release
> Mádhava·sena from bondage."

KING *(furiously)*: What? This pretentious fool proposes to barter services with me? Váhatava, the Vaidárbha is my natural enemy and now he actually provokes me.* He is ripe for an attack,* so order the strike force under Vira·sena's command to extirpate him as we had planned. 1.65

AMĀTYAḤ: yad ājñāpayati devaḥ.

RĀJĀ: atha vā kiṃ bhavān manyate?

AMĀTYAḤ: śāstra|dṛṣṭam āha devaḥ. kutaḥ:

a|cir'|âdhiṣṭhita|rājyaḥ
 śatruḥ prakṛtiṣv a|rūḍha|mūlatvāt,
nava|saṃropaṇa|śithilas
 tarur iva, su|karaḥ samuddhartum. [8]

1.70 RĀJĀ: tena hy a|vitathaṃ tantra|kāra|vacanam! idam eva nimittam ādāya samudyojyatāṃ senā|patiḥ.

AMĀTYAḤ: tathā.

iti niṣkrāntaḥ. PARIJANAŚ *ca yathā|vyāpāraṃ* RĀJĀNAM *abhitaḥ sthitaḥ.*

(praviśya)

VIDŪṢAKAḤ: ⌜āṇatto mhi tatta|hodā raṇṇā, «Godama, cintehi dāva uvāaṃ, jaha me jadicchā|diṭṭha|paḍikidī Mālaviā paccakkha|daṃsaṇā hodi» tti. mae vi taṃ taha kidaṃ. jāva se ṇivedemi.⌟

1.75 *iti parikrāmati.*

RĀJĀ *(*VIDŪṢAKAṂ *dṛṣṭvā)*: ayam aparaḥ kāry'|ântara|sacivo 'smān upasthitaḥ.

MINISTER: As Your Majesty commands.

KING: Or do you think differently?

MINISTER: Your Majesty speaks as endorsed by the *shastras*. For:

> An enemy recently established in his kingdom,
> not yet firmly rooted in his subjects,
> is as easily toppled as a newly planted,
> still-tender tree.*

KING: Well, we can't let the author's words prove untrue! 1.70
Let the general deploy the army with this matter as the *casus belli*.

MINISTER: As you say.

Exit the MINISTER. *The* RETINUE *remain, each attending the* KING *as fits his function.*

Enter the JESTER.

JESTER: His Majesty the king has commanded me, "Gáutama, why don't you think up some way for me to have an actual look at this Málavika, whose picture I've seen by chance?" I, in turn, have done as he asked. So now I'll go and report to him.

He walks about. 1.75

KING *(seeing the* JESTER*)*: Here comes my other minister, in charge of some quite different affairs.

VIDŪṢAKAḤ *(upagamya)*: ⌜vaḍḍhadu bhavaṃ!⌟

RĀJĀ *(sa|śiraḥ|kampam)*: ita āsyatām.

VIDŪṢAKA *upaviṣṭaḥ.*

RĀJĀ: kaccid upey'|ôpāya|darśane vyāpṛtaṃ te prajñā|cakṣuḥ?

VIDŪṢAKAḤ: ⌜paoa|siddhiṃ puccha.⌟

RĀJĀ: katham iva?

VIDŪṢAKAḤ *(karṇe)*: ⌜evvaṃ via.⌟

RĀJĀ: sādhu, vayasya, nipuṇam upakrāntam! idānīṃ dur|adhigama|siddhāv apy asminn ārambhe vayam āśaṃsāmahe. kutaḥ:

> arthaṃ sa|pratibandhaṃ
>   prabhur adhigantuṃ sahāyavān eva.
> dṛśyaṃ tamasi na paśyati
>   dīpena vinā sa|cakṣur api. [9]

NEPATHYE: alam, alaṃ bahu vikatthya!† rājñaḥ samakṣam ev' âvayor adhar'|ôttara|vyaktir bhaviṣyati!

RĀJĀ *(ākarṇya)*: sakhe, tvat|su|nīti|pādapasya puṣpam udbhinnaṃ.

VIDŪṢAKAḤ: ⌜phalaṃ vi a|ireṇa pekkhissasi.⌟

JESTER *(approaching)*: May you prosper, sir!

KING *(with a nod of his head)*: Sit over here.

The JESTER *sits.*

KING: I hope your shrewd mind's eye is busily looking for the means to achieve my aim?

JESTER: Better ask what it's found.

KING: How do you mean?

JESTER *(whispering in his ear)*: That's how.

KING: Bravo, comrade, that's quite a start! Not an easy venture to begin with, but I have some hope now. For:

If the goal is blocked,
you need a helper to attain it.
In the dark, eyes are not enough:
you need a lantern to see.

A VOICE OFF-STAGE: Enough, enough of all this bragging! We must take this to the king to see who is inferior and who superior!

KING *(listening)*: The tree of your cunning has burst into flower, my friend.

JESTER: Soon you shall see it bear fruit, too.

tataḥ praviśati KAÑCUKĪ.

1.90 KAÑCUKĪ: deva, amātyo vijñāpayati: «anuṣṭhitā prabhor ājñā» iti. etau punar Haradatta|Gaṇadāsau,

ubhāv abhinay'|ācāryau
  paras|para|jay'|ôdyatau
tvāṃ draṣṭum icchataḥ sākṣād—
  bhāvāv iva śarīriṇau. [10]

RĀJĀ: praveśaya tau.

KAÑCUKĪ: yad ājñāpayati devaḥ. *(niṣkramya, punas tābhyāṃ saha praviśya)* ita ito bhavantau.

HARADATTAḤ *(*RĀJĀNAM *avalokya)*: aho, dur|āsado rāja|mahimā! tathā hi:†

1.95 na ca na paricito, na c' âpy a|ramyaś,
  cakitam upaimi tath" âpi pārśvam asya.
salila|nidhir iva pratikṣaṇaṃ me
  bhavati sa eva navo navo 'yam akṣṇoḥ. [11]

GAṆADĀSAḤ: mahat khalu puruṣ'|ākāram idaṃ jyotiḥ. tathā hi:

dvāre niyukta|puruṣ'|ânumata|praveśaḥ
  siṃh'|āsan'|ântika|careṇa sah' ôpasarpan
tejobhir asya vinivartita|dṛṣṭi|pātair
  vākyād ṛte punar iva prativārito 'smi. [12]

KAÑCUKĪ: eṣa devaḥ. upasarpatāṃ bhavantau.

Enter the CHAMBERLAIN.

CHAMBERLAIN: Sire, the minister informs that Your Majesty's command has been executed. But now here are Hara·datta and Gana·dasa: 1.90

The two dance masters,
each striving to surpass the other,
wanting a personal audience with you—
like two dramatic sentiments* incarnate.

KING: Admit them.

CHAMBERLAIN: As Your Majesty commands. *(going out, then returning with the* TWO MASTERS*)* This way, gentlemen.

HARA·DATTA *(glancing at the* KING*)*: Oh, awesome is the splendor of the king! For:

Neither a stranger to me, nor unpleasant to see, 1.95
yet timidly do I approach.
Like the ocean, he is the same, yet seems
to change moment by moment before my eyes.

GANA·DASA: Indeed a great luminary he is, a man but in shape. For:

Though the guard at the door has allowed my entry,
as I approach with the attendant of the throne,
his radiance forces my gaze away
as though fending me off again without a word.

CHAMBERLAIN: There is His Majesty. Go to him, good sirs.

UBHAU *(upetya)*: vijayatāṃ devaḥ!

1.100 RĀJĀ: svāgataṃ bhavadbhyām. *(*PARIJANAṂ *vilokya)* āsane tāvad atra|bhavatoḥ!

UBHAU PARIJAN'*|ôpanītayor āsanayor upaviṣṭau.*

RĀJĀ: kim idaṃ śiṣy'|ôpadeśa|kāle yugapad ācāryayor upasthānam?

GAṆADĀSAḤ: deva, śrūyatāṃ. mayā su|tīrthād abhinaya|vidyā śikṣitā; datta|prayogaś c' âsmi; devena devyā ca parigṛhītaḥ.

RĀJĀ: dṛḍhaṃ jāne. tataḥ kim?

1.105 GAṆADĀSAḤ: so 'ham amunā Haradattena pradhāna|puruṣa|samakṣam, «n' âyaṃ me pāda|rajas" âpi tulya» ity adhikṣiptaḥ.

HARADATTA: deva, ayam eva mayi prathamaṃ parivāda|karaḥ, atra|bhavataḥ kila mama ca samudra|palvalayor iv' ântaram iti. tad atra|bhavān imaṃ māṃ ca śāstre prayoge ca vimṛśatu. deva eva nau viśeṣa|jñaḥ prāśnikaḥ.

VIDŪṢAKAḤ: ⌜samatthaṃ paḍiṇṇādaṃ.⌟

GAṆADĀSAḤ: prathamaḥ kalpaḥ! avahito devaḥ śrotum arhati.

RĀJĀ: tiṣṭha tāvat! pakṣa|pātam atra devī manyate. tad asyāḥ paṇḍita|Kauśikī|sahitāyāḥ samakṣam eva nyāyyo vyavahāraḥ.

THE TWO MASTERS *(approaching the* KING*)*: Victory to Your Majesty!

KING: And welcome to you, sirs. *(looking to the* ATTEN- 1.100
DANTS*)* Seats for the gentlemen!

The TWO MASTERS *sit down on stools brought by the* ATTENDANTS.

KING: How is it that you two masters come here together when you should be instructing your students?

GANA·DASA: Please hear me, sire. I learned the histrionic science from a worthy master. I, in turn, have taught the practice of stage performance, and Your Majesty and the queen have favored me.

KING: I'm well aware of that. So what?

GANA·DASA: So after all this, Hara·datta here has abused 1.105
me in the presence of eminent people, saying, "This one does not compare with the dust of my feet!"

HARA·DATTA: Sire, it was actually he who started reviling me by saying he was to me as the ocean is to a puddle. So Your Majesty ought to assess both him and me in theory and practice. The king alone can be our expert arbiter.

JESTER: That does make sense.

GANA·DASA: First class! May it please Your Majesty to listen attentively.

KING: Wait a minute! The queen would suspect prejudice.* So for the sake of fairness we should proceed only with her and the learned Káushiki present.

I.110 VIDŪṢAKAḤ: ⌜suṭṭhu bhavaṃ bhaṇādi.⌟

ĀCĀRYAU: yad devāya rocate.

RĀJĀ: Maudgalya, amuṃ prastāvaṃ nivedya, paṇḍita|Kauśikyā sārdham āhūyatāṃ devī.

KAÑCUKĪ: yad ājñāpayati devaḥ. *(iti niṣkramya; sa|*PARIVRĀJIKAYĀ DEVYĀ *saha praviśya)* ita ito bhavatī.

DEVĪ *(*PARIVRĀJIKĀM *vilokya)*: ⌜bhaavadi, Haradattassa Gaṇadāsassa a saṃraṃbhe kahaṃ pekkhasi?⌟

I.115 PARIVRĀJIKĀ: alaṃ sva|pakṣ'|âvasāda|śaṅkayā. na parihīyate pratidvandino Gaṇadāsaḥ.

DEVĪ: ⌜jaï vi evvaṃ, taha vi rāa|pariggaho se pahāṇattaṇaṃ uvaharaï.⌟

PARIVRĀJIKĀ: ayi, rājñī|śabda|bhājanam ātmānam api tāvac cintayatu bhavatī! paśya:

atimātra|bhāsuratvaṃ
  puṣyati bhānoḥ parigrahād analaḥ
adhigacchati mahimānaṃ
  candro 'pi niśā|parigṛhītaḥ. [13]

VIDŪṢAKAḤ: ⌜avihā, avihā! uvaṭṭhidā pīṭha|maddiaṃ paṇḍida|Kosiiṃ puro|kadua devī.⌟

I.120 RĀJĀ: paśyāmy enām, y" âiṣā

maṅgal'|âlaṅ|kṛtā bhāti Kauśikyā yati|veṣayā
trayī vigrahavaty" êva samam adhyātma|vidyayā. [14]

JESTER: Well spoken, my lord. I.110

THE TWO MASTERS: As Your Majesty pleases.

KING: Maudgálya, explain the matter to the queen and the learned Káushiki, and call them here.

CHAMBERLAIN: As Your Majesty commands. *(leaving, then returning with the* QUEEN *and* KÁUSHIKI*)* This way please, Your Highness.

QUEEN *(looking at* KÁUSHIKI*)*: Reverend lady, what is your view of the quarrel between Hara·datta and Gana·dasa?

KÁUSHIKI: No need to worry about your party's defeat. I.115
Gana·dasa is by no means inferior to his rival.

QUEEN: Nevertheless, the king's favor* would give the first prize to that one.

KÁUSHIKI: Ah but don't forget that you happen to be the queen! Consider:

> It is the sun's favor that strengthens
> the brilliance of fire* to excess,
> but the moon attains its full luster
> by the mercy of Lady Night.*

JESTER: Oh my! Here comes the queen led by her crony* the learned Káushiki.

KING: I see her, who I.120

> shines in her auspicious ornaments,
> next to Káushiki in ascetic dress,
> like the Veda accompanied
> by mystic knowledge incarnate.

PARIVRĀJIKĀ *(upetya)*: vijayatāṃ devaḥ!

RĀJĀ: bhagavati, abhivādaye.

PARIVRĀJIKĀ:

> *mahā/sāra/prasavayoḥ*
> *sadṛśa/kṣamayor* dvayoḥ
> Dhāriṇī|bhūta|dhāriṇyor
> bhava bhartā śarac|chatam. [15]

1.125 DEVĪ: ⌜jedu ajja|utto!⌟

RĀJĀ: svāgatam devyai. (PARIVRĀJIKĀṂ *vilokya)* bhagavati, kriyatām āsana|parigrahaḥ.

sarve upaviśanti.

RĀJĀ: bhagavati, atra|bhavator Haradatta|Gaṇadāsayoḥ parasparena vijñāna|saṃgharṣo jātaḥ. tad atra bhagavatyā prāśnika|padam adhyāsitavyam.

PARIVRĀJIKĀ *(sa/smitam)*: alam upālambhena! pattane vidyamāne 'pi† grāme ratna|parīkṣā?

1.130 RĀJĀ: mā, m" âivam! paṇḍita|Kauśikī khalu bhagavatī. pakṣa|pātināv anayor ahaṃ devī ca.

ĀCĀRYAU: samyag āha devaḥ. madhya|sthā bhagavatī nau guṇa|doṣataḥ paricchettum arhati.

KÁUSHIKI *(approaching)*: Victory to Your Majesty!

KING: Greetings, reverend lady.

KÁUSHIKI:

> May you remain for a hundred autumns
> the lord of both Queen Dhárini
> and the creature-supporting Earth,
> whose *offspring is of great vigor* ⁝
> *whose crop is lushly verdant* *
> and whose *ability matches their station* ⁝
> *whose tolerance is equal.*

QUEEN: Victory to my noble husband! 1.125

KING: Welcome, my queen. *(looking at* KÁUSHIKI*)* Reverend lady, please take a seat.

All sit down.

KING: Reverend lady, these two gentlemen Hara·datta and Gana·dasa have a quarrel about each other's knowledge. Would your reverence please to be their arbitrator?

KÁUSHIKI *(with a smile)*: Don't embarrass me! Would you have a jewel assayed in a village when a city is near?

KING: Do not speak so! You are justly called the learned 1.130
Káushiki. The queen and I are biased in the matter of these two.

THE TWO MASTERS: His Majesty has spoken rightly. Your reverence is impartial, and thus fit for discriminating our virtues and flaws.

RĀJĀ: tena hi prastūyatāṃ vivādaḥ.

PARIVRĀJIKĀ: deva, prayoga|pradhānaṃ nāma nāṭya|śāstram. kim atra vāg|vyavahāreṇa? kathaṃ vā devī manyate?

DEVĪ: ⌜jaï maṃ pucchasi, edāṇaṃ vivādo evva ṇa me ruccadi.⌟

1.135 GAṆADĀSAḤ: devi, na māṃ samāna|vidyataḥ paribhavanīyam anumantum arhasi.

VIDŪṢAKAḤ: ⌜bhodi, pekkhāmo urabbha†|saṃvādaṃ. kiṃ muhā veaṇa|dāṇeṇa?⌟

DEVĪ: ⌜ṇaṃ kalaha|ppio 'si.⌟

VIDŪṢAKAḤ: ⌜mā evvaṃ! aṇṇoṇṇa|kalaha|ppiāṇaṃ matta|hatthīṇaṃ ekadarassiṃ a|ṇijjide kudo uvasamo?⌟

RĀJĀ: nanu sv'|âṅga|sauṣṭhav'|âbhinayam† ubhayor dṛṣṭavatī bhagavatī?

1.140 PARIVRĀJIKĀ: atha kim.

RĀJĀ: tad idānīm ataḥ paraṃ kim ābhyāṃ pratyāyayitavyam?

PARIVRĀJIKĀ: tad eva vaktu|kām" âsmi.

> śiṣṭā kriyā kasya cid ātma|saṃsthā,
> saṃkrāntir anyasya viśeṣa|yuktā.
> yasy' ôbhayaṃ sādhu, sa śikṣakāṇāṃ
> dhuri pratiṣṭhāpayitavya eva. [16]

KING: Well then, let the dispute begin.

KÁUSHIKI: Majesty, the backbone of histrionic science is performance. So why start a verbal discussion? Or what does the queen think?*

QUEEN: If you ask me, it's their very argument I don't care for.

GANA·DASA: My queen, please do not acknowledge that I 1.135
could be defeated by one whose knowledge is no greater than mine.

JESTER: Let's see those rams clash, my lady.* No point in giving them salaries for nothing.

QUEEN: Aren't you fond of wrangling.

JESTER: Not so! When two rutting elephants are spoiling for a fight, how could there be peace unless one is defeated?

KING: I suppose your reverence has seen both of them exhibit the skill of their own limbs?

KÁUSHIKI: Of course. 1.140

KING: So what else should they demonstrate now?

KÁUSHIKI: That is just what I was about to propose.

> Some have the high art ingrained in their persons,
> others are skilled in transferring it.
> Only a man who excels in both
> should be appointed at the fore of instructors.

VIDŪṢAKAḤ: ⌜sudaṃ ajjehiṃ bhaavadīe vaaṇaṃ. eso piṇḍid'|attho: uvadesa|daṃsaṇādo ṇiṇṇao tti.⌟

HARADATTA: parama|rucitaṃ naḥ.

GAṆADĀSAḤ: devi, evaṃ sthitaṃ.

DEVĪ: ⌜jadā uṇa manda|medhā sissā uvadesaṃ maliṇedi, tadā āariassa doso ṇaṃ?⌟

RĀJĀ: evam āpadyate—

GAṆADĀSAḤ:† —vinetur a|dravya|parigraho 'pi buddhi|lāghavaṃ prakāśayati.

DEVĪ *(sva|gatam†)*: ⌜kahaṃ dāṇiṃ?⌟ (GAṆADĀSAṂ *vilokya, jan'|ântikam†)* ⌜alaṃ ajja|uttassa ussāha|kāraṇaṃ maṇo|rahaṃ pūria!⌟ *(prakāśam†)* ⌜virama ṇir|atthaādo ārambhādo.⌟

VIDŪṢAKAḤ: ⌜suṭṭhu hodī bhaṇādi. bho, Gaṇadāsa, saṃgīd'|âvadeseṇa Sarassaī|uvāaṇa|modaāiṃ khādamāṇassa kiṃ de su|laha|ṇiggaheṇa vivādeṇa?⌟

GAṆADĀSAḤ: satyam, ayam ev' ârtho devī|vacanasya. śrūyatām avasara|prāptam idam:

«labdh'|āspado 'sm'» îti vivāda|bhīros,
titikṣamāṇasya pareṇa nindām,
yasy' āgamaḥ kevala|jīvikāyai,
taṃ jñāna|paṇyaṃ vaṇijaṃ vadanti. [17]

JESTER: Gentlemen, you've heard what the reverend lady said. Boiled down, it comes to this: you show what you've taught, and then she'll judge.

HARA·DATTA: Perfectly agreeable to us. 1.145

GANA·DASA: My queen, so be it.

QUEEN: But when a dim-witted pupil spoils the instruction, would that be the fault of the teacher?

KING: It would imply that—

GANA·DASA: —if a preceptor accepts someone inadequate, that is all the more proof of his unsound intellect.

QUEEN *(to herself)*: What now? *(confidentially, to* GANA·DASA*)* 1.150
Stop playing into my husband's hands, you're only encouraging him! *(aloud)* Desist from this pointless undertaking.*

JESTER: The queen is right. Hey Gana·dasa, under the pretext of your singing you now eat the sweets offered to Sarásvati;* but what can you gain by a contest so easy to lose?

GANA·DASA: Indeed, that is what Your Majesty was implying. But let me tell you something relevant to the matter:

> The man who thinks, "I've secured my station,"
> and, shirking dispute, tolerates others' abuse
> regarding his education as but a kind of livelihood,
> is called a merchant trafficking in knowledge.

DEVĪ: ⌜a|ir'|ôvaṇīdā vo sissā—tā a|variṇiṭṭhidassa uvadesassa a|ṇṇāaṃ paāsaṇaṃ.⌟

1.155 GAṆADĀSAḤ: ata eva me nirbandhaḥ.

DEVĪ: ⌜teṇa hi duve vi bhaavadīe uvadesaṃ daṃseha.⌟

PARIVRĀJIKĀ: devi, n' âitan nyāyyam. sarva|jñasy' âpy ekākino nirṇay'|âbhyupagamo doṣāya.

DEVĪ (*jan'|ântikam*): ⌜mūḍhe parivvājie! maṃ jaggadiṃ vi suttaṃ via karesi?⌟

iti s'|âsūyaṃ parāvartate. RĀJĀ DEVĪṂ PARIVRĀJIKĀYAI *darśayati.*

1.160 PARIVRĀJIKĀ (*vilokya*):

a|nimittam, indu|vadane,
  kim atra|bhavataḥ parāṅ|mukhī bhavasi?
prabhavantyo 'pi hi bhartṛṣu
  kāraṇa|kopāḥ kuṭumbinyaḥ. [18]

VIDŪṢAKAḤ: ⌜ṇaṃ sa|kāraṇaṃ evva? attaṇo pakkho rakkhidavvo, tti.⌟ (GAṆADĀSAṂ *vilokya*) ⌜diṭṭhiā kova|vvājeṇa devīe parittādo bhavaṃ. su|sikkhido vi savvo uvadesa|daṃsaṇe ṇa ṇiuṇo hodi.⌟

āsanād utthātum icchati.

QUEEN: Your pupil has only just begun her training—and it is wrong to display skills that are not thoroughly founded.

GANA·DASA: All the more reason for me to insist. 1.155

QUEEN: Well then why don't you both show your achievements to just the reverend lady?

KÁUSHIKI: My queen, that would not be right. Even for the omniscient a conclusion reached alone is prone to be erroneous.

QUEEN *(confidentially)*: Fool of a nun! You think I'm asleep? Well I'm not.

She turns away with indignation. The KING *points her out to* KÁUSHIKI.

KÁUSHIKI *(with a glance)*: 1.160

> Why, O moon-faced lady, do you turn away
> from your good lord?
> wives, though powerful themselves, need
> a good reason to be angry at their husbands.

JESTER: She has her reason, doesn't she? She's trying to shelter her protégé. *(looking at* GANA·DASA*)* Thank heaven Her Majesty rescued you with this show of anger. Even the most erudite can't always be good at presenting what they've taught.

He prepares to stand up from his seat.

GAṆADĀSAḤ: devi, śrūyatām! evaṃ jano gṛhṇāti. tad idānīm

1.165 vivāde darśayiṣyantaṃ
 kriyā|saṃkrāntim ātmanaḥ
yadi māṃ n' ânujānāsi,
 parityakto 'smy ahaṃ tvayā. [19]

DEVĪ *(sva|gatam)*: ⌜kā gaī?⌟ *(prakāśam)* ⌜pahavadi āario sissa|jaṇassa.⌟

GAṆADĀSAḤ: ciram a|pade śaṅkito 'smi. *(*RĀJĀNAM *avalokya)* anujñātaṃ devyā. tad ājñāpayatu devaḥ: kasminn abhineya|vastuny upadeśaṃ darśayiṣyāmi?

RĀJĀ: yad ādiśati bhagavatī.

PARIVRĀJIKĀ: kim api devyā manasi vartate, tac chaṅkit" âsmi...

1.170 DEVĪ: ⌜bhaṇa vīsaddhaṃ. ṇaṃ pahavissaṃ attaṇo pariaṇassa?⌟

RĀJĀ: mama c', êti brūhi.

DEVĪ: ⌜bhaavadi, bhaṇa dāṇiṃ.⌟

PARIVRĀJIKĀ: deva, catuṣ|pad'|ôdbhavaṃ chalitaṃ duṣ|prayojam udāharanti. tatr' âik'|ârtha|saṃśrayam ubhayoḥ prayogaṃ paśyāmaḥ. tāvatā jñāyata ev' âtra|bhavator upadeś'|ântaram.

GANA·DASA: Just listen, my queen! This is how the mob sees it. So now

> If you do not allow me to display in a contest 1.165
> what I have taught,
> then indeed you have abandoned me.

QUEEN *(to herself)*: What to do? *(aloud)* A teacher can order his pupils as he likes.

GANA·DASA: I shouldn't have doubted that.* *(looking at the* KING*)* Her Majesty has given permission. Now Your Majesty shall command: in what dramatic subject shall I demonstrate my teaching?

KING: Whatever the reverend lady specifies.

KÁUSHIKI: Her Majesty has something on her mind, so I'm not sure...

QUEEN: Speak at pleasure. Surely I can keep my own retainers in hand? 1.170

KING: And me too, you should say.

QUEEN: Reverend lady, speak it out.

KÁUSHIKI: Majesty, they say it's particularly difficult to perform a *chálita* dance* to a *chatush·pada* song.* We shall watch both of them perform to the same piece of that genre. That should be enough to reveal the difference in the teaching of these two gentlemen.

ĀCĀRYAU: yad ājñāpayati bhagavatī.

1.175 VIDŪṢAKAḤ: ⌜teṇa hi duve vi vaggā pekkhā|gharae saṃgīda|raaṇaṃ karia atta|hodo dūdaṃ pesadha. aha vā mudaṅga|saddo evva ṇo uṭṭhāvaïssadi.⌟

HARADATTA: tathā.

ity uttiṣṭhati. GAṆADĀSO DEVĪM *avalokayati.*

DEVĪ *(*GAṆADĀSAṂ *vilokya)*: ⌜viaī hohi. ṇa hu viaa|paccatthiṇī ahaṃ ajjassa.⌟

ĀCĀRYAU *prasthitau.*

1.180 PARIVRĀJIKĀ: itas tāvad, ācāryau!

UBHAU *(prativṛtya)*: imau svaḥ.

PARIVRĀJIKĀ: nirṇay'|âdhikāre bravīmi. *sarv'|âṅga|sauṣṭhav'|*âbhivyaktaye vigata†|nepathyayoḥ pātrayoḥ praveśo 'stu.

UBHAU: n' êdam āvayor upadeśyam.

iti niṣkrāntau.

1.185 DEVĪ *(*RĀJĀNAM *avalokya)*: ⌜jaï rāa|kajjesu īrisī uvāa|ṇiuṇadā ajja|uttassa, tado sohaṇaṃ have.⌟

THE TWO MASTERS: As the reverend lady commands.

JESTER: Then both contestants should go to the perfor- 1.175
mance hall, and send us a messenger when they have made preparations for the concert. Or better yet, the sound of the drum shall alert us.

HARA·DATTA: Right.

He gets up. GANA·DASA *glances at the* QUEEN.

QUEEN *(looking at* GANA·DASA*)*: May you be victorious. I'm by no means adverse to Your Honor's success.

THE MASTERS *start to leave.*

KÁUSHIKI: One moment, maestros! 1.180

THE TWO MASTERS *(turning back)*: At your service.

KÁUSHIKI: I request this as arbiter. Please present the actresses without drapery so that *the skill of all their limbs : the beauty of their entire bodies* shall be discernible.

THE TWO MASTERS: No need to have told us.

Exit the TWO MASTERS.

QUEEN *(looking at the* KING*)*: If only my worthy husband 1.185
exercised the same astuteness in political matters, that would be splendid.

RĀJĀ: devi,

alam anyathā gṛhītvā.
  na khalu, manasvini, mayā prayuktam idam.
prāyaḥ samāna|vidyāḥ
  paraspara|yaśaḥ|puro|bhāgāḥ. [20]

nepathye mṛdaṅga|dhvaniḥ. sarve karṇaṃ dadati.

PARIVRĀJIKĀ: hanta, pravṛttaṃ saṃgītakam! tathā hy eṣā

jīmūta|stanita|viśaṅkibhir mayūrair
  udgrīvair anurasitasya puṣkarasya
nirhrādiny upahita|madhyama|svar'|ôtthā
  māyūrī madayati mārjanā manāṃsi. [21]

RĀJĀ: devi, sāmayikā† bhavāmaḥ.

DEVĪ *(sva|gatam)*: ⌜aho, a|viṇao ajja|uttassa!⌟

sarve uttiṣṭhanti.

VIDŪṢAKAḤ *(apavārya)*: ⌜bho, dhīraṃ gaccha! mā tatta|bhodī Dhāriṇī visaṃvādaïssadi.⌟

RĀJĀ:

dhairy'|âvalambinam api
  tvarayati māṃ muraja|vādya|rāgo† 'yam
avatarataḥ siddhi|pathaṃ
  śabdaḥ sva|mano|rathasy' êva. [22]

iti niṣkrāntāḥ sarve.
iti prathamo 'ṅkaḥ.

KING: My queen,

Abandon this misconception.
This is not my doing at all, my sharp lady.
Men of equal scholarship will ever try
to outshine each other's glory.

A drum sounds off-stage. All listen.

KÁUSHIKI: Hark, the concert has begun! For this

rumble of the membrane* maddens our minds,
sonorously rising from the middle note,
seconded by peacocks crying with head on high
taking it for the roll of thunder they are so fond of.

KING: My queen, we shouldn't be late for the rendezvous.*

QUEEN *(to herself)*: Ah, my husband's tactlessness!

All get up.

JESTER *(aside)*: What ho! Restrain your step, lest her ladyship Dhárini go back on her word.

KING:

Though I try for restraint, the passionate sound
of the drum urges me on,
as if it were the noise of the chariot of my desires
racing on the road to success.

Exeunt all.
End of the first act.

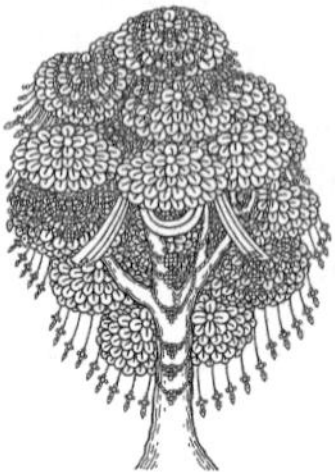

ACT TWO

2.1 *tataḥ praviśati saṃgīta|racanāyāṃ kṛtāyām āsana|sthaḥ sa|* VAYASYO RĀJĀ, DHĀRIṆĪ, PARIVRĀJIKĀ, *vibhavataś ca* PARIVĀRAḤ.

RĀJĀ: bhagavati, atra|bhavator ācāryayoḥ katarasya prathamam upadeśaṃ drakṣyāmaḥ?

PARIVRĀJIKĀ: nanu samāne 'pi jñāna|vṛddha|bhāve vayo|'dhikatvād Gaṇadāsaḥ puras|kāram arhati.

RĀJĀ: tena hi, Maudgalya, evam atra|bhavator āvedya niyogam a|śūnyaṃ kuru.

2.5 KAÑCUKĪ: yad ājñāpayati devaḥ.

iti niṣkrāntaḥ.

(praviśya)

GAṆADĀSAḤ: deva, Śarmiṣṭhāyāḥ kṛtir laya|madhyā catuṣ|padā. tasyāś caturtha|vastunaḥ prayogam eka|manāḥ śrotum arhati devaḥ.

RĀJĀ: ācārya|bahu|mānād avahito 'smi.

2.10 *iti niṣkrānto* GAṆADĀSAḤ.

RĀJĀ *(jan'|ântikam)*: vayasya,

nepathya|gṛha|gatāyāś†
  cakṣur darśana|samutsukaṃ tasyāḥ
saṃhartum a|dhīratayā
  vyavasitam iva me tiras|kariṇīm. [1]

The stage is set up for the concert. Enter the KING *seated,* accompanied by the* JESTER*; also* DHÁRINI, KÁUSHIKI, *and* ATTENDANTS *in order of rank.* 2.1

KING: Reverend lady, which of the two honorable masters shall first present his teaching?

KÁUSHIKI: They are peers in scholarship, but Gana·dasa is the senior by age, so clearly he deserves to go first.

KING: Well then, Maudgálya, say so to the two gentlemen, then go about your duties.

CHAMBERLAIN: As Your Majesty commands. 2.5

Exit the CHAMBERLAIN.

Enter GANA·DASA.

GANA·DASA: Majesty, there's a *chatush·pada* composition by Sharmíshtha in tempo moderato.* May it please Your Majesty to listen attentively to a performance of its fourth movement.*

KING: I'm riveted to the stage—because I respect you as a teacher.

Exit GANA·DASA. 2.10

KING *(confidentially)*: Comrade,

My eye is so eager to see her
standing in the back-stage*
that it is trying in its impatience
to remove the curtain, as it were.

VIDŪṢAKAḤ *(apavārya)*: ⌜uvaṭṭhidaṃ ṇaaṇa|mahu, saṃṇihida|makkhiaṃ a... tā a|ppamatto dāṇiṃ pekkha.⌟

tataḥ praviśaty ĀCĀRYA*/pratyavekṣyamāṇ'/âṅga/sauṣṭhavā* MĀLAVIKĀ.

2.15 VIDŪṢAKAḤ *(jan'/ântikam)*: ⌜pekkhadu bhavaṃ! ṇa khu se paḍicchandādo parihīadi mahuradā.⌟

RĀJĀ *(apavārya)*: vayasya,

citra|gatāyām asyāṃ
  kānti|visaṃvāda|śaṅki me hṛdayam.
saṃprati śithila|samādhiṃ
  manye, yen' êyam ālikhitā. [2]

GAṆADĀSAḤ: vatse, mukta|sādhvasā, sattva|sthā bhava!

RĀJĀ *(ātma/gatam)*: aho, sarva|sthān'|ân|a|vadyatā rūpasya! tathā hi,

2.20 dīrgh'|âkṣaṃ śarad|indu|kānti vadanaṃ;
  bāhū natāv aṃsayoḥ;
 saṃkṣiptaṃ nibiḍ'|ônnata|stanam uraḥ;
  pārśve pramṛṣṭe iva;
madhyaḥ pāṇi|mito; nitambi jaghanaṃ;
  pādāv arāl'|âṅgulī—
 chando nartayitur yath" âiva manasi,
  śliṣṭaṃ tath" âsyā vapuḥ. [3]

JESTER *(aside)*: Honey for your eyes is at hand, but the bees are near too... So keep your senses while you watch.

Enter MÁLAVIKA, *with* GANA·DASA *checking the grace* of her limbs.*

JESTER *(confidentially)*: Just look, sir! She's no less dainty than in the picture. 2.15

KING *(aside)*: Comrade,

While I knew her only from the picture,
    my heart was anxious that reality
    might disprove her allure.
Presently I think whoever painted her
    was not concentrating properly.

GANA·DASA: Daughter, let stage fright go and remain serene!

KING *(to himself)*: Wow, her beauty is impeccable all over! That is to say,

Her face gleams as the autumn moon;* 2.20
    her eyes are long;
    her arms don't jut out at the shoulder;
her chest is compact, with the breasts
    close together and arched upward;
    her flanks are smooth as if polished;
her waist measures but a hand;
    her hips sport broad buttocks;
    her toes curl—
her body is constituted
    just as the mind of a dance-master would wish.

MĀLAVIKĀ *(upagānaṃ kṛtvā catuṣ|pada|vastukaṃ gāyati)*:

⌜dul|laho pio; tassiṃ bhava, hiaa, ṇir|āsaṃ.
amho, apaṅgao me papphuraï kiṃ vi vāmao!†
eso so cira|diṭṭho kahaṃ uvaṇaïdavvo?
ṇāha, maṃ par'|âhīṇaṃ tui gaṇaa sa|tiṇhaṃ.⌟ [4]

iti yathā|rasam abhinayati.

VIDŪṢAKAḤ *(jan'|ântikam)*: ⌜bho, caü|ppada|vatthuaṃ du-vārī|kadua tui uvakkhitto via appā tatta|hodīe...⌟

2.25 RĀJĀ *(jan'|ântikam)*: sakhe, evam āvayor hṛdayam. anayā khalu

«janam imam anuraktaṃ viddhi, nāth'» êti geye
vacanam abhinayantyā sv'|âṅga|nirdeśa|pūrvam
praṇaya|gatim a|dṛṣṭvā Dhāriṇī|saṃnikarṣād
aham iva su|kumāra|prārthanā|vyājam uktaḥ. [5]

MĀLAVIKĀ *gīt'|ânte niṣkramitum ārabdhā.*

VIDŪṢAKAḤ: ⌜bhodi, ciṭṭha! kiṃ vi vo visumarido kama|bhedo. taṃ dāva pucchissaṃ.⌟

GAṆADĀSAḤ: vatse, sthīyatām! upadeśa|viśuddhā yāsyasi.

MÁLAVIKA *(sings the prelude, then sings the verse* from the* chatush·pada*)*:

> My darling is beyond reach;
> heart, hope no more for him.
> But lo, something makes my left eye's* corner throb!
> I see him now at last, but how to obtain him?
> My fate is in others' hands—but my lord,
> know that I thirst for you.

She enacts the above in the respective moods in turn.*

JESTER *(confidentially)*: Sirree, the lady's practically offered herself to you by way of that quatrain...

KING *(confidentially)*: Her heart and mine have the same desire, friend. Indeed, when she 2.25

> sang "know that I long for you, my lord,"
> acting out the words after pointing
> at her own body,
> she seems to have meant me by pretense
> of that tender entreaty,
> seeing no path for love* because
> Dhárini was present.

MÁLAVIKA *begins to withdraw at the end of the song.*

JESTER: Stop, miss! You've left out something from the proper sequence. I'd like to ask about that.

GANA·DASA: Stay, daughter! You shall go when your education has been declared free of faults.

2.30 MĀLAVIKĀ *nivṛtya sthitā.*

RĀJĀ *(ātma|gatam)*: aho, sarvāsv avasthāsu cārutā śobh"|āntaraṃ puṣyati! tathā hi

vāmaṃ saṃdhi|stimita|valayaṃ
  nyasya hastaṃ nitambe,
kṛtvā śyāmā|viṭapa|sadṛśaṃ
  srasta|muktaṃ dvitīyam,
pād'|âṅguṣṭh'|ālulita|kusume
  kuṭṭime pātit'|âkṣaṃ
nṛttād asyāḥ sthitam atitarāṃ
  kāntam ṛjv|āyat'|ârdham. [6]

DEVĪ: ⌜ṇaṃ Godama|vaaṇaṃ vi ajjo hiae karedi?⌟

GAṆADĀSAḤ: devi, mā m" âivam! *deva|pratyayāt* saṃbhāvyate sūkṣma|darśitā Gautamasya. paśya:

2.35 mando 'py a|mandatām eti
  saṃsargeṇa vipaścitaḥ,
paṅka|cchidaḥ phalasy' êva
  nikaṣeṇ' āvilaṃ payaḥ. [7]

*(*VIDŪṢAKAṂ *vilokya)* śṛṇumo vivakṣitam āryasya.

VIDŪṢAKAḤ *(*GAṆADĀSAṂ *vilokya)*: ⌜sakkhiṇiṃ dāva puccha. paccā jo mae kama|bhedo lakkhido, taṃ bhaṇissaṃ.⌟

GAṆADĀSAḤ: bhagavati, yathā|dṛṣṭam abhidhīyatāṃ—guṇo vā doṣo vā.

MÁLAVIKA *stops, turning back.* 2.30

KING *(to himself)*: Ah, her charm shines forth ever the better in different states! For now

With her left hand resting on her hip, bracelets
now motionless on the wrist,
with the other hand drooping freely
like a tassel of millet,*
with her eye cast down on the floor slabs
where her toes push the flowers about—
her stance, torso straight and erect,
is even lovelier than her dance.

QUEEN: Does Your Honor take even Gáutama seriously?

GANA·DASA: Not so, Your Majesty! Gáutama might actually be very perceptive, *what with His Majesty's faith in him ⁝ as a result of His Majesty's intellect.* Consider:

Even a dimwit may become bright 2.35
through contact with the canny,
as turbid water is made clear by rubbing
with the mud-cutter fruit.*

(looking at the JESTER*)* Let us hear what Your Honor has to say.

JESTER *(looking at* GANA·DASA*)*: Ask the arbiter first. Then I'll reveal the problem I noticed with the sequence.

GANA·DASA: Your reverence, state what you have observed—pro or contra.

PARIVRĀJIKĀ: yathā|darśanaṃ sarvam an|a|vadyam. kutaḥ:

2.40 aṅgair antar|nihita|vacanaiḥ
sūcitaḥ samyag arthaḥ;
pāda|nyāso layam anugatas;
tanmayatvaṃ raseṣu;
śākhā|yonir mṛdur abhinayas;
tad|vikalp'|ânuvṛttau
bhāvo bhāvaṃ nudati viṣayād,
rāga|bandhaḥ sa eva. [8]

GAṆADĀSAḤ: devaḥ kathaṃ manyate?

RĀJĀ: vayaṃ sva|pakṣe śithil'|âbhimānāḥ saṃvṛttāḥ.

GAṆADĀSAḤ: adya nartayit" âsmi!

upadeśaṃ viduḥ śuddhaṃ
santas tam upadeśinaḥ,
śyāmāyate na vidvatsu†
yaḥ, kāñcanam iv' âgniṣu. [9]

2.45 DEVĪ: ⌜diṭṭhiā parikkha'|ārāhaṇeṇa ajjo vaḍḍhaï.⌟

GAṆADĀSAḤ: devī|parigrahaś ca me vṛddhi|hetuḥ. *(*VIDŪṢAKAṂ *vilokya)* Gautama, vad' êdānīṃ yat te manasi vartate.

VIDŪṢAKAḤ: ⌜puḍham'|ôvadesa|daṃsaṇe puḍhamaṃ bamhaṇassa pūjā kādavvā. sā uṇa vo visumaridā?⌟

KÁUSHIKI: As far as I have observed, everything was impeccable. To wit:

> Her limbs, suffused by speech, 2.40
> perfectly expressed the message;
> her footwork stuck to the tempo;
> she identified with the moods;
> her acting was gentle, built on hand gestures;
> and in the succession of secondary emotions
> one replaced the other while the sentiment
> remained just as powerful.*

GANA·DASA: What is His Majesty's opinion?

KING: My respect for my own party is dwindling.

GANA·DASA: Now I'm a dance teacher in truth!

> Honest men know a teacher's teaching to be pure
> if, like gold in flames, it is not blackened
> in the presence of experts.

QUEEN: Fortune favors Your Honor as the judges are gratified. 2.45

GANA·DASA: Your Majesty's favor is the cause of my fortune. *(looking at the* JESTER*)* Gáutama, tell us now what's on your mind.

JESTER: Before the first presentation of what you have taught, a brahmin must be worshipped. Have you forgotten that?

PARIVRĀJIKĀ: aho, prayog'|âbhyantaraḥ praśnaḥ!

sarve prahasitāḥ. MĀLAVIKĀ *smitaṃ karoti.*

2.50 RĀJĀ *(ātma|gatam)*: upātta|sāraś cakṣuṣā me sva|viṣayaḥ. yad anena

smayamānam āyat'|âkṣyāḥ
  kiṃcid|abhivyakta|daśana|śobhi mukham
a|samagra|lakṣya|kesaram
  ucchvasad iva paṅkajaṃ dṛṣṭam. [10]

GAṆADĀSAḤ: mahā|brāhmaṇa, na khalu prathamaṃ nepathya|savanam† idam. anyathā kathaṃ tvāṃ dakṣiṇīyaṃ n' ârcayiṣyāmaḥ?

VIDŪṢAKAḤ: ⌜mae ṇāma muddha|cādaeṇa via sukkha|ghaṇa|ghajjide andarikkhe jala|pāṇaṃ icchidaṃ.⌟

PARIVRĀJIKĀ: evam eva.

2.55 VIDŪṢAKAḤ: ⌜teṇa hi paṇḍida|paridosa|paccaā mūḍha|jādī. jadi atta|bhodīe sohaṇaṃ bhaṇidaṃ, tado imaṃ se pāritosiaṃ paacchāmi.⌟

iti RĀJÑO *hastāt kaṭakam ākarṣati.*

DEVĪ: ⌜ciṭṭha dāva! guṇ'|andaraṃ a|jāṇanto kiṃ ti tumaṃ āharaṇaṃ desi?⌟

VIDŪṢAKAḤ: ⌜parakeraaṃ, ti karia.⌟

KÁUSHIKI: Ah, a question intimate with all the trade secrets of performance!

All laugh. MÁLAVIKA *smiles too.*

KING *(to himself)*: My eye has perceived the best of our 2.50
domain,* now that it has

> beheld the smiling mouth of this long-eyed girl,
> with the bright teeth somewhat exposed,
> like a lotus bud cracking
> to half-reveal its shining filaments.

GANA·DASA: Mighty brahmin, this was not a proper inaugural performance.* Else how could we have failed to worship your worthy personage?

JESTER: Yea, like a stupid *chátaka* bird* hearing the thunder, I hoped for a drink of water, but the clouds in the sky were dry.

KÁUSHIKI: Indeed.

JESTER: Then dimwits must rely* on the example of wise 2.55
people's satisfaction. Since your ladyship has called this splendid, I'll offer this reward to her.*

He pulls a bracelet off the KING*'s hand.*

QUEEN: Stop that! Why would you give a jewel when you cannot compare merits?

JESTER: Because it's not mine.

DEVĪ *(*ĀCĀRYAM *vilokya)*: ⌜ajja|Gaṇadāsa, ṇaṃ daṃsid'|ôvadesā vo sissā?⌟

2.60 GAṆADĀSAḤ: vatse, ehi, gacchāv' êdānīm.

MĀLAVIKĀ *sah'* ĀCĀRYEṆA *niṣkrāntā.*

VIDŪṢAKAḤ *(*RĀJĀNAM *vilokya, jan'|ântikam)*: ⌜ettio me madi|vihavo bhavantaṃ seviduṃ.⌟

RĀJĀ *(jan'|ântikam)*: alam, alaṃ paricchedena. ahaṃ hi

bhāgy'|âstam|ayam iv' âkṣṇor,
  hṛdayasya mah'|ôtsav'|âvasānam iva,
dvāra|pidhānam iva dhṛter
  manye tasyās tiras|karaṇaṃ. [11]

2.65 VIDŪṢAKAḤ *(jan'|ântikam)*: ⌜sāhu, tumaṃ dariddo āduro via vejjeṇa uvaṇīamāṇaṃ osahaṃ icchasi.⌟

(praviśya)

HARADATTAḤ: deva, madīyam idānīṃ prayogam avalokayituṃ kriyatāṃ prasādaḥ.

RĀJĀ *(ātma|gatam)*: avasito me darśan'|ârthaḥ. *(prakāśam, dākṣiṇyam avalambya)* nanu paryutsukā eva vayam.

HARADATTAḤ: anugṛhīto 'smi.

2.70 NEPATHYE VAITĀLIKAḤ: jayatu, jayatu devaḥ! upārūḍho madhy'|âhnaḥ. tathā hi,

QUEEN *(looking at the* DANCE TEACHER*)*: Honorable Gana·dasa, your pupil has finished demonstrating your instruction, hasn't she?

GANA·DASA: Come, daughter, let us depart now. 2.60

Exit MÁLAVIKA *with the* TEACHER.

JESTER *(looking at the* KING, *confidentially)*: That's how far my intellectual gifts could serve you, sir.

KING *(confidentially)*: No, don't draw the line here. For

> Like the fortune of my eyes dropping below
> the horizon,
> like a festival of my heart coming to an end,
> like the doors of my contentment closing
> is her disappearance to me.

JESTER *(confidentially)*: Right, so like a poor patient, you 2.65
want the doctor to bring you the medicine.*

Enter HARA·DATTA.

HARA·DATTA: Majesty, may it please you now to behold my presentation.

KING *(to himself)*: I'm done with what I had to see. *(aloud, courteously)* Why, I'm all agog.

HARA·DATTA: I am obliged.

OFF-STAGE A COURT BARD: Victory, victory to Your Majesty! 2.70
The day has risen to noon. That is to say,

patra|cchāyāsu haṃsā
mukulita|nayanā dīrghikā|padminīnāṃ;
saudhāny atyartha|tāpād
valabhi|paricaya|dveṣi|pārāvatāni;
bind'|ûtkṣepān pipāsuḥ
parisarati śikhī bhrāntimad vāri|yantraṃ;
sarvair usraiḥ samagras,†
tvam iva nṛpa|guṇair, dīpyate sapta|saptiḥ. [12]

VIDŪṢAKAḤ: ⌜avihā avihā, amhāṇaṃ bhoaṇa|velā saṃvuttā! atta|hodo vi. uida|vel"|âdikkame ciissakā dosaṃ udāharandi. Haradatta, kiṃ dāṇiṃ bhaṇasi?⌟

HARADATTAḤ: n' âsti mad|vacanasy' âvakāśo 'tra.

RĀJĀ (HARADATTAM *avalokya)*: tena hi tvadīyam upadeśaṃ śvo vayaṃ drakṣyāmaḥ. viśrāmyatu bhavān.

2.75 HARADATTAḤ: yad ājñāpayati devaḥ.

iti niṣkrāntaḥ.

DEVĪ: ⌜ṇivvattedu ajja|utto majjaṇa†|vihiṃ.⌟

VIDŪṢAKAḤ: ⌜bhodi, viseseṇa pāṇa|bhoaṇaṃ tuvarāvehi.⌟

PARIVRĀJIKĀ *(utthāya)*: svasti bhavate.

2.80 *iti sa|*PARIJANAYĀ DEVYĀ *saha niṣkrāntā.*

VIDŪṢAKAḤ: ⌜bho, ṇa kevalaṃ rūve, sippe vi a|ddudīyā Mālaviā!⌟

Eyes closed, the geese rest in the shade
of the pond's lotus leaves;
the pigeons recoil from the baking
plaster roofs of the palace;
the peacock hovers about the water-wheel*
hoping to swallow drops of the spray;
the seven-horsed sun blazes complete with all his
rays, like you with your royal virtues.*

JESTER: Oh my, it's time for me to eat! And for sir here, too. The medicos say it's wrong to disregard the proper time. What say you now, Hara·datta?

HARA·DATTA: I'm not in a position to say anything.

KING *(looking at* HARA·DATTA*)*: Well then, we shall see your instruction tomorrow. Your Honor may retire.

HARA·DATTA: As Your Majesty commands. 2.75

Exit HARA·DATTA.

QUEEN: Let my noble husband perform the ritual bath.

JESTER: Missus, make sure food and drinks are served particularly quickly.

KÁUSHIKI *(getting up)*: Fortune favor you, sire.

Exit KÁUSHIKI *along with the* QUEEN *and her* ATTENDANTS. 2.80

JESTER: What ho, this Málavika is unrivaled not just in beauty, but in skill too!

RĀJĀ: vayasya,

a|vyāja|sundarīṃ tāṃ
  vijñānena lalitena yojayatā
upakalpito vidhātrā
  bāṇaḥ Kāmasya viṣa|digdhaḥ. [13]

kiṃ bahunā? cintayitavyo 'smi te.

2.85 VIDŪṢAKAḤ: ⌜bhavadā vi ahaṃ! diḍhaṃ vipaṇi|kandū via me udar'|abbhandaraṃ dajjaï.⌟

RĀJĀ: evam eva bhavān suhṛd|arthe tvaratām.

VIDŪṢAKAḤ: ⌜gahīda|kkhaṇo mhi. kiṃ du meh'|āvalī|ṇiruddhā joṇhā via parāhīṇa|daṃsaṇā tatta|hodī Mālaviā. bhavaṃ vi sūṇā|pariaro via giddho āmisa|loluvo bhīruo a. tā aṇ|āduro bhavia kajja|siddhiṃ patthaanto me roasi.⌟

RĀJĀ: sakhe, katham an|āturo bhaviṣyāmi?

sarv'|ântaḥ|pura|vanitā|
  vyāpāra|pratinivṛtta|hṛdayasya
sā vāma|locanā me
  snehasy' âikāyanī|bhūtā. [14]

2.90 *iti niṣkrāntāḥ sarve.*

iti dvitīyo 'ṅkaḥ.

KING: Comrade,

When he imbued this innocent beauty
with the discipline of coquetry,
the creator crafted a poison-smeared arrow
for the god of love.

What else to say? Make sure you have a care for me.

JESTER: And you for me, sir! To be sure, the inside of my tummy is burning like a cauldron in the marketplace.* 2.85

KING: Kindly show the same drive in your patron's interest.

JESTER: I shall grab the first opportunity for it.* But glimpsing miss Málavika, like moonlight obscured by a bank of clouds, is controlled by other powers. While you, sir, are like a vulture hopping around the butchery, eager to snatch a gobbet but afraid. I'd much rather see you stop fretting and do something to achieve your aim.

KING: Friend, how am I to stop fretting?

My heart has turned away from dalliance
with any of the ladies in the harem,
And that pretty-eyed girl has become
the only aim of my love.

Exeunt all. 2.90

End of the second act.

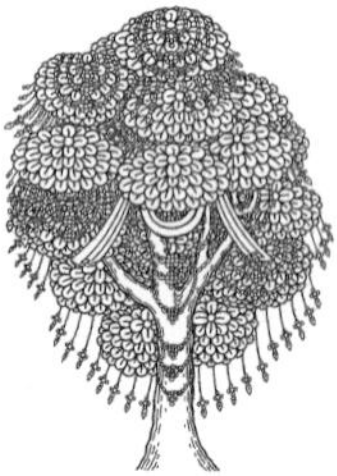

INTERLUDE

3.1 *tataḥ praviśati parivrājikāyāḥ* PARICĀRIKĀ.

PARICĀRIKĀ: ⌜āṇatta mhi bhaavadīe, «uvāaṇ'|attham bīja|pūraaṃ geṇhia āaccha» tti. tā jāva pamada|vaṇa|pāliaṃ Mahuariaṃ aṇṇesāmi.⌟ *(parikramy' âvalokya ca)* ⌜esā tavaṇī'|âsoaṃ oloantī ciṭṭhadi. jāva ṇaṃ saṃbhāvemi.⌟

tataḥ praviśaty UDYĀNA|PĀLIKĀ.

PARICĀRIKĀ *(upasṛtya)*: ⌜Mahuarie, avi suho de ujjāṇa|vvāvāro?⌟

3.5 MADHUKARIKĀ: ⌜amho, Samāhidiā! sahi, sāadaṃ de.⌟

SAMĀHITIKĀ: ⌜halā, bhaavadī āṇavedi: «a|ritta|pāṇiṇā amhārisa|jaṇeṇa tatta|hodī devī dakkhidavvā. tā bīja|pūraeṇa sussūsiduṃ icchāmi» tti.⌟

MADHUKARIKĀ: ⌜ṇaṃ saṃṇihidaṃ bīja|pūraaṃ. kahehi, aṇṇoṇṇa | saṃgharisidāṇaṃ ṇaṭṭ' | āariāṇaṃ uvadesaṃ dekkhia kadaro bhaavadīe pasaṃsido tti?⌟

SAMĀHITIKĀ: ⌜duve vi kila āamiṇo paoa|ṇipuṇā a. kiṃ du sissā|guṇa|visesena uṇṇamido Gaṇadāso.⌟

MADHUKARIKĀ: ⌜aha Mālaviā|gadaṃ kolīṇaṃ kiṃ suṇīadi?⌟

Enter SAMÁHITIKA, *the mendicant woman's handmaid.* 3.1

SAMÁHITIKA: Her reverence has ordered me to fetch her a citron* to offer as a present. So I'm now looking for Madhu·kárika, the custodian of the pleasure garden. *(walking about and looking)* There she stands, staring at the golden *ashóka* tree.* I'll just greet her.

Thereupon enter MADHU·KÁRIKA, *the custodian of the garden.*

SAMÁHITIKA *(approaching)*: Madhu·kárika, are you doing well in the garden?

MADHU·KÁRIKA: Hey, it's Samáhitika! Good to see you, my 3.5
friend.

SAMÁHITIKA: My dear, her reverence said: "The likes of me ought not to go empty-handed to see Her Majesty the queen. So I want to pay homage to her with a citron."

MADHU·KÁRIKA: Well, the citron tree is right here. But tell me, which of the two contending dance masters did her reverence approve after seeing what they had taught?

SAMÁHITIKA: Apparently both are learned, and skilful in presentation too. But Gana·dasa got a boost from the special merits of his pupil.

MADHU·KÁRIKA: And what does the grapevine* say about Málavika?

3.10 SAMĀHITIKĀ: ⌜baliaṃ khu s'|âhilāso tassiṃ bhaṭṭā. kevalaṃ devīe Dhāriṇīe cittaṃ rakkhamāṇo attaṇo pahuttaṇaṃ ṇa daṃsedi. Mālaviā vi imesu diahesu aṇuhūda|muttā via māladī|mālā milāamāṇā lakkhīadi. ado varaṃ ṇa jāṇe. visajjehi maṃ.⌟

MADHUKARIKĀ: ⌜edaṃ sāh" | âvalambidaṃ bīja | pūraaṃ geṇha.⌟

SAMĀHITIKĀ *(nāṭyena gṛhītvā)*: ⌜halā, tumaṃ vi ido† pesaladaraṃ† sāhu|jaṇa|sussūsāe phalaṃ pāehi.†⌟

iti prasthitā.

MADHUKARIKĀ: ⌜sahi, samaṃ evva gacchamha. ahaṃ vi imassa cirāamāṇa|kusum'|uggamassa tavaṇī'|âsoassa dohala|ṇimittaṃ devīe viṇṇavemi.⌟

3.15 SAMĀHITIKĀ: ⌜jujjaï. ahiāro khu tuha.⌟

iti niṣkrānte.

praveśakaḥ.

SAMÁHITIKA: Our lord is hooked on her pretty badly. The 3.10
only thing stopping him from standing up for his rights is his respect for queen Dhárini's feelings. And Málavika too seems to be wilting away these days like a used and discarded jasmine* garland. I know nothing more. You'd better let me go now.

MADHU·KÁRIKA: Grab this citron hanging down from the branch.

SAMÁHITIKA *(mimes plucking it)*: As for you, my dear, may you obtain a sweeter fruit for your service to the saintly lady.

She sets off.

MADHU·KÁRIKA: Let's go together, my dear. I'm going to report to the queen that this golden *ashóka* is still not in bloom because it's got the cravings.*

SAMÁHITIKA: Right. It's your responsibility after all. 3.15

Exeunt.

End of the interlude.

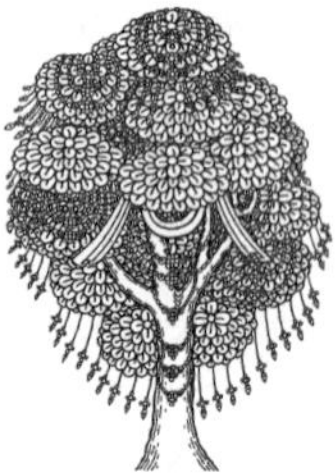

ACT THREE

tataḥ praviśati kāmayamān'|âvastho RĀJĀ VIDŪṢAKAŚ *ca.*

RĀJĀ *(ātmānaṃ vilokya)*:

3.20 śarīraṃ kṣāmaṃ syād
a|sati dayit"|āliṅgana|sukhe.
bhavet s'|âsraṃ cakṣuḥ,
kṣaṇam api na sā dṛśyata iti.
tayā sāraṅg'|âkṣyā
tvam asi na kadā cid virahitam—
prasakte nirvāṇe,
hṛdaya, paritāpaṃ vrajasi kim? [1]

VIDŪṢAKAḤ: ⌜alaṃ bhavado dhīradaṃ ujjhia paridevideṇa! diṭṭhā mae tatta|hodīe Mālaviāe pia|sahī Baülāvaliā. suṇāvidā a mae jaṃ bhavadā saṃdiṭṭhaṃ.†⌟

RĀJĀ: tataḥ kim uktavatī?

VIDŪṢAKAḤ: ⌜«viṇṇavehi bhaṭṭāraṃ: aṇugahīda mhi imiṇā ṇioeṇa. kiṃ du sā tavassiṇī devīe ahiadaraṃ rakkhīamāṇā ṇāa|rakkhido via ṇihī ṇa suhaṃ samāsādaïdavvā. taha vi ghaṭaïssaṃ» tti.⌟

RĀJĀ: bhagavan saṃkalpa|yone! pratibandhavatsv api viṣayeṣv abhiniveśya tathā praharasi, yathā jano 'yaṃ kāl'|ântara|kṣamo na bhavati! *(sa|vismayam)*

3.25 kva rujā hṛdaya|pramāthinī
kva ca te viśvasanīyam āyudham?
mṛdu tīkṣṇataraṃ yad ucyate,
tad idaṃ, Manmatha, dṛśyate tvayi. [2]

Enter the KING *in a lovelorn mood, with the* JESTER.

KING *(looking at himself)*:

My body may well be haggard, bereft of the joy 3.20
of my beloved's embrace.
My eyes may well brim with tears, never seeing her
for a moment.
But you, my heart, are ever united
with that doe-eyed girl—
why then do you burn with pain
in your ceaseless exaltation?

JESTER: Sir, will you please stop this effete moaning! I've seen Miss Málavika's friend Bakulávalika and told her your instructions.

KING: What did she say then?

JESTER: She said: "Tell our lord that this task is an honor for me. But the poor girl is now guarded even more closely by the queen, so like a trove guarded by a serpent, she won't be easy to reach. But I'll manage it anyway."

KING: My lord born in the womb of desire!* You make me fall for a goal riddled with obstacles, then whip me so I can't even bear waiting! *(bewildered)*

What's this heart-wrenching anguish 3.25
from your hope-inspiring weapons?*
They say the soft is harsher than the harsh—*
and you are the living proof of that, Love.

VIDŪṢAKAḤ: ⌜ṇaṃ bhaṇāmi, «tassiṃ sāhaṇijje† kido uvā'|ôvakkhevo» ti? tā pajjavatthāvedu bhavaṃ attāṇaṃ.⌟

RĀJĀ: ath' êmaṃ divasa|śeṣam ucita|vyāpāra|vimukhena cetasā kva nu khalu yāpayāmi?

VIDŪṢAKAḤ: ⌜ṇaṃ bhavaṃ ajja puḍhamaṃ vasand'|odāra|sūaāiṃ ratt'|âsoa|korakāiṃ uvāaṇaṃ pesia ṇava|vasand'|âvadār'|âvadeseṇa Irāvadīe Ṇiuṇiā|muheṇa patthido: «icchāmi ajja|utteṇa saha ḍol"|âhirohaṇaṃ aṇuhaviduṃ» ti. bhavadā vi se paḍiṇṇādaṃ. tā pamada|vaṇaṃ evva gacchamha.⌟

RĀJĀ: na kṣamam idam!

3.30 VIDŪṢAKAḤ: ⌜kahaṃ via?⌟

RĀJĀ: vayasya, nisarga|nipuṇāḥ striyaḥ. kathaṃ māṃ anya|saṃkrānta|hṛdayam upalālayantam api te sakhī na lakṣayiṣyati? ataḥ paśyāmi,

ucitaḥ praṇayo varaṃ vihantuṃ
  —bahavaḥ khaṇḍana|hetavo hi dṛṣṭāḥ—
upacāra|vidhir manasvinīnāṃ
  na tu pūrv' âbhyadhiko 'pi bhāva|śūnyaḥ. [3]

JESTER: Haven't I told you I've made a beginning with my strategy to achieve your aim? So why don't you compose yourself, sir.

KING: But where shall I pass the rest of the day, with no mind at all for my customary activities?

JESTER: Wasn't it just now that Irávati sent you a present of red *ashóka** buds, the first harbingers of the coming of spring? She has appealed to you through Nípunika on the occasion of the arrival of the new spring, saying, "I long to experience the pleasures of the garden swing with my noble husband." And you, sir, have promised her. So we're going straight to the pleasure garden.

KING: Impossible!

JESTER: How come? 3.30

KING: Women are perceptive by nature, comrade. How could your lady friend* not notice, even while I'm caressing her, that my heart has gone to someone else? So I deem that

it is more proper to reject the advances
of a clever woman—
for many excuses can be found for spurning her—
than merely to go through the motions
of ministering to her,
if more ardently than before, but without affection.

VIDŪṢAKAḤ: ⌜ṇ' ârihadi bhavaṃ ande|ura|paḍiṭṭhidaṃ dakkhiṇṇaṃ ekka|pade piṭṭhado kāduṃ.⌟

RĀJĀ *(vicintya)*: tena hi pramada|vana|mārgam ādeśaya.

VIDŪṢAKAḤ: ⌜ido ido bhavaṃ.⌟

ubhau parikrāmataḥ.

VIDŪṢAKAḤ: ⌜ṇaṃ edaṃ pamada|vaṇaṃ pavaṇa|bala|calāhiṃ pallav'|aṅgulihiṃ tuvaredi via bhavandaṃ pavesiduṃ.⌟

RĀJĀ *(sparśaṃ rūpayitvā)*: abhijātaḥ khalu vasantaḥ! sakhe, paśya:

āmattānāṃ śravaṇa|subhagaiḥ
  kūjitaiḥ kokilānāṃ
s'|ânukrośaṃ manasija|rujaḥ
  sahyatāṃ pṛcchat" êva
aṅge cūta|prasava|surabhir
  dakṣiṇo māruto me
sāndra|sparśaḥ kara|tala iva
  vyāpṛto mādhavena. [4]

VIDŪṢAKAḤ: ⌜pavisa ṇivvudi|lāhāa.⌟

ubhau praviśataḥ.

VIDŪṢAKAḤ: ⌜bho vaassa, avahāṇeṇa diṭṭhiṃ dehi! edaṃ khu bhavandaṃ vilohaïdu|kāmāe pamada|vaṇa|lacchīe juvaï|vesa|lajjāvaïttaaṃ vasanda|kusuma|ṇevatthaṃ gahīdaṃ.⌟

RĀJĀ: nanu vismayād avalokayāmi:

JESTER: Sir, you oughtn't to turn your heel suddenly on your customary gallantry to the ladies of the harem.

KING *(reflecting)*: Well then, lead me to the pleasure garden.

JESTER: This way, sir. 3.35

They walk about.

JESTER: Well, here's the pleasure garden, waving to you as it were with its frond-fingers swaying in the breeze, urging you to enter.

KING *(miming the feel of the breeze on his body)*: Spring is indeed noble! Look, friend:

> By the cooing of the lustful cuckoos,*
> so pleasant to the ear,
> the honeyed season all but enquires how I bear
> the pain of love;
> and caresses my body with his soothing palm,
> the southerly breeze scented with mango blossom.*

JESTER: Enter and find respite. 3.40

They enter the garden.

JESTER: What ho, comrade, look closely! Hoping to beguile you, the goddess of the pleasure garden has donned a robe of spring flowers to shame the dresses of damsels.

KING: I'm really astonished to see how

rakt'|âśoka|rucā viśeṣita|guṇo
bimb'|âdhar'|âlaktakaḥ;
pratyākhyāta|viśeṣakaṃ kurabakaṃ
śyām'|âvadāt'|âruṇam;
ākrāntā tilaka|kriy" âpi tilakair
lagna|dvireph'|âñjanaiḥ—
s'|âvajñ" êva mukha|prasādhana|vidhau
śrīr mādhavī yoṣitām. [5]

3.45 *ubhāv udyāna|śobhāṃ nirūpayataḥ. tataḥ praviśati paryutsukā* MĀLAVIKĀ.

MĀLAVIKĀ: ⌜a|viṇṇāda|hiaaṃ bhaṭṭāraṃ ahilasandī attaṇo vi dāva lajjemi. kudo vihavo siṇiddhassa sahī|aṇassa imaṃ vuttantaṃ ācakkhiduṃ? ṇa jāṇe, a|ppaḍīāra|guruaṃ veaṇaṃ kettiaṃ kālaṃ maaṇo maṃ ṇaïssadi tti.⌟ *(kati cit padāni gatvā)* ⌜kahiṃ khu patthida mhi?⌟

(vicintya) ⌜āḥ, saṃdiṭṭha mhi devīe, «Godama|cāvalādo ḍolā|paribbhaṭṭhāe sa|rujā maha calaṇā. tumaṃ dāva tavaṇī'|âsoassa dohalaṃ ṇivvaṭṭehi. jadi so pañca|ratt'|abbhantare kusumaṃ daṃsedi, tado ahaṃ tuha...⌟ *(antarā niḥśvasya)* ⌜ahilāsa|pūraïttaaṃ pasādaṃ dāissaṃ» ti. tā jāva ṇioa|bhūmiṃ puḍhamaṃ gadā homi. jāva aṇupadaṃ maha calaṇ'|âlaṅkāra|hatthāe Baülāvaliāe āandavvaṃ, paridevaïssaṃ dāva vīsaddhaṃ muhuttaaṃ.⌟

iti parikrāmati.

the luster of the red *ashóka* excels
the brightness of lac* on *bimba** lips;
the *kúrabaka,** red poised against dark,*
outclasses face marks;*
the *tílaka* flowers,* bees clinging to them
like black dots, surpass forehead designs—*
the goddess of spring seems to deride the ways
women embellish their faces.

They mime admiring the beauty of the garden. Then enter MÁLAVIKA *in a flurry.* 3.45

MÁLAVIKA: I'm actually ashamed of myself for hankering after our lord when I don't know his heart. And where do I find the strength to tell this story to my cherished friends?* And I don't know how long Love will continue to afflict me with this pain, the worse for being irremediable. *(walking a few steps)* Now where was I going?

(thinking) Ah yes, the queen has told me, "I have fallen off the swing because of Gáutama's clumsiness, and my feet hurt. So I want you to fulfill the golden *ashóka*'s craving. If its flowers appear within five days, then I'll grant you… *(sighing)* the fulfillment of your desire." So first I must go where I can carry out my task. Bakulávalika is supposed to be coming right after me, bringing the foot jewelry,* but until she arrives, I have a moment to lament undisturbed.

She walks about.

VIDŪṢAKAḤ *(dṛṣṭvā)*: ⌜hī hī! iaṃ khu sīhu|pāṇ'|uvvejidassa macchaṇḍiā uvaṇadā!⌟

RĀJĀ: aye, kim etat?

VIDŪṢAKAḤ: ⌜esā khu ṇ' âdi|pajjatta|vesā pajjussuā via eāiṇī Mālaviā a|dūre vaṭṭadi.⌟

RĀJĀ *(sa|harṣam)*: katham, Mālavikā?

VIDŪṢAKAḤ: ⌜aha iṃ?⌟

RĀJĀ: śakyam idānīṃ jīvitam avalambitum.

tvad upalabhya samīpa|gatāṃ priyāṃ
  hṛdayaṃ ucchvasitaṃ mama viklavam,
taru|vṛtāṃ pathikasya jal'|ârthinaḥ
  saritam ārasitād iva sārasāt. [6]

atha kva tatra|bhavatī?

VIDŪṢAKAḤ: ⌜esā ṇaṃ taru|rāi|majjhādo ṇikkandā ido evva āacchadi.⌟

RĀJĀ *(vilokya sa|harṣaṃ)*: vayasya, paśyāmy enām.

vipulaṃ nitamba|bimbe,
  madhye kṣāmaṃ, samunnataṃ kucayoḥ,
atyāyataṃ nayanayor—
  mama jīvitam etad āyāti. [7]

sakhe, pūrvasmād avasth"|ântaram upārūḍhā tatra|bhavatī. tathā hi,

JESTER *(seeing her)*: Hee hee! Brown sugar's at hand if you're addled with rum!*

KING: Eh, what's that?

JESTER: None other than Málavika, standing nearby on her own, wearing scant jewelry* and looking flustered.

KING *(with glee)*: What, Málavika?

JESTER: Exactly.

KING: Now I can hang on to my life.

> Learning from you that my darling is near,
> my infirm heart has found respite,
> like a parched traveler's who knows
>   by a crane's calls*
> that a river awaits beyond the trees.

But where is she?

JESTER: Don't you see her coming our way as she ambles out of that row of trees?

KING *(looking, with glee)*: I see her now, comrade.

> Here comes my very life, melon buttocks broad
>   and waist thin,
> breasts perkily rising, eyes very long.*

My friend, she's quite different* than she used to be. That is to say,

śara|kāṇḍa|pāṇḍu|gaṇḍa|
  sthal" êyam ābhāti parimit'|ābharaṇā,
mādhava|pariṇata|patrā-
  katipaya|kusum" êva kunda|latā. [8]

VIDŪṢAKAḤ: ⌜esā vi bhavaṃ via maaṇa|vvāhiṇā parāmiṭṭhā bhavissadi.⌟

RĀJĀ: sauhārdam evaṃ paśyati.

MĀLAVIKĀ: ⌜aaṃ so lalia|dohal'|âvekkhī a|gahida|kusuma|ṇevattho ukkaṇṭhidāe maha aṇukaredi asoo. jāva se pacchāa|sīdale silā|paṭṭae ṇisaṇṇā attāṇaṃ viṇodemi.⌟

3.65 VIDŪṢAKAḤ: ⌜sudaṃ bhavadā? «ukkaṇṭhida mhi» tti tatta|hodīe mantidaṃ.⌟

RĀJĀ: n' âitāvatā bhavantaṃ prasanna|tarkaṃ manye. kutaḥ:

voḍhā kurabaka|rajasāṃ
  kisalaya|puṭa|bheda|śīkar'|ânugataḥ
a|nimittām utkaṇṭhām
  api janayati Malaya|vāto 'yam. [9]

MĀLAVIK" *ôpaviṣṭā.*

RĀJĀ: vayasya, itas tāvat! āvāṃ lat"|ântaritau bhavāvaḥ.

3.70 VIDŪṢAKAḤ: ⌜Irāvadiṃ via a|dūre pekkhāmi.⌟

RĀJĀ: na hi kamalinīṃ dṛṣṭvā grāham avekṣate mataṅga|jaḥ.

iti vilokayan sthitaḥ.

With her cheeks sallow like the stalk of a reed*
and hardly wearing jewelry,
she appears like a jasmine creeper* late in the spring,*
with leaves aged* and but a few flowers left.

JESTER: She too, like you, may have been ravaged by the sickness of love.

KING: You see it that way because you're my friend.

MÁLAVIKA: This *ashóka* tree is like me in its longing, hoping for the fulfillment of its gentle craving and bereft of its flowery robe. I'll just sit down on this slab of rock, cool in the tree's shade, to while away my time.

JESTER: Did you hear that? She's talking about her longing. 3.65

KING: That isn't enough to prove your speculation. For:

Bearing *kúrabaka* pollen and bringing
dewdrops from bursting buds,
this wind from the south* can incite yearning
without any further cause.

MÁLAVIKA *sits down.*

KING: Over here, comrade! Let's hide behind the bush.

JESTER: I think I see Irávati coming. 3.70

KING: The elephant doesn't care for the crocodile when he sees a lotus plant.*

He stays there, peeking.

MĀLAVIKĀ: ⌜hiaa, ṇir|avalambādo maṇo|rahādo virama! kiṃ maṃ āāsesi?⌟

VIDŪṢAKO RĀJĀNAM *avekṣate.*

3.75 RĀJĀ: priye, paśya vāmatāṃ snehasya!

autsukya|hetuṃ vivṛṇoṣi na tvaṃ,
tattv'|âvabodh'|âika|raso† na tarkaḥ.
tath" âpi, rambh"|ōru, karomi lakṣyam
ātmānaṃ eṣāṃ paridevitānām. [10]

VIDŪṢAKAḤ: ⌜saṃpadaṃ bhavado ṇis|saṃsaaṃ bhavissadi. esā appida|maaṇa|saṃdesā vivitte ṇaṃ* Baülāvaliā uvaṭṭhidā.⌟

RĀJĀ: api smared asmad|abhyarthanām?

VIDŪṢAKAḤ: ⌜kiṃ dāṇiṃ esā dāsīe duhidā tuha guruaṃ saṃdesaṃ visumaredi? ahaṃ vi dāva ṇa visumaremi!⌟

3.80 *(praviśya caraṇ'|âlaṅkāra|hastā)*

BAKULĀVALIKĀ: ⌜avi suhaṃ sahīe?⌟

MĀLAVIKĀ: ⌜amho, Baülāvaliā! sahi, sāadaṃ de. uvavisa.⌟

BAKULĀVALIKĀ *(upaviśya†)*: ⌜halā, tumaṃ dāva dāṇiṃ devīe joggadāe ṇiuttā. tā ekkaṃ de calaṇaṃ uvaṇehi, jāva† s'|âlattaaṃ, sa|ṇeuraṃ karemi.⌟

MĀLAVIKĀ *(sva|gatam)*: ⌜hiaa, alaṃ suhidadāe, «aaṃ vihavo uvaṭṭhido» tti! kahaṃ dāṇiṃ attāṇaṃ mocaeaṃ?† aha vā edaṃ evva maha miccu|maṇḍaṇaṃ bhavissadi?⌟

MÁLAVIKA: Give up this groundless desire, my heart! Why do you nag me?

The JESTER *looks pointedly at the* KING.

KING: My dear, see how devious love is! 3.75

> Neither do you reveal the cause of your yearning,
> nor does logic, which cares only for exposing facts.
> Nonetheless I take it, lovely-legged girl,*
> that I am the object of your lamentations.

JESTER: Soon you won't doubt any more. Here comes Bakulávalika to see her in private, carrying your love message.

KING: Will she remember my request?

JESTER: How could this lowly wench forget your illustrious message? Even I can't get it out of my mind!

Enter BAKULÁVALIKA *with foot ornaments in hand.* 3.80

BAKULÁVALIKA: Are you all right, my friend?

MÁLAVIKA: Oh, it's Bakulávalika! Good to see you, dear. Sit down.

BAKULÁVALIKA *(sitting down)*: Well, my dear, at last the queen gives you a fitting task.* So put up a foot and let me paint it with lac and put an anklet on.

MÁLAVIKA *(to herself)*: Don't be so thrilled, my heart, at this promotion! How am I to get out of this? Or shall these very jewels be my funeral decoration?

BAKULĀVALIKĀ: ⌜kiṃ viāresi? ussuā khu imassa tavaṇī'|âsoassa kusum'|uggame devī.⌟

RĀJĀ: katham? aśoka|dohada|nimitto 'yam ārambhaḥ?

VIDŪṢAKAḤ: ⌜kiṃ khu ṇa jāṇāsi, a|kālaṇādo devī imaṃ ande|ura|ṇevatthena ṇa saṃjoaïssadi tti?⌟

MĀLAVIKĀ: ⌜halā, marisehi dāva ṇaṃ!⌟

iti pādam upaharati.

BAKULĀVALIKĀ: ⌜aï, sarīraṃ si me.⌟

iti nāṭyena caraṇa|saṃskāram ārabhate.

RĀJĀ:

caraṇ'|ânta|niveśitāṃ priyāyāḥ
  sa|rasāṃ paśya, vayasya, rāga|rekhām,
prathamām iva pallava|prasūtiṃ
  Hara|dagdhasya Manobhava|drumasya. [11]

VIDŪṢAKAḤ: ⌜calaṇ'|âṇurūvo khu tatta|hodīe ahiāro uvakkhitto.⌟

RĀJĀ: saṃyag āha bhavān.

nava|kisalaya|rāgeṇ' âgra|pādena bālā
  sphurita|nakha|rucā dvau hantum arhaty anena:
a|kusumitam aśokaṃ dohad'|âpekṣayā vā
  praṇamita|śirasaṃ vā kāntaṃ ārdr'|âparādham. [12]

BAKULÁVALIKA: Why are you dithering? Her Majesty is eager to see this golden *ashóka* bloom.

KING: What? So this is all about the *ashóka*'s craving?

JESTER: Surely you realize that the queen wouldn't dress her up in harem finery* for no reason.

MÁLAVIKA: Sorry about this,* my dear!

She offers up her foot.

BAKULÁVALIKA: Come on, you and I are one body.

She mimes starting to decorate her foot.

KING:

Look, my friend, this juicy line of crimson
drawn round the edge of my darling's foot
is like the first sprout bursting on the tree of Love
that has been scorched by Shiva.*

JESTER: The task the lady's been given is indeed worthy of her feet.

KING: That's right.

Two targets merit a kick from this maiden's foot,
flushed like a new sprout and
flashing with bright nails:
the flowerless *ashóka* because of its craving,
or a lover bowing his head
because of his fresh misdeed.*

VIDŪṢAKAḤ: ⌜paharissadi tatta|hodī tumaṃ avaraddhaṃ.⌟

RĀJĀ: pratigṛhītaṃ vacaḥ *siddhi|darśino* brāhmaṇasya.

tataḥ praviśati yukta|mad" ÊRĀVATĪ CEṬĪ *ca.*

IRĀVATĪ: ⌜hañje Ṇiuṇie, suṇāmi bahuso, mado kila itthiā| jaṇassa visesa|maṇḍaṇaṃ tti. avi sacco loa|vādo aaṃ?⌟

3.100 NIPUṆIKĀ: ⌜puḍhamaṃ loa|vādo evva. ajja uṇa sacco saṃvṛtto.⌟

IRĀVATĪ: ⌜alaṃ maï siṇeheṇa. kudo dāṇiṃ avagadaṃ, dolā| gharaṃ puḍhamaṃ gado bhaṭṭa tti?⌟

NIPUṆIKĀ: ⌜bhaṭṭiṇīe a|khaṇḍidādo paṇaādo.⌟

IRĀVATĪ: ⌜alaṃ sevāe! majjhatthadaṃ geṇhia bhaṇāhi.⌟

NIPUṆIKĀ: ⌜vasand'|ôvāaṇa|loluveṇa ajja|Godameṇa kahidaṃ. tuvaradu bhaṭṭiṇī.⌟

3.105 IRĀVATĪ *(avasthā|sadṛśaṃ parikramya)*: ⌜hañje,† madeṇa kilāmiamāṇaṃ attāṇaṃ ajja|utta|daṃsaṇe hiaaṃ tuvarāvedi. calaṇā uṇa ṇa magge pasarandi.⌟

NIPUṆIKĀ: ⌜ṇaṃ sampatta mha ḍolā|gharaaṃ.⌟

IRĀVATĪ: ⌜Ṇiuṇie, ṇa ettha ajja|utto dīsaï!⌟

JESTER: She'll kick you for sure if you wrong her.

KING: I acknowledge the words of the *clairvoyant* brahmin *who foresees my success.*

Enter IRÁVATI, *tipsily, with a* MAID.

IRÁVATI: Nípunika, I've often heard that tipsiness makes a woman all the more beautiful. Is this folk saying true?

NÍPUNIKA: It used to be just a folk saying, but today you 3.100
prove it true.

IRÁVATI: Away with your niceties. How do you know my husband's already gone to the swing gazebo?

NÍPUNIKA: From his unfailing love for you, mistress.*

IRÁVATI: Cut the flattery! Speak objectively.

NÍPUNIKA: Mister Gáutama told me, eager for spring gifts.* Hurry, mistress.

IRÁVATI *(walking about in a way befitting her state*)*: Girl, 3.105
my heart is languid with drink and would have me rush to see my noble husband. But my feet just won't stay on the path.

NÍPUNIKA: Why, we've just arrived at the swing gazebo.

IRÁVATI: Nípunika, I don't see my noble husband here!

NIPUṆIKĀ: ⌜oloedu bhaṭṭiṇī. parihāsa|ṇimittaṃ kahiṃ vi gūḍheṇa bhaṭṭiṇā hodavvaṃ. amhe vi imaṃ piaṅgu|la-dā|parikkhittaṃ asoa|silā|paṭṭaaṃ pavisamha.⌟

IRĀVATĪ *tathā karoti.*

3.110 NIPUṆIKĀ *(parikramya, vilokya)*: ⌜oloedu bhaṭṭiṇī! cūd'|aṅkuraṃ viciṇṇandīṇaṃ amhāṇaṃ pipīliāhiṃ daṃsidaṃ.⌟

IRĀVATĪ: ⌜kiṃ via edaṃ?⌟

NIPUṆIKĀ: ⌜esā Baülāvaliā asoa|pāava|cchāāe Mālaviāe calaṇ'|âlaṅ|kāraṃ ṇivvaṭṭedi.⌟

IRĀVATĪ *(śaṅkāṃ rūpayitvā)*: ⌜a|bhūmī iaṃ Mālaviāe. kathaṃ ettha takkesi?⌟

NIPUṆIKĀ: ⌜takkemi, dolā|paribbhaṃsidāe sa|ruja|calaṇāe devīe asoa|dohad'|âhiāre Mālaviā ṇiutta tti. aṇṇahā kahaṃ devī saaṃ dhāriaṃ ṇeura|jualaṃ pariaṇassa abbhaṇujāṇissadi?⌟

3.115 IRĀVATĪ: ⌜mahadī khu se saṃbhāvaṇā.⌟

NIPUṆIKĀ: ⌜kiṃ ṇa aṇṇesīadi bhaṭṭā?⌟

IRĀVATĪ: ⌜hañje, ṇa me calaṇā aṇṇado pavaṭṭandi, maṇo vi kiṃ vi† viāredi. āsaṅkidassa dāva antaṃ gamissaṃ.⌟ *(*MĀLAVIKĀṂ *nirvarṇya, ātma|gatam)* ⌜ṭhāṇe khu kādaraṃ me hiaaṃ.⌟

NÍPUNIKA: Look around, mistress. His Majesty must have hidden somewhere for a laugh. We should just sit down under the *ashóka* tree on this slab of rock surrounded by *priyángu* plants.*

IRÁVATI *does so.*

NÍPUNIKA *(walking about, looking)*: Look out, mistress! The 3.110
ants have bitten while we were busy looking for mango sprouts.*

IRÁVATI: What are you nattering about?

NÍPUNIKA: Here's Bakulávalika decorating Málavika's feet in the shade of the *ashóka* tree.

IRÁVATI *(miming suspicion)*: Málavika shouldn't be here. What do you think?

NÍPUNIKA: What I think is that when Her Majesty had fallen off the swing and her foot was hurt, she commissioned Málavika to fulfill the *ashóka*'s craving. Why else would she have permitted a maid to use that pair of anklets she usually wears herself?

IRÁVATI: A great honor to her indeed. 3.115

NÍPUNIKA: Shouldn't we look for His Majesty?

IRÁVATI: Girl, my legs just won't carry me anywhere. And I'm having funny thoughts. First I'll find out about my suspicions. *(looking at* MÁLAVIKA, *to herself)* She's certainly one to be wary of.

BAKULĀVALIKĀ *(caraṇaṃ darśayantī)*: ⌜avi roadi de aaṃ rāa|rehā|viṇṇāso?⌟

MĀLAVIKĀ: ⌜attaṇo calaṇa|gado tti lajjemi ṇaṃ pasaṃsiduṃ. kahehi, keṇa pasāhaṇa|kalāe ahiviṇīd" âsi?⌟

BAKULĀVALIKĀ: ⌜ettha khu bhaṭṭiṇo sissa mhi.⌟

VIDŪṢAKAḤ: ⌜tuvarehi dāṇiṃ guru|dakkhiṇāe.⌟

MĀLAVIKĀ: ⌜diṭṭhiā ṇa gavvidā si.⌟

BAKULĀVALIKĀ: ⌜uvades'|âṇurūve calaṇe lambhia ajja gavvidā bhavissaṃ.⌟ *(ātma/gatam)* ⌜hanta, siddhaṃ me doccaṃ.⌟ *(prakāśaṃ, rāgaṃ vilokya†)* ⌜sahi, ekkassa de calaṇassa avasido rāga|ṇikkhevo.† kevalaṃ muha|mārudo lambhaïdavvo. aha vā... pavādaṃ evva edaṃ ṭhāṇaṃ.⌟

RĀJĀ: sakhe, paśya, paśya!

ārdr'|âlaktakam asyāś
  caraṇaṃ mukha|mārutena vījayitum
pratipannaḥ prathamataraḥ
  samprati sev"|âvakāśo me. [13]

VIDŪṢAKAḤ: ⌜kudo de aṇusao? ciraṃ bhavadā edaṃ kameṇa aṇuhodavvaṃ.⌟

BAKULĀVALIKĀ: ⌜sahi, aruṇa|sada|pattaṃ via sohadi de calaṇaṃ. savvahā *bhaṭṭiṇo aṅka/parivaṭṭiṇī* hohi.⌟

IRĀVATĪ NIPUṆIKĀ/*mukham avekṣate.*

RĀJĀ: mam' êyam āśīḥ.

BAKULÁVALIKA *(pointing at* MÁLAVIKA*'s foot)*: Do you like the pattern I painted?

MÁLAVIKA: I'm only shy to praise it because it's on my own foot. Tell me, who instructed you in the art of makeup?

BAKULÁVALIKA: Actually I learned from His Majesty.

JESTER: Hurry, ask for the teacher's fee.

MÁLAVIKA: I applaud your lack of arrogance.

BAKULÁVALIKA: I shall be proud now that I have worked on feet worthy of what I learned. *(to herself)* Right, that takes care of my mission. *(aloud, inspecting the paint)* I've finished painting one foot, my friend. Now I just need to blow on it. Or... we have a breeze here, anyway.

KING: Look, my friend, look!

> This could be a prime opportunity to serve her:
> to blow with my mouth on the wet paint
> on her foot.

JESTER: Why so sorry? In due course you'll have plenty of opportunity to do so.

BAKULÁVALIKA: My friend, your foot is as pretty as a red waterlily. May you ever *remain by our lord's side : rock on your husband's lap.*

IRÁVATI *glances at* NÍPUNIKA*'s face.*

KING: Just what I pray for.

3.130 MĀLAVIKĀ: ⌜halā, a|vaaṇīaṃ mantesi!⌟

BAKULĀVALIKĀ: ⌜mantidavvaṃ evva mae mantidaṃ.⌟

MĀLAVIKĀ: ⌜piā khu ahaṃ tuha.⌟

BAKULĀVALIKĀ: ⌜ṇa kevalaṃ maha...⌟

MĀLAVIKĀ: ⌜kassa vā aṇṇassa?⌟

3.135 BAKULĀVALIKĀ: ⌜guṇesu ahiṇivesiṇo bhaṭṭiṇo vi.⌟

MĀLAVIKĀ: ⌜alīaṃ mantesi. edaṃ evva maï ṇ' atthi.⌟

BAKULĀVALIKĀ: ⌜saccaṃ tui ṇ' atthi? bhaṭṭiṇo kisesu dara†|paṇḍuresu aṅgesu dīsaï!⌟

NIPUṆIKĀ: ⌜puḍhama|gaṇidaṃ via had'|āsāe uttaraṃ.⌟

BAKULĀVALIKĀ: ⌜aṇurāo aṇurāeṇa parikkhidavvo tti su|jaṇa|vaaṇaṃ pamāṇī|karehi.⌟

3.140 MĀLAVIKĀ: ⌜kiṃ attaṇo chandeṇa mantesi?⌟

BAKULĀVALIKĀ: ⌜ṇa hi! bhaṭṭiṇo edāiṃ paṇaa|miduāiṃ akkharāiṃ bimb'|andaridāiṃ.⌟

MÁLAVIKA: You mustn't say things like that, my dear! 3.130

BAKULÁVALIKA: I only said what was right and proper.

MÁLAVIKA: You're really fond of me.

BAKULÁVALIKA: Not only I...

MÁLAVIKA: But who else?

BAKULÁVALIKA: Our lord who is partial to special charms. 3.135

MÁLAVIKA: That isn't true. He isn't... like that about me.

BAKULÁVALIKA: Isn't he indeed? But his emaciated and pallid body shows it!

NÍPUNIKA: The hussy's answer sounds ready-made.

BAKULÁVALIKA: You should go by what good folk say: that love's test is love.

MÁLAVIKA: Are you saying what you hope to be so? 3.140

BAKULÁVALIKA: No way! What I say is a reflection of our lord's words tender with love.

MĀLAVIKĀ: ⌜halā, deviṃ vicintia ṇa me hiaaṃ vissasidi.⌟

BAKULĀVALIKĀ: ⌜muddhe, bhamara|saṃbādho† tti vasand'|âvadāra|savvassaṃ kiṃ ṇa cūda|ppasavo odaṃsidavvo?⌟

MĀLAVIKĀ: ⌜tumaṃ dāva duj|jāde maha accanda|sahāiṇī hohi.⌟

3.145 BAKULĀVALIKĀ: ⌜vimadda|surahī Baülāvaliā khu ahaṃ.⌟

RĀJĀ: sādhu, Bakulāvalike, sādhu!

bhāva|jñān'|ânantaraṃ prastutena,
 pratyākhyāne datta|yukt'|ôttareṇa
vākyen' êyaṃ sthāpitā sve nideśe.
 sthāne prāṇāḥ kāmināṃ dūty|adhīnāḥ. [14]

IRĀVATĪ: ⌜hañje, pekkha! kāridā evva edassiṃ Baülāvaliāe padaṃ Mālaviā!⌟

NIPUṆIKĀ: ⌜bhaṭṭiṇi, ṇivviārassa vi ussuattaṇa|jaṇao uvadeso.⌟

3.150 IRĀVATĪ: ⌜ṭhāṇe khu saṃkidaṃ me hiaaṃ. gahid'|atthā aṇ|antaraṃ cintaïssaṃ.⌟

BAKULĀVALIKĀ: ⌜eso dudīo vi de ṇivutta|paḍikammo calaṇo. jāva duve vi sa|ṇeure karemi.⌟ *(nāṭyeṇa nūpura|yugalam āmucya)* ⌜halā, uṭṭhehi. aṇuciṭṭha devīe asoa|viāsaïttaaṃ ṇioaṃ.⌟

MÁLAVIKA: My heart despairs when I think of the queen, my dear.

BAKULÁVALIKA: Silly girl, the mango flower, the very essence of the coming of spring, is thronged by bees, but who would hesitate to use it for an ear ornament?*

MÁLAVIKA: Then you must help me by all means if the going gets rough.

BAKULÁVALIKA: I'm justly named after the *bákula* flower,* 3.145
whose scent only grows stronger when bruised.

KING: Bravo, Bakulávalika, bravo!

She sounded her out, then introduced the message;
she cancelled her objections by witty replies;
her speech brought her under her sway.
True indeed: the lives of lovers depend
on the go-between.

IRÁVATI: Just look at that, girl! Bakulávalika has practically pushed Málavika toward him!

NÍPUNIKA: Majesty, her counsel would awaken desire even if there were none to begin with.

IRÁVATI: So my heart did have reason to suspect. I shall fig- 3.150
ure out what to do next when I've got the details.

BAKULÁVALIKA: There, I'm done with your other foot. I'll just put anklets on both. *(She mimes putting a pair of anklets on* MÁLAVIKA.*)* Get up, my dear. Do the queen's command and make the *ashóka* bloom.*

ubhe uttiṣṭhataḥ.

IRĀVATĪ: ⌜sudaṃ, devīe ṇioo tti. hodu dāṇiṃ.⌟

BAKULĀVALIKĀ: ⌜eso uvārūḍha|rāo uvabhoa|kkhamo purado de vaṭṭadi—⌟

3.155 MĀLAVIKĀ *(sa|harṣam)*: ⌜kiṃ bhaṭṭā?⌟

BAKULĀVALIKĀ *(sa|smitam)*: ⌜ṇa dāva bhaṭṭā. eso asoa|sāh''|âvalambī pallava|guccho. odaṃsehi dāva ṇaṃ.⌟

VIDŪṢAKAḤ: ⌜avi sudaṃ bhavadā?⌟

RĀJĀ: sakhe, paryāptam etāvatā kāminām.

an|ātur'|ôtkaṇṭhitayoḥ prasidhyatā
samāgamen' âpi ratir na māṃ prati;
paraspara|prāpti|nirāśayor varaṃ
śarīra|nāśo 'pi sam'|ânurāgayoḥ. [15]

3.160 MĀLAVIKĀ *racita|pallav'|âvataṃsā sa|līlam aśokāya pādaṃ prahinoti.*

RĀJĀ: vayasya,

ādāya karṇa|kisalayam
asmād iyam atra caraṇam arpayati.
ubhayoḥ sadṛśa|vinimayād
ātmānaṃ vañcitaṃ manye. [16]

They stand up.

IRÁVATI: Now we know it's the queen's command. Let it be for now.

BAKULÁVALIKA: Right before you, flushed with passion, ready to be ravished—

MÁLAVIKA *(with delight)*: The king?

BAKULÁVALIKA *(with a smile)*: Well no, not the king. This spray of leaves hanging down from the *ashóka* branch. Why don't you use it for an ear ornament?

JESTER: Did you hear that, sir?

KING: That much is enough for any lover, my friend.

> If one of a pair were enamored
> and the other unafflicted,
> their union, though successful,
> would seem joyless to me.
> Better if both perish, equally in love,
> but each hopeless to attain the other.

After attaching the sprout to her ear, MÁLAVIKA *playfully swings her foot at the tree.*

KING: Comrade,

> She accepts a twig to put behind her ear,
> and offers her foot in return.
> I feel she's broken faith with me, for they have
> exchanged equal pledges.

MĀLAVIKĀ: ⌜avi ṇāma amhāṇaṃ saṃbhāvaṇā sa|phalā have?⌟

BAKULĀVALIKĀ: ⌜halā, ṇ' atthi de doso. ṇig|guṇo aaṃ asoo, jaï kusum|ubbheda|manthara bhave, jo īrisaṃ calaṇa| sak|kāraṃ lahei.⌟

RĀJĀ:

3.165 anena tanu|madhyayā
mukhara|nūpur'|ārāviṇā
nav'|âmbu|ruha|komale-
na caraṇena saṃbhāvitaḥ,
aśoka, yadi sadya e-
va kusumair na saṃpatsyase
vṛthā vahasi dohadaṃ-
lalita|kāmi|sādhāraṇam. [17]

sakhe, vacan'|âvasara|pūrvakaṃ praveṣṭum icchāmi.

VIDŪṢAKAḤ: ⌜ehi, ṇaṃ parihāsaïssaṃ!⌟

ubhau praveśaṃ kurutaḥ.

NIPUṆIKĀ: ⌜bhaṭṭiṇi, bhaṭṭā ettha evva pavisadi!⌟

3.170 IRĀVATĪ: ⌜evvaṃ puḍhamaṃ mama cintidaṃ hiaeṇa.⌟

VIDŪṢAKAḤ *(upasṛtya)*: ⌜hodi, juttaṃ† ṇāma atta|hodo pia| vaasso asoo *vāma*|pādeṇa tāḍeduṃ?⌟

UBHE *(sa|saṃbhramam)*: ⌜amho, bhaṭṭā!⌟

VIDŪṢAKAḤ: ⌜Baülāvalie, gahid'|atthāe tue atta|hodī īrisaṃ a|viṇaaṃ karandī kīsa ṇa ṇivāridā?⌟

MÁLAVIKA: I wonder if our worship will be fruitful.

BAKULÁVALIKA: My dear, you are not at fault. It would be disgraceful of the *ashóka* to dawdle with flowering when he's been honored by such a foot.

KING:

Ashóka, if you don't burst out in flowers 3.165
this very instant
after this slender-waisted girl has honored you
with her foot—
tender as a fresh lotus and
jingling with noisy anklets—
then your craving, so like a playful lover's,*
is pointless.

My friend, I need an opportunity to join them.

JESTER: Come, I'll play a joke on them.

They enter. *

NÍPUNIKA: Mistress, His Majesty is coming right here!

IRÁVATI: My heart suspected that from the beginning. 3.170

JESTER *(approaching the girls)*: Lady, do you really call it proper to strike his lordship's dear friend the *ashóka* tree with your *left : lovely* foot?*

THE TWO GIRLS *(in a flurry)*: Look, the king!

JESTER: Bakulávalika, you know how things stand.* Why didn't you prevent this lady from committing such a breach of propriety?

MĀLAVIKĀ *bhayaṃ rūpayati.*

3.175 NIPUṆIKĀ: ⌜bhaṭṭiṇi, pekkha, kiṃ paüttaṃ ajja|Godameṇa!⌟

IRĀVATĪ: ⌜kahaṃ bamha|bandhū aṇṇahā jīvissadi?⌟

BAKULĀVALIKĀ: ⌜ajja, esā devīe ṇioaṃ aṇuciṭṭhadi. edassiṃ adikkame paravadī iaṃ. pasīdadu bhaṭṭā.⌟

ātmanā samam enāṃ praṇipātayati.

RĀJĀ: yady evam, an|aparāddh" âsi. uttiṣṭha, bhadre.

3.180 *hastena gṛhītv" ôtthāpayati.*

VIDŪṢAKAḤ: ⌜jujjaï. devī ettha māṇaïdavvā.⌟

RĀJĀ *(vihasya)*:

kisalaya|mṛdor, vilāsini,
 kaṭhine nihitasya pādapa|skandhe
caraṇasya na te bādhā
 samprati, vām'|ōru, vāmasya? [18]

MĀLAVIKĀ *lajjāṃ nāṭayati.*

3.185 IRĀVATĪ: ⌜aho, ṇavaṇīda|kappa|hidao ajja|utto!⌟

MÁLAVIKA *mimes dismay.*

NÍPUNIKA: Majesty, see what Mister Gáutama is up to! 3.175

IRÁVATI: How else could the son-of-a-brahmin* make a living?

BAKULÁVALIKA: Mister, she's following the queen's orders. She did not commit this transgression of her own will. May our lord relent.

She falls to the ground and makes MÁLAVIKA *do the same.*

KING: In that case you are not at fault. Stand, fair maid.

He takes MÁLAVIKA *by the hand and pulls her to her feet.** 3.180

JESTER: Fair's fair. Got to respect the queen here.*

KING *(laughing)*:

> Playful girl, I hope the touch of the tree's hard trunk
> Has not left your left foot, tender as a frond, in pain.

MÁLAVIKA *mimes coyness.*

IRÁVATI: Ah, my noble husband with his heart like butter! 3.185

MĀLAVIKĀ: ⌜Baülāvalie, ehi. aṇuṭṭhidaṃ attaṇo ṇioaṃ devīe ṇivedemha.⌟

BAKULĀVALIKĀ: ⌜teṇa hi viṇṇavehi bhaṭṭāraṃ, «visajjehi» tti.⌟

RĀJĀ: bhadre, yāsyasi. mama tāvad utpann'|âvasaram arthitvaṃ śrūyatām.

BAKULĀVALIKĀ: ⌜avahidā suṇāhi! āṇavedu bhaṭṭā.⌟

RĀJĀ:

3.190 dhṛti|puṣpam ayam api jano
  badhnāti na tādṛśaṃ cirāt prabhṛti.
sparś'|âmṛtena pūraya
  dohadam asy' âpy an|anya|ruceḥ! [19]

IRĀVATĪ *(sahas" ôpasṛtya)*: ⌜pūrehi, pūrehi! asoo kusumaṃ ṇa daṃsedi: aaṃ uṇa pupphaï phalaï a!⌟

sarve IRĀVATĪṂ *dṛṣṭvā saṃbhrāntāḥ.*

RĀJĀ *(apavārya)*: vayasya, kā pratipattir atra?

VIDŪṢAKAḤ: ⌜kiṃ aṇṇaṃ? jaṅghā|balaṃ evva!⌟

3.195 IRĀVATĪ: ⌜Baülāvalie, sāhu tue uvakkandaṃ! Mālavie, tumaṃ dāva ajja|uttaṃ sa|phala|patthaṇaṃ karehi!⌟

UBHE: ⌜pasīdadu bhaṭṭiṇī! kā vaaṃ† bhaṭṭiṇo paṇaa|pariggahassa?⌟

MÁLAVIKA: Come on, Bakulávalika. Let's go report to the queen that we've carried out her order.

BAKULÁVALIKA: Then ask our lord's leave to withdraw.

KING: You shall go in a moment. But first listen to my entreaty now that I have an opportunity for it.

BAKULÁVALIKA: You listen sharp! Command us, sire.

KING:

> I too have not worn the blossom of satisfaction,
> passionate as the tree's, for a long time.
> I have no interest in anything else: fulfill my
> craving too with the nectar of your touch!

IRÁVATI *(approaching suddenly)*: Fulfill indeed! The *ashóka* may not bloom, but this one is sure to flower, and fruit, too!

All are bewildered to see IRÁVATI.

KING *(aside)*: What to do now, comrade?

JESTER: What else? Leg it!

IRÁVATI: Bakulávalika, nice job! Málavika, better make sure you satisfy my noble husband's request!

THE TWO GIRLS: Mercy, my lady! Who are we to deserve the king's affection?

iti niṣkrānte.

IRĀVATĪ: ⌜aho, a|vissasaṇīā purisā! mae khu attaṇo vañcaṇā|vaaṇaṃ pamāṇī|karia vāha|gīda|rattāe hariṇīe via a|saṅkidāe idaṃ ṇa viṇṇādaṃ.⌟

VIDŪṢAKAḤ *(jan'|ântikam)*: ⌜bho, paḍivajjehi kiṃ vi! kamma|gahideṇa kumbhīlaeṇa «saṃdhi|ccheaṇe sikkhido mhi» tti vattavvaṃ hodi.⌟

3.200 RĀJĀ: sundari, na me Mālavikayā kaś cid arthaḥ. mayā «tvaṃ cirāyas'» îti yathā|kathaṃ|cid ātmā vinoditaḥ.

IRĀVATĪ: ⌜vissasaṇīo si! mae ṇa viṇṇādaṃ, «īrisaṃ viṇoda|vatthuaṃ ajja|utteṇa uvaladdhaṃ» ti. aṇṇahā manda|bhāiṇīe evvaṃ ṇa karīadi.⌟

VIDŪṢAKAḤ: ⌜mā dāva atta|hodī atta|hodo dakkhiṇṇassa uvarohaṃ bhaṇadu. samāvatti|diṭṭheṇa devīe pariaṇeṇa saṃkahā vi jaï avarāho ṭhāviadi… ettha tumaṃ evva pamāṇaṃ.⌟

IRĀVATĪ: ⌜ṇaṃ saṃkahā ṇāma hodu! kiṃ tti attāṇaṃ āasaïssaṃ?⌟

iti ruṣā prasthitā.

3.205 RĀJĀ *(anusaran)*: prasīdatu bhavatī!

IRĀVATĪ *raśanā|saṃdita|caraṇā vrajati eva.*

Exeunt THE TWO GIRLS.

IRÁVATI: Oh, never trust a man! I believed your perfidious message and suspected nothing of all this, like a doe attracted by a hunter's singing.

JESTER *(confidentially)*: Hey, find some riposte! When an adulterer is caught in the act, what else can he say but: "I'm just practicing conjugation."*

KING: My pretty, I have no business with Málavika at all. It's just because you were late that I had to find something to amuse myself. 3.200

IRÁVATI: Very believable! I'm so sorry I didn't know my noble husband had found such a pretty thing to amuse himself with. Else my humble self wouldn't have been so lowly as to intrude.

JESTER: Please, my lady, don't say you intruded when his lordship was just being civil to these girls. If you consider it a sin to engage in conversation with the queen's maids, whom we met by chance… then you alone know best.

IRÁVATI: Call it conversation if you will! Why should I fret any more?

She sets off in a huff.

KING *(hurrying after her)*: Relent, my lady! 3.205

IRÁVATI*'s girdle* entangles her legs, but she goes on nonetheless.*

RĀJĀ: sundari, na śobhate praṇayi|jane nirapekṣatā!

IRĀVATĪ: ⌜saṭha, a|vissasaṇīa|hiao si!⌟

RĀJĀ:

śaṭha iti mayi tāvad astu
  te paricayavaty avadhīraṇā, priye.
caraṇa|patitayā na, caṇḍi,
  tāṃ visṛjasi mekhalay" âpi yācitā? [20]

3.210 IRĀVATĪ: ⌜iaṃ vi had'|āsā tumaṃ evva aṇusaradi!⌟

iti raśanām ādāya RĀJĀNAṂ *tāḍayitum icchati.*

RĀJĀ: eṣā

bāṣp'|āsārā hema|kāñcī|guṇena
  śroṇī|bimbād a|vyapekṣā|cyutena
caṇḍī caṇḍaṃ hantum abhyudyatā māṃ,
  vidyud|dāmnā megha|rāj" îva Vindhyam. [21]

IRĀVATĪ: ⌜kiṃ maṃ evva bhūo vi avaraddhaṃ karesi?⌟

3.215 *iti sa|raśanaṃ hastam avalambate.*

RĀJĀ:

aparādhini mayi daṇḍaṃ
  saṃharasi kim udyataṃ, kuṭila|keśi?
vardhayasi vilasitaṃ tvaṃ,
  dāsa|janāy' âtra kupyasi ca. [22]

KING: My pretty, it isn't worthy of you to disregard one who is besotted with you!

IRÁVATI: You're a fickle-hearted rascal!

KING:

Darling, you may well call me a rascal
with contempt bred by our familiarity.*
But will you not release that contempt, fierce lady,
when even your girdle falls at your feet to beg you?

IRÁVATI: Even the blasted girdle takes your side!

She removes the girdle and makes to hit the KING *with it.*

KING: Behold

the fierce lady raining tears,
    about to strike me fiercely
with a whip of the golden girdle
carelessly slipped from her swelling hips—
like a cloud bank about to strike
the Vindhya mountain with a cord of lightning.

IRÁVATI: So even that is my fault?

She lets down her hand holding the girdle.

KING:

Why do you revoke the intended punishment
    when I have offended you, tangle-haired lady?
You are ever more graceful, yet you're still angry
    with your servant here.

(ātma|gatam) nūnam idam idānīm anujñātam.

iti pādayoḥ patati.

IRĀVATĪ: ⌜ṇa khu ime Mālaviā|calaṇā, jā de pharisa|dohalaṃ pūraïssandi!⌟

iti niṣkrāntā saha CEṬYĀ.

VIDŪṢAKAḤ: ⌜bho, uṭṭhehi. kida|pasādo si.⌟

RĀJĀ *(utthāy'* ÊRĀVATĪM *a|paśyan)*: kathaṃ, gat" âiva priyā?

VIDŪṢAKAḤ: ⌜vaassa, diṭṭhiā imassa a|viṇaassa a|ppasaṇṇā gadā. tā vaaṃ sigghaṃ avakkamāma, jāva Aṅgārao rāsiṃ via sā aṇuvakkaṃ ṇa karedi.⌟

RĀJĀ: aho Manasija|vaiṣamyam!

manye priy"|āhṛta|manās
tasyāḥ praṇipāta|laṅghanaṃ sevām:
evaṃ hi praṇayavatī
sā śakyaṃ upekṣituṃ kupitā. [23]

iti parikramya niṣkrāntāḥ sarve. *

iti tṛtīyo 'ṅkaḥ.

(to himself) Surely she'll let me now.

With that he falls at her feet.

IRÁVATI: It's Málavika's feet that should fulfill your craving, not these!

Exit IRÁVATI *with her* MAID.

JESTER: Hey, stand up. You've been absolved.

KING *(standing up to see* IRÁVATI *gone)*: What, my darling has left?

JESTER: Comrade, fortunately she left impolitely,* without forgiving you. So let's be off quickly before she returns, like the fiery planet Mars entering a sign of the zodiac in retrograde.*

KING: Ah, the perversity of Love!

Because my mind dwells on Málavika, I consider
Irávati's rejection of my entreaty a kindness:
This way, though she loves me,
I can now ignore her because she's angry.

They walk about and leave.

End of the third act.

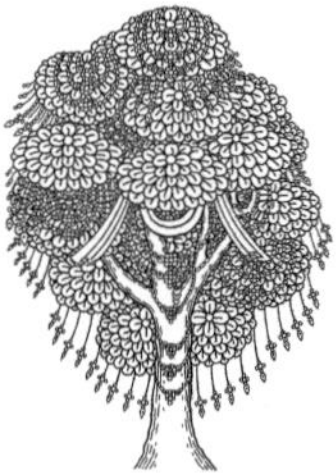

ACT FOUR

4.1 *tataḥ praviśati paryutsuko* RĀJĀ PRATĪHĀRĪ *ca.*

RĀJĀ *(ātma|gatam)*:

tām āśritya śruti|patha|gatām
  āsthayā baddha|mūlaḥ,
saṃprāptāyāṃ nayana|viṣayaṃ
  rūḍha|rāga|pravālaḥ,
hasta|sparśair mukulita iva
  vyakta|rom'|ôdgamatvāt—
kuryāt klāntaṃ† manasija|tarur
  māṃ rasa|jñaṃ phalasya! [1]

(prakāśam) sakhe Gautama!

4.5 PRATĪHĀRĪ: ⌜jedu, jedu bhaṭṭā! a|saṃṇihido Godamo.⌟

RĀJĀ *(ātma|gatam)*: āḥ, Mālavikā | vṛttānta | jñānāya mayā preṣitaḥ.

VIDŪṢAKAḤ *(praviśya)*: ⌜jedu bhavaṃ!⌟

RĀJĀ: Jayasene, jānīhi tāvat kva devī Dhāriṇī, kathaṃ vā sa|ruja|caraṇatvād vinodyata iti.

PRATĪHĀRĪ: ⌜jaṃ devo āṇavedi.⌟

4.10 *iti niṣkrāntā.*

RĀJĀ: sakhe, ko vṛttāntas tatra|bhavatyās te sakhyāḥ?

VIDŪṢAKAḤ: ⌜jo biḍāla|gahidāe parahudiāe.⌟

Enter the KING *in agitation, with* JAYA·SENA *the usheress.* 4.1

KING *(to himself)*:

It took root on the strength of my hope for her
when I first heard of her.
It blushed with the new growth of passion
when she came within reach of my eyes.
It burst out in buds as it were when I was covered
in goose bumps at the touch of her hand.
May that tree of love permit me, fatigued with
desire, to savor its fruit!

(aloud) My dear Gáutama!

JAYA·SENA: Victory, victory, sire! Gáutama is not here. 4.5

KING *(to himself)*: Ah, I sent him to find out what had happened to Málavika.

JESTER *(entering)*: Victory, sir!

KING: Jaya·sena, please find out where Queen Dhárini is and how she is being diverted from the pain in her feet.

JAYA·SENA: As Your Majesty commands.

Exit. 4.10

KING: What's befallen your lady friend, comrade?

JESTER: Just what befalls the cuckoo in the cat's paws.

RĀJĀ *(sa|viṣādam)*: katham iva?

VIDŪṢAKAḤ: ⌜sā khu tāvassiṇī tāe piṅgal'|acchīe sāra|bhaṇḍa|bhū|gharae miccu|muhe via ṇikkhittā.⌟

4.15 RĀJĀ: nanu mat|saṃparkam upalabhya?

VIDŪṢAKAḤ: ⌜aha iṃ?⌟

RĀJĀ: ka evaṃ vimukho 'smākaṃ, yena caṇḍī|kṛtā devī?

VIDŪṢAKAḤ: ⌜suṇādu bhavaṃ. parivvājiā me kahedi: hio kila tatta|hodī Irāvadī ruj"|akkanta|calaṇaṃ deviṃ suha|pucchiā āadā.⌟

RĀJĀ: tatas tataḥ?

4.20 VIDŪṢAKAḤ: ⌜tado sā devīe pucchidā: «kiṃ ṇu ṇ' āloido jaṇo vallaho?» tti. tado tāe uttaṃ: «maṃdo† vā de uvaāro, jaṃ de parianassa vallahattaṇaṃ jāṇantī vi pucchasi» tti.⌟

RĀJĀ: nirbhedād ṛte 'pi Mālavikāyām ayam upanyāsaḥ śaṅkayati. tatas tataḥ?†

VIDŪṢAKAḤ: ⌜tado tāe aṇubandhijjamāṇāe bhavado a|viṇaaṃ andareṇa parigahid'|atthā kidā devī.⌟

RĀJĀ: aho dīrgha|roṣatā tatra|bhavatyāḥ! ataḥ paraṃ kathaya.

VIDŪṢAKAḤ: ⌜ado varaṃ kiṃ? Mālaviā Baülāvaliā a ṇiala|vādīo a|diṭṭha|sujja|pādaṃ pādāla|vāsaṃ ṇāa|kaṇṇaāo via aṇuhonti.⌟

KING *(dejectedly)*: What do you mean?

JESTER: The yellow-eyed predator has cast the poor creature in the underground strongroom as if into the jaws of death.

KING: Because she found out I had met her, right? 4.15

JESTER: Obviously.

KING: Who hates us enough to have incensed the queen?

JESTER: Listen, sir. The mendicant woman tells me she heard that yesterday the lady Irávati came to the queen, who was incapacitated by pain, to ask if she was any better.

KING: And then?

JESTER: Then the queen asked her: "Hasn't he met you, 4.20
his favorite?" She replied: "Not too polite, are you, to ask when you know full well that his favorite is your maidservant."*

KING: The way she put that casts suspicion on Málavika without actually speaking it out. What then?

JESTER: Then Her Majesty kept insisting until she explained everything about your misconduct.

KING: Ah, the lady is relentless in her anger! Carry on with the story.

JESTER: What's there to carry on? Málavika and Bakulávalika have been fettered and cast into the sunless netherworld to live like *naga* girls.*

4.25 RĀJĀ: kaṣṭaṃ, kaṣṭam!

madhura|ravā† parabhṛtikā†
  bhramarī ca vibuddha|cūta|saṃginyau
koṭaram a|kāla|vṛṣṭyā
  prabala|puro|vātayā gamite. [2]

vayasya, apy atra kasya cid upakramasya gatiḥ syāt?

VIDŪṢAKAḤ: ⌜kahaṃ bhavissadi? jaṃ sāra|bhaṇḍa|vāudā Māhaviā devīe saṃdiṭṭhā: «maha aṅgulīaa|muddaṃ a|dekkhia ṇa mottavvā tue had'|āsā Mālaviā Baülāvaliā a» tti.⌟

RĀJĀ *(niḥśvasya, sa|parāmarśam)*: sakhe, kim atra pratikartavyam?

4.30 VIDŪṢAKAḤ *(vicintya)*: ⌜atthi ettha uvāo…⌟

RĀJĀ: ka iva?

VIDŪṢAKAḤ *(sa|dṛṣṭi|kṣepam)*: ⌜ko vi a|diṭṭho suṇādi. kaṇṇe de kahemi.⌟ *(upaśliṣya, karṇe)* ⌜evvaṃ via!⌟

RĀJĀ: suṣṭhu cintitam! prayujyatāṃ siddhaye!

praviśya

4.35 PRATĪHĀRĪ: ⌜deva, pavāda|saaṇe devī ṇisaṇṇā ratta|candaṇa|dhāriṇā pariaṇa|hattha|gadeṇa calaṇeṇa bhaavadīe kahāhiṃ viṇodīamāṇā ciṭṭhadi.⌟

KING: Dreadful! 4.25

> The sweet-voiced cuckoo and the little bee
> came to the quickened mango tree,
> and have been driven into a hollow
> by an untimely gale and rain.

Can any stratagem succeed now, comrade?

JESTER: How could it? This is what the queen commanded Mádhavika, the lady in charge of the strongroom: "You mustn't release this wretched Málavika and Bakulávalika unless you see the seal of my signet ring."

KING *(with a sigh, thoughtfully)*: How could we counter that, my friend?

JESTER *(reflecting)*: There is a way... 4.30

KING: How's that?

JESTER *(glancing around)*: Someone we can't see might hear. I'll whisper in your ear. *(bending close to the king, whispering)* That's how!

KING: Great idea! Go about it and may you succeed!

Enter JAYA·SENA.

JAYA·SENA: Majesty, the queen is resting on a bed placed 4.35
in the breeze, her feet covered in red sandal paste* and held in the hands of her attendants. The reverend lady is diverting her with stories.

RĀJĀ: asmat|praveśa|yogyo 'yam avasaraḥ.

VIDŪṢAKAḤ: ⌜tā gacchadu bhavaṃ. ahaṃ vi deviṃ pekkhi-dum a|ritta|pāṇī bhavissaṃ.⌟

RĀJĀ: Jayasenāyās tāvat saṃvedya gaccha!

VIDŪṢAKAḤ: ⌜taha.⌟ *(karṇe)* ⌜hodi, evvaṃ via.⌟

4.40 *iti niṣkrāntaḥ.*

RĀJĀ: Jayasene, pravāta|śayana|mārgam ādeśaya.

PRATĪHĀRĪ: ⌜ido, ido devo.⌟

tataḥ praviśati śayana|sthā DEVĪ, PARIVRĀJIKĀ, *vibhavataś ca* PARIVĀRAḤ.

DEVĪ: ⌜bhaavadi, ramaṇijjaṃ kahā|vatthu. tado tado?⌟

4.45 PARIVRĀJIKĀ *(sa|dṛṣṭi|kṣepam)*: ataḥ paraṃ punaḥ kathayi-ṣyāmi. atra|bhavān Vidiś"|ēśvaraḥ prāptaḥ.

DEVĪ: ⌜amho, bhaṭṭā!⌟

abhyutthātum icchati.

KING: Then it's proper for me to visit her now.

JESTER: Go ahead, sir. Me, I'll just pick up something so I don't come before the queen empty-handed.

KING: Fill in Jaya·sena before you go!

JESTER: Right. *(whispering in her ear)* Lady, that's the plan.

Exit. 4.40

KING: Jaya·sena, lead me to that bed in the breeze.

JAYA·SENA: This way, Your Majesty.

Enter the QUEEN *reclining on a bed,** KÁUSHIKI, *and* ATTENDANTS *in order of rank.*

QUEEN: Reverend lady, I enjoy the plot of this story. Do carry on.

KÁUSHIKI *(glancing around)*: I'll tell you the rest another 4.45
time. The king of Vídisha has come.

QUEEN: Ah, it's my husband!

She attempts to stand.

RĀJĀ: alam, alam upacāra|yantraṇayā.

an|ucita|nūpura|viraham
  n" ârhasi tapanīya|pīṭhik"|ālambi
caraṇaṃ rujā parītaṃ,
  kala|bhāṣiṇi, māṃ ca pīḍayitum. [3]

4.50 DEVĪ: ⌜jedu ajja|utto!⌟

PARIVRĀJIKĀ: vijayatāṃ devaḥ.

RĀJĀ (PARIVRĀJIKĀṂ *praṇamya, upaviśya)*: devi, api sahyā te vedanā?

DEVĪ: ⌜atthi me viseso.⌟

tataḥ praviśati yajñ'|ôpavīta|saṃvīt'|âṅguṣṭhaḥ, saṃbhrānto VIDŪṢAKAḤ.

4.55 VIDŪṢAKAḤ: ⌜parittāadu! sappeṇa daṭṭho mhi!⌟

sarve viṣaṇṇāḥ.

RĀJĀ: kaṣṭaṃ, kaṣṭam! kva bhavān paribhrāntaḥ?

VIDŪṢAKAḤ: ⌜deviṃ pekkhissaṃ tti āāra|puppha|ggahaṇa|kālaṇādo pamada|vaṇaṃ gado mhi—⌟

DEVĪ: ⌜haddhī, haddhī! ahaṃ evva bamhaṇassa jīvita|saṃsaa|ṇimittaṃ jādā.⌟

KING: Enough, stop exerting yourself with formality.

Sweet-voiced lady, please do not torment me
by tormenting your aching foot:
it's unused to being divested of its anklets,
and worthy of a golden stool to rest on.

QUEEN: Victory to my noble husband! 4.50

KÁUSHIKI: May Your Majesty be victorious.

KING *(bowing to* KÁUSHIKI *and taking a seat)*: My queen, is your pain bearable?

QUEEN: I do feel better.

Enter the JESTER *in distress, with his sacrificial thread* wrapped around his thumb.*

JESTER: Save me! I've been bitten by a snake! 4.55

All despair.

KING: What a calamity! Where have you been traipsing, sir?

JESTER: I was going to visit the queen, so I went to the pleasure garden to grab some flowers to offer—

QUEEN: Alas, alas! It's because of me that a brahmin is now in danger of his life.

VIDŪṢAKAḤ: ⌜tahiṃ asoa|tthavaa|kālaṇādo pasāride dakkhiṇa|hatthe koḍara|ṇiggadeṇa sappa|rūviṇā kāleṇa daṭṭho mhi. ṇaṃ edāiṃ† duve dasaṇa|padāiṃ.⌟

iti daṃśaṃ darśayati.

PARIVRĀJIKĀ: tena hi «daṃśa|cchedaḥ pūrva|karma» iti śrūyate. sa tāvad asya kriyatām.

chedo daṃśasya, dāho vā,
  kṣater vā rakta|mokṣaṇam—
etāni daṣṭa|mātrāṇām
  āyuṣyāḥ pratipattayaḥ. [4]

RĀJĀ: samprati viṣa|vaidyānāṃ karma. Jayasene, kṣipram ānīyatāṃ Dhruvasiddhiḥ.

PRATĪHĀRĪ: ⌜jaṃ devo āṇavedi.⌟

iti niṣkrāntā.

VIDŪṢAKAḤ: ⌜aho, pāveṇa miccuṇā gahido mhi!⌟

RĀJĀ: mā kātaro bhūḥ! a|viṣo 'pi kadā cid daṃśo bhavet.

VIDŪṢAKAḤ: ⌜kahaṃ ṇa bhāissaṃ? simasimāanti me aṅgāiṃ!⌟

iti viṣa|vegaṃ rūpayati.

DEVĪ: ⌜hā, daṃsidaṃ a|suhaṃ viāreṇa. halā, avalambaha ṇaṃ!⌟

JESTER: There as I reached out with my right hand to pluck 4.60
a cluster of *ashóka* blossoms, death—in the form of a snake—emerged from a hollow* and bit it. Look, here are the two fang-marks.

He shows the bite.

KÁUSHIKI: Well, textbooks say the first thing to do is to cut the bite. Do that to him first.

> Cutting the bite, cauterization
> or bleeding the wound out—*
> These are the life-saving procedures to apply
> immediately after a bite.

KING: That's a job for poison specialists. Jaya·sena, get Dhruva·siddhi at once.

JAYA·SENA: As Your Majesty commands. 4.65

Exit.

JESTER: Oh no, I'm in the clutches of vile death!

KING: Don't be faint! Sometimes the bite is without venom.

JESTER: How could I not be scared? My limbs are all aquiver!

*He mimes the effects of poisoning.** 4.70

QUEEN: Alas, the symptoms portend no good. Girls, support him!

PARIJANAḤ *sa|sambhramam avalambate.*

VIDŪṢAKAḤ *(*RĀJĀNAM *avalokya)*: ⌜bho, bhavado bālattaṇādo pia|vaasso mhi. taṃ viāria a|puttāe me jaṇaṇīe joga|kkhemaṃ vahehi.⌟

RĀJĀ: mā bhaiṣīḥ! a|cirāt tvāṃ viṣa|vaidyaś cikitsate. sthiro bhava!

4.75 PRATĪHĀRĪ *(praviśya)*: ⌜deva, āṇāvido Dhuvasiddhī viṇṇavedi, «iha evva āṇīadu Godamo» tti.⌟

RĀJĀ: tena hi varṣavara|parigṛhītam enaṃ tatra|bhavataḥ sakāśaṃ prāpaya.

PRATĪHĀRĪ: ⌜taha.⌟

VIDŪṢAKAḤ *(*DEVĪṂ *vilokya)*: ⌜bhodi, jīveaṃ vā, ṇa vā: jaṃ mae atta|bhavantaṃ sevamāṇeṇa de avaraddhaṃ, taṃ marissehi.⌟

DEVĪ: ⌜dīh'|āū hohi.⌟

4.80 *iti niṣkrānto* VIDŪṢAKAḤ PRATĪHĀRĪ *ca.*

RĀJĀ: prakṛti|bhīrus tapasvī. Dhruvasiddher api yath"|ârtha|nāmnaḥ siddhiṃ na manyate.

praviśya

PRATĪHĀRĪ: ⌜jedu bhaṭṭā! Dhuvasiddhī viṇṇavedi: «uda|kumbha|vihāṇe sappa|muddiaṃ kiṃ vi kappaïdavvaṃ. taṃ aṇṇesīadu» tti.⌟

The ATTENDANTS *hastily support him.*

JESTER *(looking at the* KING*)*: Sir, I've been your faithful sidekick since our childhood. Please consider that and endow my mother with some maintenance when she no longer has a son.

KING: Fear not! The poison-doctor will soon heal you. Steady!

JAYA·SENA *(entering)*: Majesty, I've called Dhruva·siddhi but 4.75
he asks to have Gáutama brought to him.

KING: Then have the eunuchs carry him to the master's place.

JAYA·SENA: As you say.

JESTER *(looking at the* QUEEN*)*: Lady, whether I survive or not, please forgive me whatever sin I've committed against you while serving his lordship.

QUEEN: May you live long.

Exit the JESTER *and* JAYA·SENA. 4.80

KING: Poor thing, he's timid by nature. He doesn't believe even our aptly named Dhruva·siddhi* can succeed.

Enter JAYA·SENA.

JAYA·SENA: Victory, sire! Dhruva·siddhi says that some item with the likeness of a snake must be procured for the waterpot rite.* So please find one.

DEVĪ: ⌜idaṃ sappa|muddiaṃ aṅgulīaaṃ. pacchā mama hatthe dehi ṇaṃ.⌟

4.85 *iti prayacchati.* PRATĪHĀRĪ *nāṭyena gṛhṇāti.*

RĀJĀ: Jayasene, karma|siddhāv āśu pratipattim ānaya.

PRATĪHĀRĪ: ⌜jaṃ devo āṇavedi.⌟

iti niṣkrāntā.

PARIVRĀJIKĀ: yathā me hṛdayam ācaṣṭe, tathā nir|viṣo Gautamaḥ.

4.90 RĀJĀ: bhūyād evam!

(praviśya)

PRATĪHĀRĪ: ⌜jedu bhaṭṭā! ṇivutta|visa|veo Godamo muhuttaeṇa pakidi|ttho saṃvutto.⌟

DEVĪ: ⌜diṭṭhiā vaaṇīādo mutta mhi.⌟

PRATĪHĀRĪ: ⌜eso uṇa amacco Vāhadavo viṇṇavedi: «rāja|kajjaṃ bahu mantidavvaṃ. daṃsaṇeṇa aṇuggahaṃ icchāmi» tti.⌟

4.95 DEVĪ: ⌜gacchadu ajja|utto kajja|siddhīe.⌟

QUEEN: Here's my ring with a snake seal. Hand it back to me afterward.

She offers the ring. JAYA·SENA *mimes taking it.* 4.85

KING: Jaya·sena, inform us as soon as the task* has succeeded.

JAYA·SENA: As Your Majesty commands.

Exit.

KÁUSHIKI: My heart tells me that Gáutama should be free of poison.*

KING: May it be so! 4.90

Enter JAYA·SENA.

JAYA·SENA: Victory, sire! The poison's power has been overcome and Gáutama returned to his normal state soon after.

QUEEN: Thanks to fate, I'm freed from reproach.

JAYA·SENA: Also, the minister Váhatava entreats you: "There are many state affairs to be discussed. I beg to be granted an audience."

QUEEN: My noble husband is free to go, and may he succeed in his affairs. 4.95

RĀJĀ *(utthāya)*: devī, ātap'|ākrānto 'yam uddeśaḥ. śīta|kriyā c" âsya praśastā. tad anyatra nīyatāṃ śayanīyam.

DEVĪ: ⌜bāliāo, ajja|utta|vaaṇaṃ aṇuciṭṭhaha.⌟

PARIJANAḤ: ⌜taha.⌟

iti niṣkrāntā DEVĪ, PARIVRĀJIKĀ PARIJANAŚ *ca.*

4.100 RĀJĀ: Jayasene, gūḍha|pathena māṃ pramada|vanaṃ prāpaya.

PRATĪHĀRĪ: ⌜ido, ido devo.⌟

RĀJĀ *(parikramya)*: Jayasene, nanu samāpta|kṛtyo Gautamaḥ?

PRATĪHĀRĪ: ⌜aha iṃ?⌟

RĀJĀ:

iṣṭ'|âdhigama|nimittaṃ
prayogam ek'|ânta|sādhum api matvā
saṃdigdham eva siddhau
kātaram āśaṅkate cetaḥ. [5]

4.105 *(praviśya)*

VIDŪṢAKAḤ: ⌜jedu bhavaṃ! siddhāiṃ me maṅgala|kammāiṃ.⌟

KING *(standing)*: My queen, the sun is now shining on this area. Cooling is prescribed for your condition, so have your bed taken elsewhere.

QUEEN: Girls, do as my noble husband says.

ATTENDANTS: As you say.

Exeunt the QUEEN, KÁUSHIKI *and the* ATTENDANTS.

KING: Jaya·sena, take me to the pleasure garden by the secret 4.100
path.

JAYA·SENA: This way, Your Majesty.

KING *(walking about)*: Jaya·sena, Gáutama has completed his task, hasn't he?

JAYA·SENA: Of course.

KING:

Even though I know the plan is certain
to bring about the desired goal,
my anxious mind still hesitates,
doubtful of our success.

Enter the JESTER. 4.105

JESTER: Victory, sir! My pious labors have succeeded.

RĀJĀ: Jayasene, tvam api niyogam a|śūnyaṃ kuru.

PRATĪHĀRĪ: ⌜jaṃ devo āṇavedi.⌟

iti niṣkrāntā.

4.110 RĀJĀ: vayasya, kṣudrā Mādhavikā. na khalu kiṃ cid vicāritam anayā?

VIDŪṢAKAḤ: ⌜devīe aṅgulīaa|muddiaṃ dekkhia kahaṃ viāredi?⌟

RĀJĀ: na khalu mudrām adhikṛtya bravīmi. «tayor baddhayoḥ kiṃ|nimitto 'yaṃ mokṣaḥ? kiṃ vā devyāḥ parijanam atikramya bhavān saṃdiṣṭa?» ity evam anayā praṣṭavyam.

VIDŪṢAKAḤ: ⌜ṇaṃ pucchido mhi. puṇo mandeṇ' âvi paccuppaṇṇa|buddhiṇā mae kahidaṃ...⌟

RĀJĀ: kathyatām.

4.115 VIDŪṢAKAḤ: ⌜«devva|cintaehiṃ viṇṇāvido rāā, ‹s'|ôvasaggaṃ vo ṇakkhattaṃ. savva|bandhaṇa|mokkho karīadu› tti. taṃ suṇia devīe Irāvadīe cittaṃ rakkhantīe ‹rāā kila modi› tti ahaṃ saṃdiṭṭho mhi» tti. tado «jujjadi» tti tāe saṃpādido attho.⌟

RĀJĀ (VIDŪṢAKAṂ *pariṣvajya*): sakhe, priyo 'haṃ tava!

na hi buddhi|guṇen' âiva
    suhṛdām artha|darśanam:
kārya|siddhi|pathaḥ sūkṣmaḥ
    snehen' âpy upalabhyate. [6]

KING: Jaya·sena, you may go about your duties now.

JAYA·SENA: As Your Majesty commands.

Exit.

KING: Didn't Mádhavika hesitate at all, comrade? She's a mean one. 4.110

JESTER: How could she have when she saw the queen's signet ring?

KING: I don't mean about the signet. She could have asked, "Why are these two being released from bondage? Why were you sent rather than the queen's servants?"

JESTER: She sure did. I may be dull, but I had my wits about me and said...

KING: Tell me.

JESTER: "The soothsayers have told the king that his horoscope had developed a negative aspect and that he should release all captives to counterbalance its influence. When the queen heard that, to spare Irávati's feelings she gave the errand to me to make it obvious that it's the king who's freeing them." She said, "fair enough" and did what we wanted. 4.115

KING *(embracing the* JESTER*)*: Friend, I see that I'm indeed dear to you!

> Friends do not only use their intellectual talent
> to envision the goal,
> but affection actually finds the intricate way
> to accomplish success in the venture.

VIDŪṢAKAḤ: ⌜tuvaradu bhavaṃ! samudda|gharae sahī|sahidaṃ Mālaviaṃ ṭhāvia bhavandaṃ paccuggado mhi.⌟

RĀJĀ: aham enāṃ saṃbhāvayāmi. gacch' âgrataḥ.

4.120 VIDŪṢAKAḤ: ⌜edu bhavaṃ.⌟ *(parikramya)* ⌜edaṃ samudda|gharaaṃ.⌟

RĀJĀ *(s'|āśaṅkam)*: eṣā kusum'|âvacaya†|vyagra|hastā sakhyās te Irāvatyāḥ paricārikā Candrikā samāgacchati. itas tāvad āvāṃ bhitti|gūḍhau bhavāvaḥ.

VIDŪṢAKAḤ: ⌜aho, kumbhīlaehiṃ kāmuehiṃ a pariharaṇijjā candiā!⌟

ubhau yath"|ôktaṃ kurutaḥ.

RĀJĀ: Gautama, kathaṃ nu te sakhī māṃ pratipālayati? ehy, enāṃ gav'|âkṣaṃ āśrity' âvalokayāvaḥ.

4.125 VIDŪṢAKAḤ: ⌜taha.⌟

iti vilokayantau sthitau.

tataḥ praviśati MĀLAVIKĀ BAKULĀVALIKĀ *ca.*

BAKULĀVALIKĀ: ⌜halā, paṇama bhaṭṭāraṃ!⌟

JESTER: Hurry, sir! I had left Málavika and her friend in the water pavilion* before I came to you.

KING: I'll greet her. Lead the way.

JESTER: Come, sir. *(walking about)* Here's the water pavilion. 4.120

KING *(anxiously)*: Here comes your lady friend Irávati's handmaid Chándrika, busily picking flowers. Let's just hide behind this wall.

JESTER: Ah, thieves and lovers must avoid moonlight!*

Both do as the KING *suggests.*

KING: Gáutama, I wonder how your lady friend is waiting for me. Come, let's peek at her through this window.

JESTER: Right. 4.125

They stand and look.

Enter MÁLAVIKA *and* BAKULÁVALIKA.

BAKULÁVALIKA: Bow to your lord, my dear!

RĀJĀ: manye, pratikṛtiṃ me darśayati.

4.130 MĀLAVIKĀ *(sa|harṣam)*: ⌜ṇamo de!⌟ *(dvāram avalokya sa|viṣādam)* ⌜halā, vippalabbhesi maṃ!⌟

RĀJĀ: sakhe, harṣa|viṣādābhyām atra|bhavatyāḥ prīto 'smi.

> sūry'|ôdaye bhavati yā,
> sūry'|âstam|aye ca puṇḍarīkasya,
> vadanena su|vadanāyās
> te samavasthe kṣaṇād ūḍhe. [7]

BAKULĀVALIKĀ: ⌜ṇaṃ eso citta|gado bhaṭṭā.⌟

UBHE *(praṇipatya)*: ⌜jedu bhaṭṭā!⌟

4.135 MĀLAVIKĀ: ⌜halā, tadā saṃmuha|ṭṭhidā bhaṭṭiṇo rūva|daṃsaṇeṇa ṇa taha vitiṇha mhi, jaha ajja mae vibhāvido citta|gada|daṃsaṇo bhaṭṭā.⌟

VIDŪṢAKAḤ: ⌜sudaṃ bhavatā? atta|hodīe jaha diṭṭho citte, ṇa taha diṭṭho bhavaṃ ti mantidaṃ. muhā dāṇiṃ mañjūsā via radaṇa|bhaṇḍaṃ jovvaṇa|gavvaṃ vahesi.⌟

RĀJĀ: sakhe, kutūhalavān api nisarga|śālīnaḥ strī|janaḥ. paśya:

> kārtsnyena nirvarṇayituṃ ca rūpam
> icchanti tat|pūrva|samāgatānām;†
> na ca priyeṣv āyata|locanānāṃ
> samagra|pātīni vilocanāni. [8]

MĀLAVIKĀ: ⌜halā, kā esā pāsa|pariutta|vaaṇeṇa† bhaṭṭiṇā siṇiddhāe diṭṭhīe ṇijjhāīadi?⌟

KING: I suppose she's showing her a picture* of me.

MÁLAVIKA *(joyfully)*: Greetings! *(looking to the door, sadly)* 4.130
You're deceiving me, my dear!

KING: My friend, I'm pleased by the lady's joy and sorrow.

> The face of the pretty-faced girl had
> in one moment put on
> two aspects of the white lotus: the one it bears
> at sunrise and the one at sunset.

BAKULÁVALIKA: But your lord *is* here, in a picture.

THE TWO GIRLS *(bowing low)*: Victory, sire!

MÁLAVIKA: My dear, back when I was actually facing him I 4.135
could not drink my fill of my lord's beauty as much as I can now when I admire him in a picture.

JESTER: Did you hear that? The lady says you looked different in life than you do in the picture.* Like a casket* containing a trove of jewels, you have no use for your treasured youthfulness.*

KING: Though curious, womenfolk are shy by nature, my friend. Don't you see:

> They wish to observe thoroughly
> the looks of men they meet for the first time,
> yet the eyes of wide-eyed girls
> do not fall fully upon their lovers.

MÁLAVIKA: Who's this woman, my dear, that my lord is looking at so lovingly with his face turned to the side?

4.140 BAKULĀVALIKĀ: ⌜ṇaṃ iaṃ bhaṭṭiṇo passa|gadā Irāvadī.⌟

MĀLAVIKĀ: ⌜sahi, a|dakkhiṇo via bhaṭṭā me paḍibhādi, jo savvaṃ devī|jaṇaṃ ujjhia ekkāe muhe baddha|lakkho.⌟

BAKULĀVALIKĀ *(ātma|gatam)*: ⌜citta|gadaṃ bhaṭṭāraṃ param'|atthado saṃkappia asūadi. bhodu, kīḍissaṃ dāva edāe.⌟ *(prakāśam)* ⌜halā, bhaṭṭiṇo vallahā esā.⌟

MĀLAVIKĀ: ⌜tado kiṃ dāṇiṃ attāṇaṃ āāsemi?⌟

iti s'|âsūyaṃ parāvartate.

4.145 RĀJĀ: sakhe, paśya, paśya!

bhrū|bhaṅga|bhinna|tilakaṃ, sphurit'|âdhar'|oṣṭhaṃ
s'|âsūyam ānanam itaḥ parivartayantyā
kānt'|âparādha|kupiteṣv anayā vinetuḥ
saṃdarśit" êva lalit'|âbhinayasya śikṣā. [9]

VIDŪṢAKAḤ: ⌜aṇuṇaa|sajjo dāṇiṃ hohi.⌟

MĀLAVIKĀ: ⌜ajja|Godamo vi ettha evva sevadi ṇaṃ!⌟

punaḥ sthān'|ântar'|âbhimukhī bhavitum icchati.

4.150 BAKULĀVALIKĀ (MĀLAVIKĀM *ruddhvā)*: ⌜ṇa khu kuvidā dāṇiṃ tumaṃ?⌟

MĀLAVIKĀ: ⌜jaï ciraṃ kuvidaṃ evva maṃ maṇṇesi, eso paccāṇīadi kovo!⌟

BAKULÁVALIKA: Why, that's Irávati by the lord's side. 4.140

MÁLAVIKA: My friend, I guess that's not very polite of my lord, to disregard all his queens and keep looking at the face of just one.

BAKULÁVALIKA *(to herself)*: She takes the lord's picture for reality and she's getting jealous. All right, let me play a joke on her. *(aloud)* She *is* the lord's favorite, my dear.

MÁLAVIKA: Then why do I take the trouble?

She turns away jealously.

KING: Look, friend, look! 4.145

> Forehead mark crumpled by her knitting brow,
> lower lip trembling, as she turns her face
>   jealously aside,
> she seems to be showing off how well she learned
>   from her teacher
> the coquettish expression of anger
>   at a lover's offense.

JESTER: Get ready to conciliate her.

MÁLAVIKA: And Mister Gáutama is helping him with *that*!*

She makes to turn away again.

BAKULÁVALIKA *(stopping* MÁLAVIKA*)*: You aren't still angry, are you? 4.150

MÁLAVIKA: If you think I can persist so long in anger, I will be again!

RĀJĀ *(upetya)*:

> kupyasi, kuvalaya|nayane,
> citr'|ârpita|ceṣṭayā kim evam, ayi?
> nanu tava sākṣād ayam aham
> an|anya|sādhāraṇo dāsaḥ! [10]

BAKULĀVALIKĀ: ⌜jedu bhaṭṭā!⌟

4.155 MĀLAVIKĀ *(ātma|gatam)*: ⌜kahaṃ? citta|gado bhaṭṭā mae asūido?⌟

sa|vrīḍa|vadan" âñjaliṃ karoti. RĀJĀ *madana|kātaryaṃ rūpayati.*

VIDŪṢAKAḤ: ⌜kiṃ bhavaṃ udāsīṇo via?⌟

RĀJĀ: a|viśvasanīyatvāt sakhyās tava.

VIDŪṢAKAḤ: ⌜mā dāva, atta|hodīe tuha a|vissāso?⌟

4.160 RĀJĀ: śrūyatāṃ:

> pathi nayanayoḥ sthitvā svapne
> tiro|bhavati kṣaṇāt.
> sarati sahasā bāhvor madhyaṃ
> gat" âpy a|balā satī.†
> manasija|rujā kliṣṭasy' âivaṃ
> samāgama|māyayā
> katham iva, sakhe, visrabdhaṃ syād
> imām prati me manaḥ? [11]

BAKULĀVALIKĀ: ⌜sahi, bahuso kila bhaṭṭā vippaladdho. tā dāva attā vissasaṇijjo karīadu!⌟

KING *(approaching)*:

> Hey lotus-eyed lady,* why so angry
> at what I do in a picture?
> Here I stand in the flesh,
> your servant and no one else's!

BAKULÁVALIKA: Victory, sire!

MÁLAVIKA *(to herself)*: What? Was I really jealous at a picture of my lord? 4.155

She folds her hand in greeting with an embarrassed face. The KING *mimes a lover's timidity.*

JESTER: Why are you looking so dejected?

KING: Because your lady friend is so fickle.

JESTER: You don't say you don't trust her?

KING: I'll explain: 4.160

> In my dreams she crosses the path of my eyes, then
> disappears the next moment.
> Limp in my arms, she runs away with sudden vigor.
> When the fever of love so torments me
> with illusory union,
> how could I, my friend, bring my mind
> to trust her?

BAKULÁVALIKA: It seems you've tricked our lord time and again, my dear. Now prove yourself reliable!

MĀLAVIKĀ: ⌜sahi, mama uṇa manda|bhāāe siviṇa|samāgamo vi bhaṭṭiṇo dul|laho āsī!⌟

BAKULĀVALIKĀ: ⌜bhaṭṭā, dehi se uttaraṃ.⌟

RĀJĀ:

4.165 uttareṇa kim? ātm" âiva pañca|bāṇ'|âgni|sākṣikam
tava sakhyai mayā datto, na sevyaḥ, sevitā rahaḥ! [12]

BAKULĀVALIKĀ: ⌜aṇugahida mha.†⌟

VIDŪṢAKAḤ *(parikramya, sa|saṃbhramam)*: ⌜Baülāvalie, eso bāl'|âsoa|rukkhassa pallavāiṃ hariṇo laṅghiduṃ āacchadi! ehi, ṇivārema ṇaṃ.⌟

BAKULĀVALIKĀ: ⌜taha.⌟

iti prasthitā.

4.170 RĀJĀ: evam asmad|rakṣaṇe 'vahitena bhavitavyam.

VIDŪṢAKAḤ: ⌜evaṃ vi Godamo ṇaṃ saṃdissīadi?⌟

BAKULĀVALIKĀ: ⌜ajja Godama, ahaṃ a|ppaāse ciṭṭhāmi. tumaṃ duāra|rakkhao hohi.⌟

VIDŪṢAKAḤ: ⌜jujjaï.⌟

MÁLAVIKA: But my dear, I'm the one worse off: I couldn't meet him even in my dreams!*

BAKULÁVALIKA: Sire, will you give her an answer?

KING:

An answer? I've given my very self, 4.165
with love's fire as my witness,*
To be your friend's intimate servant, not her master!

BAKULÁVALIKA: Thank you.

JESTER *(walking about, urgently)*: Bakulávalika, there's a deer coming to nibble the shoots of that *ashóka* sapling! Come, let's chase him away.

BAKULÁVALIKA: Right.

She begins to go.

KING: It's me you should guard* as diligently as you guard 4.170
that tree.

JESTER: Does Gáutama need to be told so?

BAKULÁVALIKA: Mister Gáutama, I'll hide over there. You guard the door.

JESTER: Right.

niṣkrāntā BAKULĀVALIKĀ.

4.175 VIDŪṢAKAḤ: ⌜idaṃ dāva phaliha|tthalaṃ assido homi.⌟ *(iti tathā kṛtvā)* ⌜aho suha|ppharisadā silā|visesassa!⌟

nidrāyate. MĀLAVIKĀ *sa|sādhvasā tiṣṭhati.*

RĀJĀ:

visṛja, sundari, saṃgama|sādhvasaṃ
  tava cirāt prabhṛti praṇay'|ônmukhe!
parigṛhāṇa gate† sahakāratāṃ
  tvam atimukta|latā|caritaṃ mayi! [13]

MĀLAVIKĀ: ⌜devīe bhaeṇa attaṇo vi piaṃ kāduṃ ṇa pāremi.⌟

RĀJĀ: ayi, na bhetavyam.

4.180 MĀLAVIKĀ *(s'|ôpālambham)*: ⌜jo ṇa bhāedi, so mae bhaṭṭiṇī| daṃsaṇe diṭṭha|sāmattho bhaṭṭā!⌟

RĀJĀ:

dākṣiṇyaṃ nāma, bimb'|ôṣṭhi,
  Baimbikānāṃ† kula|vratam.
tan me, dīrgh'|âkṣi, ye prāṇās,
  te tvad|āśā|nibandhanāḥ. [14]

tad anugṛhyatāṃ cir'|ânurakto 'yaṃ janaḥ.

iti saṃśleṣam abhinayati. MĀLAVIKĀ *nāṭyena pariharati.*

RĀJĀ *(ātma|gatam)*: ramaṇīyaḥ khalu nav'|âṅganānāṃ madana|viṣay'|âvatāraḥ!

Exit BAKULÁVALIKA.

JESTER: I'll sit down on this crystal floor here. *(doing so)* 4.175
Gosh, it feels like a particularly pleasant kind of stone!

He falls asleep. MÁLAVIKA *stands in apprehension.*

KING:

> Forget your fear of union with me, who have
> long been longing for you, my pretty!
> I've become your mango tree;
> now you be my *atimúkta* vine!*

MÁLAVIKA: I'd like to, but I can't, because I'm afraid of the queen.

KING: Come now, nothing to fear.

MÁLAVIKA *(reproachfully)*: My lord may well have no fear, 4.180
but I've seen how assertive he is when Her Ladyship is around!

KING:

> There is such a thing as courtliness, which
> happens to be a family tradition
> with Báimbikas,* my *bimba*-lipped girl.
> But my life, long-eyed lady, depends altogether
> on my hopes for you.

So please, please this creature who's longed for you so long.

He mimes trying to embrace her. MÁLAVIKA *dances away.*

KING *(to himself)*: Pleasant indeed to see a young woman's first venture into the realms of love!

4.185 hastaṃ kampavatī ruṇaddhi raśanā|
vyāpāra|lol'|âṅguliṃ,
hastau svau nayati stan'|āvaraṇatām
āliṅgyamānā balāt,
pātuṃ pakṣmala|cakṣur† unnamayataḥ
sācī|karoty ānanaṃ:
vyājen' âpy abhilāṣa|pūraṇa|sukhaṃ
nirvartayaty eva me. [15]

tataḥ praviśat' ÎRĀVATĪ NIPUṆIKĀ *ca.*

IRĀVATĪ: ⌜hañje Ṇiuṇie, saccaṃ tumaṃ parigad'|atthā, Candiāe samudda|ghara'|âlindae ajja|Godamo eāī diṭṭho tti?⌟

NIPUṆIKĀ: ⌜aṇṇahā kahaṃ bhaṭṭiṇī viṇṇavīadi?⌟

IRĀVATĪ: ⌜teṇa hi tahiṃ evva gacchamha saṃsaādo muttaṃ ajja|uttassa pia|vaassaṃ pucchiduṃ ca...⌟

4.190 NIPUṆIKĀ: ⌜s'|âvasesaṃ via bhaṭṭiṇīe vaaṇaṃ.⌟

IRĀVATĪ: ⌜aṇṇaṃ ca... citta|gadaṃ bhaṭṭāraṃ pasādeduṃ.⌟

NIPUṆIKĀ: ⌜aha dāṇiṃ bhaṭṭā evva kiṃ ṇa paccaṇuṇīadi?⌟

IRĀVATĪ: ⌜muddhe, jāriso citta|gado, ṇa tāriso evva aṇṇa|saṃkanta|hidao ajja|utto. kevalaṃ uvaār'|âdikkamaṃ pamajjiduṃ aaṃ ārambho.⌟

NIPUṆIKĀ: ⌜ido, ido bhaṭṭiṇī.⌟

She trembles as she restrains my hand 4.185
engaged with her belt,
draws her palms to cover her breasts
when I try hard to embrace her,
turns her feathery-eyed face aside *in defense*
when I tilt her head up *to kiss it*:
she grants my desire even by trying to evade it.

Enter IRÁVATI *and* NÍPUNIKA.

IRÁVATI: Nípunika, are you sure you got this right? Chándrika has seen Mister Gáutama alone on the terrace of the water pavilion?

NÍPUNIKA: Else I would not have told your ladyship so.

IRÁVATI: Well then, let's go there to ask if my noble husband's dear companion is past the crisis, and…

NÍPUNIKA: Were you going to say something else, mistress? 4.190

IRÁVATI: And… to apologize to our lord's picture.

NÍPUNIKA: But why not to His Majesty himself?

IRÁVATI: Now that his heart has gone to another, I prefer the picture version, silly. We're only doing this to wash off the stain of my breach of good manner.

NÍPUNIKA: This way, mistress, this way.

4.195 *iti parikrāmataḥ.*

(praviśya)

CEṬĪ: ⌜jedu bhaṭṭiṇī! devī bhaṇādi: «ṇa me eso maccharassa kālo. tuha khu bahu|māṇaṃ vaḍḍheduṃ vaassiāe saha ṇiala|bandhaṇe kidā Mālaviā. jaï aṇumaṇṇesi, ajja|uttaṃ vi tuha kide viṇṇāvaïssaṃ. jaṃ tuha icchidaṃ, taṃ bhaṇāhi» tti.⌟

IRĀVATĪ: ⌜Ṇāarie, viṇṇavehi deviṃ: «kā vaaṃ bhaṭṭiṇiṃ ṇiojeduṃ? pariaṇa|ṇiggaheṇa maï daṃsido aṇuggaho. kassa vā aṇṇassa pasādeṇa aaṃ jaṇo vaḍḍhadi?» tti.⌟

CEṬĪ: ⌜taha.⌟

4.200 *iti niṣkrāntā.*

NIPUṆIKĀ *(parikramy' âvalokya ca)*: ⌜eso duvār'|uddese samudda|gharassa vipaṇi|gado via vusaho ajja|Godamo āsīṇo evva ṇiddāadi.⌟

IRĀVATĪ: ⌜accāhidaṃ! ṇa khu s'|âvasesa|visa|viāro have?⌟

NIPUṆIKĀ: ⌜pasaṇṇa|muha|vaṇṇo dīsaï. avi a Dhuvasiddhiṇā ciicchido. tā se a|saṅkaṇīaṃ pāvaṃ.⌟

VIDŪṢAKAḤ *(utsvapnāyate)*: ⌜bhodi Mālavie!⌟

4.205 NIPUṆIKĀ: ⌜sudaṃ bhaṭṭiṇīe? kassa eso attaṇīṇo had'|āso kidavo? savva|kālaṃ ido evva sotthi|vāaṇa|modaehiṃ kukkhiṃ pūria, saṃpadaṃ Mālaviaṃ ussiviṇāadi!⌟

They walk about. 4.195

Enter the maid NÁGARIKA.

NÁGARIKA: Victory, mistress! The queen sends this message: "I do not care for strife right now. To augment your standing, I have put Málavika and her friend in chains. Now if you consent, I will solicit our husband for your sake. Tell me what you wish."

IRÁVATI: Nágarika, inform the queen: "Who are we to send Your Majesty on errands? You have already shown your grace to me by binding those menials. Who else's favor can the likes of me count on?"

NÁGARIKA: As you say.

Exit NÁGARIKA. 4.200

NÍPUNIKA *(walking about and looking)*: There's Mister Gáutama at the entrance to the water pavilion, sitting on his haunches and dozing like a bull in the marketplace.

IRÁVATI: What a tragedy! Could he be stricken by the after-effect of the poison?

NÍPUNIKA: His face looks happy enough. And anyway, it was Dhruva·siddhi, Mister Certain Success, who cured him, so we needn't fear anything's wrong with him.

JESTER *(talking in his sleep)*: Miss Málavika!

NÍPUNIKA: Did you hear, mistress? Whose side is the 4.205
wretched scoundrel on? All this time he's been filling his belly with sweets *we* gave him for his blessings, and now he talks to Málavika in his sleep!

VIDŪṢAKAḤ: ⌜Irāvadiṃ adikkamandī hohi!⌟

NIPUṆIKĀ: ⌜edaṃ accāhidaṃ! bhujaṃga|bhīruaṃ brahma|bandhuṃ imiṇā bhujaṃga|kuḍileṇa daṇḍa|kaṭṭheṇa tambh'|andaridā bhāaïssaṃ.⌟

IRĀVATĪ: ⌜aruhadi kida|gghoᵻ uvaddavassa.⌟

NIPUṆIKĀ VIDŪṢAKASY' *ôpari daṇḍa|kāṣṭhaṃ pātayati.*

4.210 VIDŪṢAKAḤ *(sahasā prabudhya)*: ⌜avihā! avihā! bho, davvīkaro me uvari paḍido!⌟

RĀJĀ *(sahas" ôpasṛtya)*: sakhe, na bhetavyaṃ, na bhetavyam!

MĀLAVIKĀ *(anusṛtya)*: ⌜bhaṭṭā, mā dāva sahasā ṇikkama! sappo tti bhaṇādi.⌟

IRĀVATĪ: ⌜haddhī, haddhī! bhaṭṭā ido evva dhāvadi.⌟

VIDŪṢAKAḤ *(sa|prahāsam)*: ⌜kahaṃ? daṇḍa|kaṭṭhaṃ edaṃ! ahaṃ uṇa jāṇe, jaṃ mae kedaī|kaṇṭaehiṃ daṃsaṃ karia sappassa via daṃso kido, taṃ phalidaṃ tti.⌟

4.215 *(praviśya paṭ'|ākṣepeṇa)*

BAKULĀVALIKĀ: ⌜mā dāva bhaṭṭā pavisadu! iha kuḍila|gaī sappo via dīsadi.⌟

IRĀVATĪ (RĀJĀNAM *upasṛtya)*: ⌜avi ṇivviggha|maṇoraho divā|saṃkedo mihuṇassa?⌟

JESTER: May you surpass Irávati!

NÍPUNIKA: Outrageous! Let me hide behind a pillar and frighten this poor excuse for a brahmin with this stick: it's sinuous as a snake, and he's scared of snakes.

IRÁVATI: He deserves a shock for being a turncoat.

NÍPUNIKA *throws the stick at the* JESTER.

JESTER *(awakening suddenly)*: Help! Help! Sir, a cobra has 4.210
fallen on me!

KING *(dashing toward him)*: Fear not, my friend, fear not!

MÁLAVIKA *(running after the* KING*)*: Don't you step so carelessly, my lord! He says there's a snake.

IRÁVATI: Oh damn! The king's running right this way.

JESTER *(laughing out loud)*: What? It's a stick! And I thought it was my reward for the way I imitated a snake bite, wounding myself with *kétaki* thorns.*

Enter BAKULÁVALIKA *with a toss of the curtain.** 4.215

BAKULÁVALIKA: Don't go any closer, sire! I see something twisted like a snake.

IRÁVATI *(approaching the* KING*)*: I trust the little couple's daytime tryst was satisfactory and unimpeded?

sarve IRĀVATĪM *dṛṣṭvā saṃbhrāntāḥ.*

RĀJĀ: priye, a|pūrvo 'yam upacāraḥ.

IRĀVATĪ: ⌜Baülāvalie, diṭṭhiā docc'|âhiāra|visaā saṃpuṇṇā de paḍiṇṇā.⌟

BAKULĀVALIKĀ: ⌜pasīdadu bhaṭṭiṇī! kiṃ ṇu khu daddurā vāharandi tti devo puḍhavīe varisiduṃ sumaredi?⌟

VIDŪṢAKAḤ: ⌜mā dāva! hodīe daṃsaṇa|metteṇa atta|bhavaṃ paṇipāda|laṅghaṇaṃ visumarido. hodī uṇa ajja vi pasādaṃ ṇa geṇhedi?⌟

IRĀVATĪ: ⌜kuvidā vi dāṇiṃ kiṃ karissaṃ?⌟

RĀJĀ: a|sthāne kopa ity etad an|upapannaṃ tvayi. tathā hi:

kadā mukhaṃ, vara|tanu, kāraṇād ṛte
tav' āgataṃ kṣaṇam api kopa|pātratām?
a|parvaṇi graha|kaluṣ'|êndu|maṇḍalā
vibhāvarī, kathaya, kathaṃ bhaviṣyati? [16]

IRĀVATĪ: ⌜«a|ṭṭhāṇe» tti suṭṭhu vāharidaṃ ajja|utteṇa. aṇṇa|saṃkandesu amhāṇaṃ bhāa|heesu jaï uṇa kuppeaṃ, tado hassā bhavissaṃ.⌟

All are shocked to see IRÁVATI.

KING: That's a strange way to greet me, my dear.

IRÁVATI: Bakulávalika, congratulations on fulfilling your promise to play the go-between. 4.220

BAKULÁVALIKA: Forgiveness, Your Majesty! Does the god* need the frogs' croaking to remember to shower rain on the earth?*

JESTER: Come on, mistress! As soon as he saw you, His Majesty has forgotten that you scorned him when he fell at your feet. And you still can't find forgiveness in yourself?

IRÁVATI: What does it matter if I'm angry? There's nothing I can do.

KING: It does not become you to be angry when you shouldn't. Listen:

When, O gorgeous lady, has your face 4.225
    ever been obscured
    by pointless anger, even for a moment?
Say, how could Lady Night's face,
    the moon's orb, ever be dulled
    by an eclipse, except on a full-moon day?

IRÁVATI: "Pointless"—my noble husband has put that well. If what should have been my lot has passed to another, my anger only turns me into a laughing stock.

RĀJĀ: tvam anyathā kalpayasi. ahaṃ punaḥ satyam ev' âtra kopa|sthānaṃ na paśyāmi. kutaḥ:

> «n' ârhati kṛt'|âparādho 'py
> utsava|divaseṣu parijano bandham.»
> iti mocite may" âite,
> praṇipatituṃ māṃ upagate ca. [17]

IRĀVATĪ: ⌜Ṇiuṇie, gaccha, deviṃ viṇṇavehi: «diṭṭhaṃ devīe pakkha|vādittaṇaṃ ajja» tti.⌟

4.230 NIPUṆIKĀ: ⌜taha.⌟

iti niṣkrāntā.

VIDŪṢAKAḤ *(ātma|gatam)*: ⌜aho, aṇ|attho saṃpaḍido! bandhaṇa|bbhaṭṭo giha|kavodo biḍāli"|āloe paḍido.⌟

praviśya

NIPUṆIKĀ *(apavārya)*: ⌜bhaṭṭiṇi, jadicchā|diṭṭhāe Māhaviāe ācakkhidaṃ: «evvaṃ khu edaṃ ṇivuttaṃ» tti.⌟

4.235 *iti karṇe kathayati.*

IRĀVATĪ *(ātma|gatam)*: ⌜uvavaṇṇaṃ evva. saccaṃ aaṃ ettha bamha|bandhuṇo† ubbhiṇṇo dup|paogo.⌟ *(*VIDŪṢAKAṂ *vilokya, prakāśam)* ⌜iaṃ imassa kāma|tanta|sacivassa ṇīdī!⌟

VIDŪṢAKAḤ: ⌜bhodi, jadi ṇīdīe ekkaṃ vi akkharaṃ paḍheaṃ, tado Gāattiṃ vi visumareaṃ.⌟

RĀJĀ *(ātma|gatam)*: kathaṃ nu saṃkaṭād asmād ātmānaṃ mocayiṣyāmi?

KING: You're misinterpreting me. But seriously, I see no reason for you to be angry. Let me explain:

> "Even if guilty, servant folk
> should not be bound on holidays."
> With this in mind, I've set these two free,
> and they've come to salute me.

IRÁVATI: Nípunika, go and tell the queen: "Now I have seen where Your Majesty's favor truly lies."

NÍPUNIKA: As you say.

Exit NÍPUNIKA.

JESTER *(to himself)*: Gosh, what a disaster! No sooner did the dove get out of the cage than the cat set eyes on her.*

Enter NÍPUNIKA.

NÍPUNIKA *(aside)*: Mistress, I happened to meet Mádhavika, and she told me how this has come to pass.

She whispers in her ear.

IRÁVATI *(to herself)*: All clear now. The subterfuge of that son-of-a-brahmin is truly laid bare now. *(*LOOKING *at the jester, aloud)* Such polity from this Minister of Amorous Affairs!

JESTER: Mistress, if I were to study a single syllable of polity, I might even forget the Gayátri.*

KING *(to himself)*: How am I to get out of this quandary?

(praviśya)

4.240 PRATĪHĀRĪ *(s'|āvegam)*: ⌜deva, kumārī Vasulacchī kanduaṃ aṇudhāvandī piṅgala|vāṇareṇa baliaṃ uttāsidā, aṅka|ṇisaṇṇā devīe pavāda|kisalaaṃ via vevamāṇā ṇa kiṃ vi pakidiṃ paḍivajjaï.⌟

RĀJĀ: kaṣṭam! kātaro bāla|bhāvaḥ.

IRĀVATĪ *(s'|āvegam)*: ⌜tuvaradu ajja|utto ṇaṃ samassāsaïduṃ! mā se saṃtāsa|jaṇido viāro vaḍḍhadu.⌟

RĀJĀ: aham enāṃ saṃjñāpayāmi.

iti sa|tvaraṃ parikrāmati.

4.245 VIDŪṢAKAḤ *(ātma|gatam)*: ⌜sāhu, re piṅgala|vāṇara, sāhu! parittādo tue sa|vakkho.⌟

niṣkrānto RĀJĀ VIDŪṢAKAŚ *ca;* IRĀVATĪ, NIPUṆIKĀ PRATĪHĀRĪ *ca.*

MĀLAVIKĀ: ⌜halā, deviṃ cintia vevadi me hiaaṃ. ṇa āṇe ado varaṃ kiṃ aṇuhodavvaṃ havissadi tti.⌟

NEPATHYE: ⌜accariaṃ, accariaṃ! a|puṇṇe evva pañca|ratte dohalassa, muulehiṃ saṇṇaddho tavaṇī'|âsoo! jāva devīe ṇivedemi.⌟

UBHE *śrutvā prahṛṣṭe bhavataḥ.*

4.250 BAKULĀVALIKĀ: ⌜āsasidu sahī. sacca|ppaïṇṇā devī.⌟

Enter JAYA·SENA.

JAYA·SENA *(in distress)*: Majesty, the princess Vasu·lakshmi 4.240
was terrified by a ginger monkey* while she was running after her ball. She's sitting on the queen's lap now, but trembles like a leaf in a gale and won't be herself again.

KING: Blast it! Children are always so sensitive.

IRÁVATI *(in distress)*: Hurry, my noble husband, hurry to comfort her, lest her shock worsen!

KING: I'll bring her round.

He walks about in a hurry.

JESTER *(to himself)*: Kudos to you, ginger monkey, well 4.245
done! You've just managed to save your kin.*

Exeunt the KING *with the* JESTER, *and* IRÁVATI *with* NÍPUNIKA *and* JAYA·SENA.

MÁLAVIKA: When I think of the queen, my dear, my heart trembles. I don't know what more I'll have to endure.

A VOICE OFF-STAGE: What a surprise! Even before the fifth night of the craving rite, the golden *ashóka* is covered in buds! I'll report to the queen right away.

Hearing this, THE TWO GIRLS *become delighted.*

BAKULÁVALIKA: Take heart, my friend. The queen is true to 4.250
her promises.

MĀLAVIKĀ: ⌜teṇa hi pamada|vaṇa|pāliāe piṭṭhado homma.⌟

BAKULĀVALIKĀ: ⌜taha.⌟

iti niṣkrāntāḥ sarve.

iti caturtho 'ṅkaḥ.

MÁLAVIKA: Then let's go after the custodian of the pleasure garden.

BAKULÁVALIKA: As you say.

Exeunt all.

End of the fourth act.

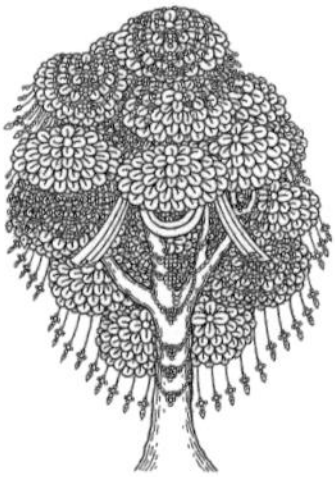

INTERLUDE

5.1 *tataḥ praviśaty* UDYĀNA|PĀLIKĀ.

UDYĀNA|PĀLIKĀ: ⌜uvakkhitto mae kida|sakkāra|vihiṇo tavaṇī'|âsoassa vediā|bandho. jāva aṇuṭṭhida|ṇioaṃ attāṇaṃ devīe ṇivedemi.⌟ *(parikramya)* ⌜aho, devvassa aṇukampaṇīā Mālaviā! tassiṃ taha caṇḍiā devī imiṇā asoa|kusuma|vuttanteṇa pasāda|sumukhī bhavissadi. kahiṃ ṇu khu devī have?⌟ *(vilokya)* ⌜amho, eso devīe pariaṇ'|abbhandaro kiṃ vi jadu|muddā|lañchidaṃ mañjūsiaṃ geṇhia caüs|sālādo kujjo Sārasao ṇikkāmadi. pucchissaṃ dāva ṇaṃ.⌟

tataḥ praviśati yathā|nirdiṣṭaḥ KUBJAḤ.

UDYĀNA|PĀLIKĀ *(upasṛtya)*: ⌜Sārasaa, kahiṃ patthido si?⌟

5.5 SĀRASAKAḤ: ⌜Mahuarie, vijjā|pāra|āṇaṃ bamhaṇāṇaṃ ṇicca|dakkhiṇā dādavvā. tā ajja|purohidassa hatthaṃ pāvaïssaṃ.⌟

MADHUKARIKĀ: ⌜kiṃ|ṇimittaṃ?⌟

SĀRASAKAḤ: ⌜jadā pahudi sudaṃ, «seṇā|vaïṇā jaṇṇa|turaa|rakkhaṇe ṇiutto bhaṭṭi|dārao Vasumitto» tti, tadā pahudi tassa āuso ṇimittaṃ aṭṭhādasa|suvaṇṇa|parimāṇaṃ dakkhiṇaṃ devī dakkhiṇīehiṃ paḍiggāhedi.⌟

MADHUKARIKĀ: ⌜jujjaï. aha kahiṃ devī? kiṃ v" âṇuciṭṭhadi?⌟

Enter the custodian of the garden, MÁDHU·KARIKA. 5.1

MADHU·KÁRIKA: I've knocked together a platform* around the golden *ashóka* now that it's been worshipped.* Now I'll report to the queen that I'm done with my errand. *(walking about)* Oh, fate is merciful to Málavika! The queen was ever so furious, but surely she'll forgive her thanks to the *ashóka*'s flowering. Now where could the queen be? *(looking)* Ah, here's the hunchback Sárasaka, one of the queen's personal attendants, just stepping out of the courtyard, carrying of all things a casket with a lac seal. I'll just ask him.

Enter SÁRASAKA *the hunchback as described.*

MADHU·KÁRIKA *(going up to him)*: Sárasaka, where are you off to?

SÁRASAKA: Madhu·kárika, it's time to hand the regular gifts to the brahmins versed in the Vedas. I am to present this to His Honor the head priest. 5.5

MADHU·KÁRIKA: On what occasion?

SÁRASAKA: Since she heard that the General* has charged His Majesty's son Vasu·mitra with guarding the sacrificial horse,* the queen's been giving worthy priests a regular donation of eighteen gold pieces to ensure long life for the prince.

MADHU·KÁRIKA: That makes sense. So where's the queen? And what is she doing?

SĀRASAKAḤ: ⌜maṅgala|ghare āsaṇa|tthā bhavia Vidabbha|visaādo bhāduṇā Vīraseṇeṇa pesidaṃ livi|arehiṃ vāiamāṇaṃ lehaṃ suṇādi.⌟

5.10 MADHUKARIKĀ: ⌜ko uṇa Vidabbha|rāja|vuttanto?⌟

SĀRASAKAḤ: ⌜vasī|kido kila Vīraseṇa|ppamuhehiṃ bhaṭṭiṇo viaa|daṇḍehiṃ Vidabbha|ṇāho. moido se dāādo Māhavaseṇo. dūdo a teṇa mahā|sārāiṃ raaṇāiṃ, vāhaṇāiṃ, sippa|āriā|bhūiṭṭhaṃ pariaṇaṃ a uvāaṇī|karia bhaṭṭiṇo saāsaṃ pesido, suvo kila bhaṭṭāraṃ pekkhissadi tti.⌟

MADHUKARIKĀ: ⌜gaccha, aṇuciṭṭha attaṇo ṇioaṃ. ahaṃ vi deviṃ pekkhissaṃ.⌟

iti niṣkrāntau.

praveśakaḥ.

SÁRASAKA: She's sitting in the house shrine,* having the scribes read out to her a letter her brother Vira·sena sent from Vidárbha country.

MADHU·KÁRIKA: And what's up with the king of Vidárbha? 5.10

SÁRASAKA: Apparently His Majesty's victorious forces, under the command of Vira·sena, have vanquished the Lord of Vidárbha. They've set free his rival Mádhava·sena. I hear he's sent to His Majesty a messenger who brings gifts of valuable jewels and vehicles and a troop of servants, most of them skilled women. He's to meet our king tomorrow.

MADHU·KÁRIKA: Go then, and carry on with your task. As for me, I'll see the queen.

Exeunt.

End of the interlude.

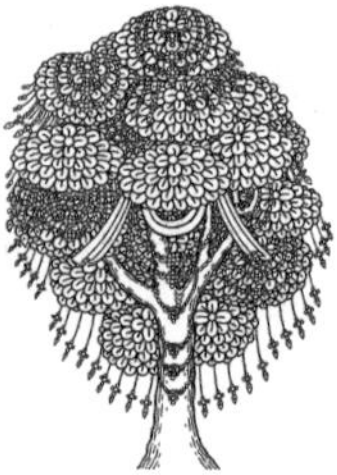

ACT FIVE

5.15 *tataḥ praviśati* PRATĪHĀRĪ.

PRATĪHĀRĪ: ⌜āṇatta mhi asoa|sakkāra|vvāvudāe devīe: «viṇṇavehi ajja|uttaṃ, ‹icchāmi ajja|utteṇa saha asoa|rukkhassa pasūṇa|lacchiṃ paccakkhī|kāduṃ› tti.» jāva dhamm'|āsaṇa|gadaṃ devaṃ paḍivālemi.⌟

iti parikrāmati.

(nepathye) VAITĀLIKAU: diṣṭyā daṇḍen' âiv' âri|śiraḥsu vartate devaḥ!

PRATHAMAḤ:

> *parabhṛta|kala|vyāhāreṣu*
> tvam *ātta|Ratir* madhuṃ
> nayasi Vidiśā|tīr'|ôdyāneṣv,
> Anaṅga iv' *âṅgavān.*
> vijaya|kariṇām ālān'|âṅkair
> *upoḍha|balasya* te,
> vara|da, Varadā|rodho|vṛkṣaiḥ
> sah' âvanato ripuḥ. [1]

DVITĪYAḤ:

5.20
> viracita|padaṃ vīra|prītyā,
> sur'|ôpama, sūribhiś
> caritam ubhayor madhye|kṛtya
> sthitaṃ Krathakaiśikān:

Enter JAYA·SENA. 5.15

JAYA·SENA: While she was paying her respect to the *ashóka* tree, the queen has commanded me to tell her husband that she wishes to inspect the beauty of the *ashóka* blossoms together with him. The king is dealing with matters of state, so I'll wait for him.

She walks about.

TWO COURT BARDS *(off-stage)*: Congratulations to Your Majesty whom his enemies know only as their punisher!

FIRST BARD:

Like disembodied Love
embodied : with your shapely body,
you while away the spring
*in the company of Rati : blissfully**
to the dulcet
cooing of the cuckoos : words of your retainers
in the gardens along the banks of the Vídisha.
O bounteous king *of aggregated power*, the trees
on the bank of the bounteous Várada—*
bent down along with your enemies—
serve your *invading army*
as pickets for your victorious elephants.

SECOND BARD:

O godlike king, when it comes to the Kratha· 5.20
káishika people, the acts of two men
shall endure, bound in verse by literati
with a penchant for heroics:
of you who with your punishing troops robbed

tava hṛtavato daṇḍ'|ânīkair
Vidarbha|pateḥ śriyam,
parigha|gurubhir dorbhiḥ Śaureḥ
prasahya ca Rukmiṇīm. [2]

PRATĪHĀRĪ: ⌜eso jaa|sadda|sūcida|patthāṇo bhaṭṭā ido evva āacchadi. ahaṃ vi dāva imassa pamuhādo kiṃ vi osaria edaṃ muh'|âlinda|toraṇaṃ samassidā homi.⌟

ek'|ânte sthitā.

*tataḥ praviśati sa|*VAYASYO RĀJĀ.

RĀJĀ:

kāntāṃ vicintya su|labh'|êtara|saṃprayogāṃ,
śrutvā Vidarbha|patim ānamitaṃ balaiś ca,
dhārābhir ātapa iv' âbhihataṃ saro|jaṃ,
duḥkhāyate ca hṛdayaṃ sukham aśnute ca. [3]

5.25 VIDŪṢAKAḤ: ⌜jaha ahaṃ pekkhāmi, taha ekk'|anda|suhido bhavaṃ bhavissadi.⌟

RĀJĀ: katham iva?

VIDŪṢAKAḤ: ⌜ajja kila devīe Dhāriṇīe paṇḍida|Kosiī bhaṇidā: «jaï tumaṃ pasāhaṇa|gavvaṃ vahesi, tā daṃsehi Mālaviāe sarīre Vedabbhaṃ vivāha|ṇevacchaṃ» tti. tāe vi sa|vises" âlaṃ|kidā Mālaviā. tatta|hodī kadā vi pūrae bhavado maṇo|rahaṃ.⌟

the Vidárbha king of a goddess: his glory;
and of Krishna, who with his arms* like iron bars
abducted the goddess Rúkmini.*

JAYA·SENA: The eulogies mean the king is coming out, and he's headed just this way. So I'll move a little way off his path and stand under this archway of the front porch.

She stands aside.

Enter the KING *with the* JESTER.

KING:

Hearing that my troops have
humbled the Vidárbha king
while I brood on how hard it is to find
union with my beloved,
my heart rejoices even while it suffers,
like a lotus struck by torrents of rain
in blazing sunlight.

JESTER: As far as I can see, sir, you're going to be happy 5.25
through and through.

KING: How's that?

JESTER: It's rumored that today Queen Dhárini said to the learned Káushiki: "If you pride yourself on your skill in adornment, then show me a Vidárbhan wedding costume:* dress Málavika in it." Whereupon she ornamented Málavika with particular care. It's quite possible that the lady will fulfill your desire.

RĀJĀ: sakhe, mad|apekṣ"|ânuvṛttyā nivṛtt'|ērṣyāyā Dhāriṇyāḥ pūrva|caritaiḥ saṃbhāvyata ev' âitat.

PRATĪHĀRĪ *(upagamya)*: ⌜jedu bhaṭṭā! devī viṇṇavedi: «tavaṇī'|âsoassa kusuma|sohagga|daṃsaṇeṇa maha āraṃbho sa|phalī|karīadu» tti.⌟

5.30 RĀJĀ: nanu tatr' âiva devī?

PRATĪHĀRĪ: ⌜aha iṃ. jah'|âruha|saṃmāṇa|suhidaṃ ande|uraṃ visajjia Mālaviā|puro|eṇa attaṇo parijaṇeṇa saha devaṃ paḍivāledi.⌟

RĀJĀ *(sa|harṣam* VIDŪṢAKAṂ *vilokya)*: Jayasene, gacch' âgrataḥ.

PRATĪHĀRĪ: ⌜ido, ido devo.⌟

iti parikrāmanti.

5.35 VIDŪṢAKAḤ *(vilokya)*: ⌜bho vaassa, kiṃ ci parivutta|jovvaṇo via vasando pamada|vaṇe lakkhīadi.⌟

RĀJĀ: yath" āha bhavān.

agre vikīrṇa|kurabaka|
  phala|jāla|vibhidyamāna|sahakāram,
pariṇām'|âbhimukham ṛtor
  utsukayati yauvanaṃ cetaḥ. [4]

VIDŪṢAKAḤ *(parikramya)*: ⌜bho, aaṃ so diṇṇa|ṇevaccho via kusuma|tthavaehiṃ tavaṇī'|âsoo. oloedu bhavaṃ!⌟

KING: That's indeed possible, my friend, for Dhárini has more than once quelled her jealousy to defer to my wishes.

JAYA·SENA *(approaching)*: Victory, sire! Her Majesty asks you: "Please reward my labors by inspecting the glamour of the *ashóka* blossoms."

KING: Is the queen right there? 5.30

JAYA·SENA: To be sure. She's released the rest of the ladies of the harem after honoring them with gifts according to their merits, and is now waiting for Your Majesty with only her own attendants—Málavika first among them.

KING *(glancing gleefully at the* JESTER*)*: Jaya·sena, show the way.

JAYA·SENA: This way, Your Majesty, this way.

They walk about.

JESTER *(looking around)*: What ho, comrade, spring seems 5.35
to be a little way past its first youth in the pleasure garden.

KING: You're quite right.

> Coming first with a scattering of *kúrabaka* blossoms
> and a lace of fruit bursting on the mango trees,
> the youth of the season now approaches its climax
> and fills the heart with longing.

JESTER *(walking about)*: What ho, here is the golden *ashóka*, blanketed as it were in clusters of flowers. Look, sir!

RĀJĀ: sthāne khalv ayaṃ prasava|mantharo 'bhūt. yad ayam idānīm an|anya|sādhāraṇīṃ śobhām udvahati. paśya:

5.40 sarv'|âśoka|tarūṇāṃ
  prathamaṃ sūcita|vasanta|vibhavānām
nirvṛtta|dohade 'smin
  saṃkrāntān' îva kusumāni. [5]

VIDŪṢAKAḤ: ⌜bho, vīsaddho hohi! amhesu saṃṇihidesu vi Dhāriṇī passa|parivaṭṭiṇiṃ Mālaviaṃ aṇumaṇṇedi.⌟

RĀJĀ *(sa|harṣam)*: sakhe, paśya:

mām iyam abhyuttiṣṭhati
  devī vinayād anūtthitā priyayā
vismṛta†|hasta|kamalayā
  nar'|êndra|Lakṣmyā Vasumat" îva. [6]

tataḥ praviśati DHĀRIṆĪ, MĀLAVIKĀ, PARIVRĀJIKĀ, *vibhavataś ca* PARIVĀRAḤ.

5.45 MĀLAVIKĀ *(ātma|gatam)*: ⌜jāṇāmi ṇimittaṃ kodu'|âlaṃkārassa. taha vi bisiṇī|patta|gadaṃ salilaṃ via vevadi me hiaaṃ. avi a dakkhiṇ'|êdaraṃ vi me ṇaaṇaṃ bahuso phuradi.⌟

VIDŪṢAKAḤ: ⌜bho vaassa, vivāha|ṇevaccheṇa sa|visesaṃ khu sohadi atta|hodī Mālaviā!⌟

RĀJĀ: paśyāmy enām, y" âiṣā

an|ati|lambi|dukūla|nivāsinī
  bahubhir ābharanaiḥ pratibhāti me,
uḍu|gaṇair uday'|ônmukha|candrikā
  gata|himair iva Caitra|vibhāvarī. [7]

KING: He was right to delay his flowering. For now his brilliance is quite unparalleled. See:

> Now that his craving has been satisfied, it seems 5.40
> as if the flowers of all *ashóka* trees,
> those first harbingers of the bounty of spring,
> had been transferred to this one.

JESTER: What ho, trust your luck! Dhárini is permitting Málavika to remain at her side even though we're around.

KING *(joyfully)*: Look, my friend:

> The noble lady stands to greet me, my beloved
> rising modestly after her,
> like the very goddess Earth joined by royal Glory,
> who's lost the lotus from her hand.*

Enter DHÁRINI, MÁLAVIKA, KÁUSHIKI, *and* ATTENDANTS *in order of rank.*

MÁLAVIKA *(to herself)*: I know the simple reason why I was 5.45
dressed in marriage jewelry. But even so my heart quivers like water on a lotus leaf. And my left eye twitches so much, too.*

JESTER: What ho, comrade, I dare say the lady Málavika looks rather good in wedding dress!

KING: I see her, who,

> wearing a short, pale veil
> and bedecked with a host of jewels,
> looks like a hazeless spring night
> with stars and a rising moon.*

DEVĪ *(upetya)*: ⌜jedu ajja|utto!⌟

5.50 VIDŪṢAKAḤ: ⌜vaḍḍhadu hodī.⌟

PARIVRĀJIKĀ: vijayatāṃ devaḥ.

RĀJĀ: bhagavati, abhivādaye.

PARIVRĀJIKĀ: abhimata|siddhir astu.

DEVĪ *(sa|smitam)*: ⌜eso de amhehiṃ taruṇī|jaṇa|sahāassa asoo saṃketa|gharaaṃ saṃkappido.⌟

5.55 VIDŪṢAKAḤ: ⌜bho, ārāhio si!⌟

RĀJĀ *(sa|vrīḍam aśokam abhitaḥ parikrāman)*:

n' âyaṃ devyā bhājanatvaṃ na neyaḥ
  sat|kārāṇām īdṛśānām aśokaḥ,
yaḥ s'|âvajño mādhava|śrī|niyoge
  puṣpaiḥ śaṃsaty ādaraṃ tvat|prayatne. [8]

VIDŪṢAKAḤ: ⌜bho, vīsaddho bhavia tumaṃ jovvaṇavadiṃ imaṃ pekkha.⌟

DEVĪ: ⌜kaṃ?⌟

5.60 VIDŪṢAKAḤ: ⌜tavaṇī'|âsoassa kusuma|sohaṃ.⌟

QUEEN *(approaching)*: Victory, my noble husband!

JESTER: May you prosper, my lady. 5.50

KÁUSHIKI: May Your Majesty triumph.

KING: Greetings, reverend lady.

KÁUSHIKI: May you achieve what you have in mind.

QUEEN *(with a smile)*: We've set up this ashóka tree for you as a place to meet your young ladies.

JESTER: Wow, she's very kind to you! 5.55

KING *(shyly walking around the ashóka)*:

> Verily he, this joyful *ashóka*, deserves to be honored
> by Your Highness in this manner,
> for he has ignored the command of the vernal
> goddess, and shows, by blooming,
> his respect for your efforts.*

JESTER: Sir, now you can admire this virginal beauty to your heart's content.

QUEEN: Who do you mean?

JESTER: The splendor of the blooming golden *ashóka*. 5.60

sarve upaviśanti.

RĀJĀ *(MĀLAVIKĀṂ vilokya, ātma|gatam)*: kaṣṭaḥ khalu saṃnidhi|viprayogaḥ!

aham rath'|âṅga|nām" êva, priyā saha|car" îva me;
an|anujñāta|saṃparkā Dhāriṇī rajan" îva nau. [9]

KAÑCUKĪ: jayatu devaḥ! amātyo vijñāpayati: «tasmin Vidarbha|viṣay'†|ôpāyane dve śilpa|kārike mārga|pariśramād alasa|śarīre iti pūrvaṃ na praveśite. saṃprati dev'|ôpasthāna|yogye. tad ājñāṃ devo dātum arhat'» îti.

5.65 RĀJĀ: praveśaya te.

KAÑCUKĪ: yad ājñāpayati devaḥ.

(iti niṣkramya, tābhyāṃ saha punaḥ praviśya)

ita, ito bhavatyau.

PRATHAMĀ *(jan'|ântikam)*: ⌜halā Raaṇīe, a|puvvaṃ vi edaṃ rāa|ulaṃ pavisantīe pasīdadi me abbhandara|gado appā.⌟

5.70 DVITĪYĀ: ⌜Josiṇie, maha vi evvaṃ. atthi khu loa|vādo: «āāmi suhaṃ vā dukkhaṃ vā hiaa|samavatthā kahedi» tti.⌟

PRATHAMĀ: ⌜so dāṇiṃ sacco hodu!⌟

All sit down.

KING *(looking at* MÁLAVIKA, *to himself)*: Oh but it's hard to bear separation even while we are together!

> I'm like the *chakra* gander,*
> my beloved like his mate;
> and Dhárini, frowning on our union,
> is like the night to us.

CHAMBERLAIN: Victory, sire! The minister sends this message: "In the booty from Vidárbha land there were two skilled maids whom I had not brought to your audience because I deemed them too exhausted from their journey. They are now fit to attend Your Majesty. They await your command."

KING: Bring them. 5.65

CHAMBERLAIN: As Your Majesty commands.

(Exit, then reenter with the two women, JYÓTSNIKA *and* RÁJANIKA.*)*

This way, ladies.

JYÓTSNIKA *(confidentially)*: Rájanika my dear, even though I'm a stranger to this kingdom, my inner soul is unruffled as I enter.

RÁJANIKA: Same with me, Jyótsnika. The proverb says, "The 5.70
state of the heart tells you of joy and sadness to come."

JYÓTSNIKA: May it be so now!

KAÑCUKĪ: eṣa devyā saha devas tiṣṭhati. upasarpatāṃ bhavatyau.

ubhe upasarpataḥ. MĀLAVIKĀ PARIVRĀJIKĀ *ca ceṭyau dṛṣṭvā parasparam avalokayataḥ.*

UBHE *(praṇipatya)*: ⌜jedu bhaṭṭā! jedu bhaṭṭiṇī!⌟

5.75 RĀJĀ: niṣīdatam.

ubhe upaviṣṭe.

RĀJĀ: kasyāṃ kalāyām abhivinīte bhavatyau?

UBHE: ⌜bhaṭṭā, saṃgīde abbhandara mha.⌟

RĀJĀ: devi, gṛhyatām anayor anyatarā.

5.80 DEVĪ: ⌜Mālavie, ido pekkha! kadarā de saṃgīda|saaāriṇī ruccaï?⌟

UBHE (MĀLAVIKĀṂ *dṛṣṭvā)*: ⌜amho, bhaṭṭi|dāriā!⌟ *(iti praṇamya)* ⌜jedu, jedu bhaṭṭi|dāriā!⌟

iti tayā saha bāṣpaṃ visṛjataḥ. sarve sa|vismayam ālokayanti.

RĀJĀ: ke bhavatyau, kā v" êyam?

CHAMBERLAIN: Here stands the king with the queen. You may approach, ladies.

The women approach. MÁLAVIKA *and* KÁUSHIKI *glance at one another after seeing the two maids.*

THE TWO MAIDS *(prostrating themselves)*: Victory, sire! Victory, Your Highness!

KING: Sit.

THE MAIDS *sit down.*

KING: In which art are you proficient, good women?

THE TWO MAIDS: Sire, we're skilled in music.

KING: Choose one of them for yourself, my lady.

QUEEN: Málavika, look here! Which of them would you like to accompany you with music?

THE TWO MAIDS *(noticing* MÁLAVIKA*)*: Ah, the princess! *(bowing)* Victory, victory, princess!

They burst out in tears along with MÁLAVIKA. *Everyone stares in amazement.*

KING: Who are you and who is she?

PRATHAMĀ: ⌜deva, iaṃ amhāṇaṃ bhaṭṭi|dāriā!⌟

5.85 RĀJĀ: katham iva?

UBHE: ⌜suṇādu bhaṭṭā. jo so bhaṭṭiṇo vijaa|daṇḍehiṃ Vidabbha|ṇāhaṃ vasī|karia bandhaṇādo moido kumāro Māhavaseṇo ṇāma, tassa iaṃ kaṇīasī bhaïṇī, Mālaviā ṇāma.⌟

DEVĪ: ⌜kahaṃ? rāa|dāriā iaṃ? candaṇaṃ khu mae pādu"|ôvaogeṇa dūsidaṃ!⌟

RĀJĀ: ath' âtra|bhavatī katham itthaṃ|bhūtā?

MĀLAVIKĀ *(niśvasy' ātma|gatam)*: ⌜vihiṇo ṇioeṇa.⌟

5.90 DVITĪYĀ: ⌜suṇādu bhaṭṭā. dāāda|vasaṃ gade amhāṇaṃ bhaṭṭi|dārae Māhavaseṇe, tassa amacceṇa ajja|Sumadiṇā amhārisaṃ pariaṇaṃ ujjhia gūḍhaṃ avaṇīdā esā.⌟

RĀJĀ: śruta|pūrvaṃ may" âitāvat. tatas tataḥ?

UBHE: ⌜ado varaṃ ṇa āṇīmo.⌟

PARIVRĀJIKĀ: ataḥ param ahaṃ manda|bhāgyā kathayiṣyāmi.

UBHE: ⌜ajja|Kosiïe via sara|saṃjoo!⌟

5.95 MĀLAVIKĀ: ⌜ṇaṃ sā evva.⌟

JYÓTSNIKA: Sire, she's our king's daughter!

KING: How can that be? 5.85

THE TWO MAIDS: Listen, sire. You know Prince Mádhava·sena, whom your victorious troops released from captivity when they overthrew the king of Vidárbha. She is his younger sister, named Málavika.

QUEEN: What? So she's a princess? Then I've defiled sandalwood by using it to make slippers!

KING: So how did she end up like this?

MÁLAVIKA *(sighing, to herself)*: By the ordinance of fate.

RÁJANIKA: Listen, sire. When Mádhava·sena, the son of our 5.90
king, fell captive to his rival, his minister Mister Súmati carried her away in secret, leaving us and the other servants behind.

KING: I've heard as much. And then?

THE TWO MAIDS: We know no more.

KÁUSHIKI: I—woe unto me—shall tell the rest.

THE TWO MAIDS: This inflection sounds like Lady Káushiki's!

MÁLAVIKA: That's just who she is. 5.95

UBHE: ⌜jadi|vesa|dhāriṇī ajja|Kosiī dukkheṇa vibhāvīadi. bhaavadi, vandāmo.⌟

PARIVRĀJIKĀ: svasti bhavatībhyām.

RĀJĀ: katham, āpta|vargo 'yaṃ bhagavatyāḥ?

PARIVRĀJIKĀ: evam etat.

5.100 VIDŪṢAKAḤ: ⌜teṇa hi kahedu bhaavadī atta|hodīe vuttanda|sesaṃ.⌟

PARIVRĀJIKĀ *(sa|vaiklavyam)*: śrūyatāṃ tāvat. Mādhavasena|sacivaṃ Sumatiṃ mam' âgra|jam avagaccha.

RĀJĀ: upalabdham. tatas tataḥ?

PARIVRĀJIKĀ: sa imāṃ tathā|gata|bhrātṛkāṃ mayā sārdham apavāhya bhavat|saṃbandh'|âpekṣayā pathika|sārthaṃ Vidiśā|gāminam anupraviṣṭaḥ.

RĀJĀ: tatas tataḥ?

5.105 PARIVRĀJIKĀ: sa c' âṭavy|ante niviṣṭo gat'|âdhvā vaṇig|jano 'dhva|śram'|ārto viśramituṃ.

RĀJĀ: tatas tataḥ?

PARIVRĀJIKĀ: tataś ca,

THE TWO MAIDS: It's hard to imagine Mistress Káushiki wearing an ascetic's dress. Lady, we salute you.

KÁUSHIKI: Blessings on you, ladies.

KING: What? So your reverence is familiar with these people?

KÁUSHIKI: Indeed.

JESTER: Then let your reverence tell us the remainder of 5.100
Málavika's story.

KÁUSHIKI *(unsteadily)*: Listen, then. Know that Súmati, the minister of Mádhava·sena, is my elder brother.

KING: I see. Carry on.

KÁUSHIKI: When the princess's brother ended up the way he did, Súmati gathered her and me up, and joined a caravan traveling to Vídisha, planning to form an alliance with you.

KING: And then?

KÁUSHIKI: Having traveled some distance, the fatigued mer- 5.105
chant troop settled down to rest at the edge of a forest.

KING: And then?

KÁUSHIKI: And then,

tūṇīra|paṭṭa|pariṇaddha|bhuj'|ântarālam
  ā|pārṣṇi|lambi|śikhi|barha|kalāpa|dhāri
kodaṇḍa|pāṇi ninadat pratirodhakānām
  āpāta|duṣ|prasaham āvir abhūd anīkam. [10]

MĀLAVIKĀ *bhayaṃ rūpayati.*

5.110 VIDŪṢAKAḤ: ⌜mā bhāāhi! adikkantaṃ khu tatta|hodī kahedi.⌟

RĀJĀ: tatas tataḥ?

PARIVRĀJIKĀ: tato muhūrtaṃ baddha|yuddhās te parāṅmukhī|kṛtāḥ sārtha|vāha|yoddhāras taskaraiḥ.

RĀJĀ: bhagavati, ataḥ param idānīṃ kaṣṭaṃ śrotavyam...

PARIVRĀJIKĀ: hanta, tataḥ sa mat|sodaryaḥ

5.115 imāṃ parīpsur dur|jāte
  par'|âbhibhava|kātarām
bhartṛ|priyaḥ priyair bhartur
  ānṛṇyam asubhir gataḥ. [11]

PRATHAMĀ: ⌜hā, hado Sumadī!⌟

DVITĪYĀ: ⌜ado khu bhaṭṭi|dāriāe iaṃ samavatthā saṃvuttā.⌟

PARIVRĀJIKĀ *bāṣpaṃ visṛjati.*

RĀJĀ: bhagavati, tanu|bhṛtām īdṛśī loka|yātrā. na śocyas tatra|bhavān saphalī|kṛta|bhartṛ|piṇḍaḥ. tatas tataḥ?

Chests girt with baldrics for their quivers,
wearing peacock feather bundles
  hanging to their heels,
bows in their hands, a yelling host of brigands
  appeared and rushed upon us inexorably.

MÁLAVIKA *mimes fear.*

JESTER: Fear not! The lady's talking about the past.

KING: And then?

KÁUSHIKI: Then the fighters with the caravan engaged them in battle, but presently they were routed by the robbers.

KING: Reverend lady, the rest must be a sorry tale…

KÁUSHIKI: Well, my brother then

In an attempt to rescue from distress
the lady who dreaded falling into enemy hands,
putting love of his lord before love of his life,
paid his debt to his lord with his beloved life.

JYÓTSNIKA: Oh no, Súmati's dead!

RÁJANIKA: So that's how the princess has come to this state.

KÁUSHIKI *weeps.*

KING: Reverend lady, that's the way all who have a body must go. Do not lament that gentleman who proved true to his master's salt. What then?

5.120 PARIVRĀJIKĀ: tato 'haṃ moham upagatā yāvat saṃjñāṃ upalabhe, tāvad iyaṃ dur|labha|darśanā saṃvṛttā.

RĀJĀ: mahat khalu kṛcchram anubhūtaṃ bhagavatyā!

PARIVRĀJIKĀ: tato bhrātṛ|śarīram agnisāt kṛtvā punar navī|kṛta|vaidhavya|duḥkhayā mayā tvadīyaṃ deśam avatīry' ême kāṣāye gṛhīte.

RĀJĀ: yuktaḥ saj|janasy' âiṣa panthāḥ. tatas tataḥ?

PARIVRĀJIKĀ: s" êyam āṭavikebhyo Vīrasenaṃ, Vīrasenāc ca devīṃ gatā, devī|gṛhe labdha|praveśayā mayā punar dṛṣṭ"—êty etad avasānaṃ kathāyāḥ.

5.125 MĀLAVIKĀ *(ātma|gatam)*: ⌜kiṃ ṇu khu saṃpadaṃ bhaṭṭā bhaṇādi?⌟

RĀJĀ: aho, paribhav'|ôpahāriṇo vinipātāḥ! kutaḥ:

preṣya|bhāvena nām' êyaṃ
  devī|śabda|kṣamā satī,
snānīya|vastra|kriyayā
  patr'|ōrṇ" êv' ôpayujyate.† [12]

DEVĪ: ⌜bhaavadi, tue abhijaṇavadiṃ Mālaviaṃ aṇ|ācakkhandīe a|saṃpadaṃ kidaṃ.⌟

PARIVRĀJIKĀ: śāntaṃ pāpam! kāraṇen' âiva khalu mayā naibhṛtyam avalambitam.

5.130 DEVĪ: ⌜kiṃ via taṃ kāraṇaṃ?⌟

RĀJĀ: yadi vaktavyaṃ, kathyatām.

KÁUSHIKI: I fainted, and by the time I came round, she was nowhere to be seen. 5.120

KING: Indeed your reverence has suffered greatly!

KÁUSHIKI: Then, once I had consigned my brother's body to fire, I came, my pain at widowhood renewed, to your country and donned the russets.*

KING: That course is proper for gentlefolk. What then?

KÁUSHIKI: She was meanwhile passed from the jungle folk to Vira·sena, and from Vira·sena in turn to the queen. I saw her again when I was allowed into Her Majesty's quarters. That's the dénouement of the story.

MÁLAVIKA *(to herself)*: I wonder what my lord will say now. 5.125

KING: Alas, adversities breed disgrace! For:

> Though she deserves the title "Majesty,"
> I've actually employed her as a servant,
> as though I had used
> a silken kerchief for a bath towel.

QUEEN: Reverend lady, it was not right that you failed to announce that Málavika is of high birth.

KÁUSHIKI: Perish the thought! I stuck to secrecy for a good reason.

QUEEN: Pray what reason? 5.130

KING: Out with it unless it's a secret.

PARIVRĀJIKĀ: śrūyatām. iyaṃ pitari jīvati ken' âpi deva|yātrā|gatena siddh'|ādeśena sādhunā mat|samakṣaṃ ādiṣṭā: «saṃvatsara|mātraṃ preṣya|bhāvam anubhūya, tataḥ sadṛśa|bhartṛ|gāminī bhaviṣyat'» îti. tam avaśyaṃ|bhāvinam ādeśam asyās tvat|pāda|śuśrūṣayā pariṇamantam avekṣya kāla|pratīkṣayā mayā sādhu kṛtam iti paśyāmi.

RĀJĀ: yukt" ôpekṣā.

(praviśya)

5.135 KAÑCUKĪ: deva, kath"|ântareṇ' ântaritam idam amātyo vijñāpayati: «Vidarbha|gatam anuṣṭheyam avadhāritam asmābhiḥ. devasya tāvad abhiprāyaṃ śrotum icchām'» îti.

RĀJĀ: Maudgalya, tatra|bhavator bhrātror Yajñasena|Mādhavasenayor dvairājyam idānīm avasthāpayitu|kāmo 'smi.

tau pṛthag Varadā|kūle
 śiṣṭām uttara|dakṣine,
naktaṃ|divaṃ vibhajy' ôbhau
 śīt'|ôṣṇa|kiraṇāv iva. [13]

KAÑCUKĪ: deva, evam amātya|pariṣade nivedayāmi.

RĀJ" *âṅguly" ânumanyate. niṣkrāntaḥ* KAÑCUKĪ.

KÁUSHIKI: Hear me. While her father was still alive, an ascetic whose prophecies are known to come true happened by on a pilgrimage and told her in my presence that she'd first experience servitude for a year, then be married to a worthy husband. So when I beheld the prophecy carried out by her obeying your majesties, I decided to bide my time;* and I deem that I have done what was proper.

KING: You were right to forbear.

Enter the CHAMBERLAIN.

CHAMBERLAIN: Majesty, while you were occupied with this 5.135
other story, the minister sent you this message: "We have pondered what to do about Vidárbha. But first we wish to hear Your Majesty's intention."

KING: Maudgálya, henceforth I wish to establish a double kingship* of those two honorable cousins, Yajña·sena and Mádhava·sena.

Let them severally rule
the northern and southern bank of the Várada,
as the moon and sun divide
and rule the night and the day.

CHAMBERLAIN: Majesty, I shall inform the cabinet of ministers.

The KING *waves his finger in consent. Exit the* CHAMBERLAIN.

5.140 PRATHAMĀ *(jan'|ântikam)*: ⌜bhaṭṭi|dārie, diṭṭhiā bhaṭṭi|dārao addha|rajje paḍiṭṭhaṃ gamissadi!⌟

MĀLAVIKĀ: ⌜etthiaṃ dāva bahu mantavvaṃ, jaṃ jīvida|saṃsaādo mutto.⌟

(praviśya)

KAÑCUKĪ: vijayatāṃ devaḥ! amātyo vijñāpayati: «aho, kalyāṇī devasya buddhiḥ! mantri|pariṣado 'py evam eva darśanam. kutaḥ:

dvidhā vibhaktāṃ śriyam udvahantau,
dhuraṃ rath'|âśvāv iva saṃgrahītuḥ,
tau sthāsyatas te nṛpatī nideśe
paraspar'|âvagraha†|nirvikārau.» [14]

5.145 RĀJĀ: tena hi mantri|pariṣadaṃ brūhi: «senā|nye Vīrasenāya likhyatām, ‹evaṃ kriyatām› iti.»

KAÑCUKĪ: yad ājñāpayati devaḥ. *(iti niṣkramya sa|prābhṛtakaṃ lekhaṃ gṛhītvā punaḥ praviśya)* anuṣṭhitā prabhor ājñā. ayaṃ punar idānīṃ devasya senā|pateḥ Puṣpamitrasya sakāśāt sa|prābhṛtako lekhaḥ prāptaḥ. pratyakṣī|karotv enaṃ devaḥ.

RĀJĀ *sahas" ôpasṛtya, prābhṛtakaṃ s'|ôpacāraṃ śirasi kṛtvā* PARIJANĀY' *ârpayati, lekhaṃ ca nāṭyen' ôdveṣṭayati.*

DEVĪ *(ātma|gatam)*: ⌜amhahe, tado|muhaṃ evva ṇo hiaaṃ! suṇissaṃ dāva guru|aṇa|kusal'|âṇandaraṃ puttassa Vasumittassa vuttantaṃ. adi|bhāre khu me puttao seṇā|vaïṇā ṇiutto.⌟

JYÓTSNIKA *(confidentially)*: Princess, thank heaven the prince 5.140
will be established in half the kingdom!

MÁLAVIKA: The simple fact that his life is no longer in danger is a great thing.

Enter the CHAMBERLAIN.

CHAMBERLAIN: Victory, sire! The minister says to tell: "Ah, Your Majesty's idea is excellent! The cabinet of ministers sees it the same way. For:

Bearing their shares of royal dignity,
the two kings shall remain
compliant to your dictates,
as a pair of horses yoked to a chariot obey the driver
each checking the other's pace.

KING: Then tell the cabinet of ministers to write to general 5.145
Vira·sena that he should arrange it so.

CHAMBERLAIN: As Your Majesty commands. *(exit, then reenter bearing a letter and a present)* I've done as you commanded, sire. Now here is a letter and a present sent to Your Majesty by General Pushpa·mitra. Have a look at it, sire.

The KING *approaches hurriedly, lifts the present ceremoniously to his forehead, hands it to his* ATTENDANTS, *then mimes unfolding the letter.*

QUEEN *(to herself)*: Ah, that's where my heart turns! Now I shall hear if my father-in-law is well, and learn how my son Vasu·mitra fares. The general surely assigned a great burden to my little son.

RĀJĀ *(upaviśya vācayati)*: svasti. yajña|śaraṇāt senā|patiḥ Puṣpamitro Vaidiśa|sthaṃ putram āyuṣmantam Agnimitraṃ snehāt pariṣvajy' ânudarśayati: «viditam astu, yo 'sau rāja†|yajña|dīkṣitena mayā rāja|putra|śata|parivṛtaṃ Vasumitraṃ goptāram ādiśya saṃvatsar'|ôpāvartanīyo nir|argalas turago visṛṣṭaḥ, sa Sindhor dakṣiṇe rodhasi carann aśv'|ânīkena Yavanānāṃ prārthitaḥ. tata ubhayoḥ senayor mahān āsīt saṃmardaḥ.»

5.150 DEVĪ *viṣādaṃ nirūpayati.*

RĀJĀ: katham īdṛśaṃ saṃvṛttaṃ? *(śeṣaṃ punar vācayati.)*

«tataḥ parān parājitya Vasumitreṇa dhanvinā
prasahya hriyamāṇo me vāji|rājo nivartitaḥ» [15]

DEVĪ: ⌜imiṇā assasidaṃ me hiaaṃ.⌟

RĀJĀ *(lekha|śeṣam vācayati)*: «so 'ham idānīṃ Aṃśumat" êva Sagaraḥ pautreṇa pratyāhṛt'|âśvo yakṣye. tad idānīm a|kāla|hīnaṃ vigata|roṣa|cetasā bhavatā vadhū|janena saha yajña|sevanāy' āgantavyam» iti.

KING *(sits down and reads it out)*: Hail. General Pushpa·mitra sends his fond embrace from the sacrificial hut to his son Agni·mitra (may his life be long) in the land of Vídisha, and informs him: "Let it be known that a regiment of Greek* cavalry has made an attempt against the horse—which I, after being consecrated for the royal sacrifice,* had released to go unfettered and to be returned after a year, appointing Vasu·mitra and his company of a hundred princes to protect it—while it was roaming on the southern bank of the Indus.* A great clash then ensued between the two armies."

The QUEEN *mimes despair.* 5.150

KING: How could such a thing have happened? *(He continues reading.)*

"Vasu·mitra then grabbed his bow,
defeated the foe,
and brought back the royal horse
that they were dragging away."

QUEEN: That puts my heart at rest.

KING *(reads out the rest of the letter)*: "So now that my grandson has returned my horse just as Ánshumat had returned Ságara's,* I shall perform the sacrifice. Please come therefore without delay, emptying your mind of anger,* accompanied by your wives, to attend to the sacrifice."

5.155 RĀJĀ: anugṛhīto 'smi.

PARIVRĀJIKĀ: diṣṭyā putra|vijayena dampatī vardhete. (DEVĪṂ *vilokya)*

bhartr" âsi vīra|patnīnāṃ
  ślāghyāyāṃ sthāpitā dhuri.
«vīra|sūr» iti śabdo 'yam
  tanayāt tvām upasthitaḥ. [16]

VIDŪṢAKAḤ: ⌜hodi, parituṭṭho mhi jaṃ pidaraṃ aṇujādo vaccho tti.⌟

RĀJĀ: Maudgalya, nanu kalabhena yūtha|patir anukṛtaḥ.

KAÑCUKĪ:

5.160 n' âitāvatā vīra|vijṛmbhitena
  cittasya no vismayam ādadhāti,
yasy' â|pradhṛṣyaḥ prabhavas tvam uccair,
  agner apāṃ dagdhur iv' ōru|janmā. [17]

RĀJĀ: Maudgalya, Yajñasena|śyālam urarī|kṛtya mucyantāṃ sarve bandhana|sthāḥ.

KAÑCUKĪ: yad ājñāpayati devaḥ.

iti niṣkrāntaḥ.

DEVĪ: ⌜Jaaseṇe, gaccha, Irāvadi|ppamuhāṇaṃ ande|urāṇaṃ puttassa viaa|vuttandaṃ ṇivedehi.⌟

KING: I'm obliged. 5.155

KÁUSHIKI: Congratulations to the couple on the victory of their son. *(looking at the* QUEEN*)*

> Your husband gave you the exalted rank
> of first among the wives of heroes.
> Now your son has granted you
> the title "mother of heroes."

JESTER: Mistress, I'm pleased that the son takes after his father.*

KING: Maudgálya, it appears the elephant calf is imitating the prime bull.

CHAMBERLAIN:

> It is no surprise to my mind 5.160
> that his heroism burgeons thus far,
> for he comes from lofty and unconquerable stock
> —you—
> as the fire that burns water came
> from the thigh-born sage.*

KING: Maudgálya, let all prisoners be released, including Yajña·sena's brother-in-law.*

CHAMBERLAIN: As Your Majesty commands.

Exit.

QUEEN: Go, Jaya·sena, and tell Irávati and the rest of the harem this news of my son's victory.

5.165 PRATĪHĀRĪ: ⌜taha.⌟

iti prasthitā.

DEVĪ: ⌜ehi dāva!⌟

PRATĪHĀRĪ *(pratinivṛtya)*: ⌜iaṃ mhi.⌟

DEVĪ *(jan'|ântikam)*: ⌜jaṃ mae asoa|dohala|ṇioe Mālaviāe paḍiṇṇādaṃ, taṃ se ahiaṇaṃ a ṇivedia, maha vaaṇeṇa Irāvadiṃ aṇuṇehi, «tue ahaṃ saccādo ṇa paribbhaṃsaï-davv"» êtti.†⌟

5.170 PRATĪHĀRĪ: ⌜jaṃ devī āṇavedi.⌟ *(iti niṣkramya, punaḥ praviśya)* ⌜bhaṭṭiṇi, putta|vijaa|ṇimitteṇa paritoseṇa ande|urāṇaṃ āharaṇāṇaṃ maṃjūsa mhi saṃvuttā!⌟

DEVĪ: ⌜kiṃ ettha accariaṃ? sāhāraṇo khu tāṇaṃ maha a aaṃ abbhudao.⌟

PRATĪHĀRĪ *(jan'|ântikam)*: ⌜bhaṭṭiṇi, Irāvadī viṇṇavedi: «sarisaṃ khu devīe pahavantīe. tuha vaaṇaṃ puḍhama|saṃkappidaṃ ṇa jujjaï aṇṇahā kāduṃ» tti.⌟

DEVĪ: ⌜bhaavadi, tue aṇumadā icchāmi ajja|Sumadiṇā puḍhama|saṃkappidaṃ Mālaviaṃ ajja|uttassa paḍivādeduṃ.⌟

PARIVRĀJIKĀ: idānīm api tvam ev' âsyāḥ prabhavasi.

5.175 DEVĪ (MĀLAVIKĀṂ *haste gṛhītvā)*: ⌜ajja|utto idaṃ pia|ṇivedaṇ'|âṇurūvaṃ pāritosiaṃ paḍicchadu.⌟

JAYA·SENA: Right. 5.165

She sets off.

QUEEN: Wait a moment!

JAYA·SENA *(turning back)*: Yes?

QUEEN *(confidentially)*: Tell Irávati what I promised Málavika when I appointed her to fulfill the *ashóka*'s craving; tell her also of her high birth, and beseech her on my behalf not to let me down by making my promise untrue.

JAYA·SENA: As Your Majesty commands. *(exit, then reenter)* 5.170
Mistress, the victory of your son made the harem ladies so happy they've turned me into a veritable jewel box with the ornaments they gave me!

QUEEN: What's the surprise in that? Obviously they share my happiness.

JAYA·SENA *(confidentially)*: Mistress, Irávati says to tell you: "Your request befits a queen mother. Once you have promised something, you mustn't go back on your word."

QUEEN: Reverend lady, with your permission I wish to give Málavika to my noble husband, for whom the noble Súmati had originally intended her.

KÁUSHIKI: It is still you alone who has authority over her.

QUEEN *(holding* MÁLAVIKA *by the hand)*: Let my noble hus- 5.175
band accept this gift worthy of the good news we just received.

RĀJĀ *sa/vrīḍaṃ joṣam āste.*

DEVĪ *(sa/smitam)*: ⌜kiṃ avadhīredi maṃ ajja|utto?⌟

VIDŪṢAKAḤ: ⌜hodi, eso loa|vvavahāro: savvo vi ṇava|varo lajj'|āduro hodi tti.⌟

RĀJĀ VIDŪṢAKAM *avekṣate.*

5.180 VIDŪṢAKAḤ: ⌜aha vā, devīe evva kida|ppaṇaa|visesaṃ diṇṇa|devī|saddaṃ Mālaviaṃ atta|bhavaṃ paḍiggahīduṃ icchadi.⌟

DEVĪ: ⌜edāe rāja|dāriāe ahiaṇeṇa evva diṇṇo devī|saddo. kiṃ puṇar|utteṇa?⌟

PARIVRĀJIKĀ: mā, m" âivam!

> apy ākara|samutpannā maṇi|jātir a|saṃskṛtā
> jāta|rūpeṇa, kalyāṇi, na hi saṃyogam arhati. [18]

DEVĪ: ⌜marisedu bhaavadī, abbhudaa|kahāe mae ṇa lakkhidaṃ. Jaaseṇe, gaccha dāva! kosea|patt'|ôṇṇaṃ uvaṇehi.⌟

5.185 PRATĪHĀRĪ: ⌜jaṃ devī āṇavedi.⌟ *(iti niṣkramya, patr'/ōrṇaṃ gṛhītvā punaḥ praviśya)* ⌜devi, edaṃ.⌟

DEVĪ (MĀLAVIKĀM *avaguṇṭhya)*: ⌜dāṇiṃ ajja|utto paḍicchadu.⌟

RĀJĀ: devi, tvac|chāsanād a|pratyuttarā vayam.

The KING *stays bashfully silent.*

QUEEN *(smiling)*: Does my noble husband just ignore me?

JESTER: Mistress, that's the way of the world: all new bridegrooms are shy.

The KING *looks pointedly at the* JESTER.

JESTER: Or rather, Sire here wishes to accept Málavika after 5.180
you, the queen, have shown her special favor by giving her the title "Queen."

QUEEN: She's the daughter of a king, so the title "Queen" is her birthright. What's the point in reiterating it?

KÁUSHIKI: Not so, not so!

> Though produced in a jewel mine,
> no gemstone of any kind is worthy
> of union with gold, noble lady,
> unless it is polished first.

QUEEN: Forgive me, reverend lady, for neglecting that because of the happy news. Jaya·sena, off you go! Bring a silken shawl.

JAYA·SENA: As the queen commands. *(exit, then re-enter with* 5.185
a silken shawl) Here, Your Majesty.

QUEEN *(enrobing* MÁLAVIKA*)*: Now accept her, my noble husband.

KING: My lady, if that's your command, I have no more to say.

PARIVRĀJIKĀ: hanta, pratigṛhītā!

VIDŪṢAKAḤ: ⌜amho devīe aṇuūladā!⌟

DEVĪ PARIJANAM *avalokayati.*

PARIJANAḤ (MĀLAVIKĀM *upetya)*: ⌜jedu bhaṭṭiṇī!⌟

DEVĪ PARIVRĀJIKĀṂ *nirvarṇayati.*

PARIVRĀJIKĀ: n' âitac citraṃ tvayi. kutaḥ:

pratipakṣeṇ' âpi patiṃ
  sevante bhartṛ|vatsalāḥ sādhvyaḥ;
anya|saritāṃ śatāni hi
  samudra|gāḥ prāpayanty abdhim. [19]

(praviśya)

NIPUṆIKĀ: ⌜jedu bhaṭṭā! Irāvadī viṇṇavedi: «jaṃ uvaār'|âdikkameṇa tadā bhaṭṭiṇo avaraddhaṃ, taṃ saaṃ bhaṭṭiṇo aṇuūlaṃ mae āaridaṃ. saṃpadaṃ puṇṇa|maṇoraheṇa bhaṭṭiṇā pasāda|metteṇa saṃbhāvaïdavv"» êtti.⌟

DEVĪ: ⌜Ṇiuṇie, avassaṃ tāe saṃdesaṃ sevidum ajja|utto jāṇissadi.⌟

NIPUṆIKĀ: ⌜jaṃ devī āṇavedi.⌟

iti niṣkrāntā.

KÁUSHIKI: Accepted, at last!

JESTER: Oh, gracious is the queen!

The QUEEN *glances at her* ATTENDANTS. 5.190

ATTENDANTS *(approaching* MÁLAVIKA*)*: Victory, Your Highness!

The QUEEN *looks at* KÁUSHIKI.

KÁUSHIKI: This is no surprise, coming from you. For:

> A good woman devoted to her husband
> will serve him even by giving him rival wives;
> after all a river joining the ocean
> also brings him hundreds of other streams.

Enter NÍPUNIKA. 5.195

NÍPUNIKA: Victory, sire! Irávati says to tell you: "When I offended my husband by scorning his courtesy, I actually did what was favorable for my husband. Now that his desire has been fulfilled, I expect him to honor me with his forgiveness."

QUEEN: Nípunika, I'm sure my noble husband will know how to react to her message.

NÍPUNIKA: As the queen commands.

Exit.

5.200 PARIVRĀJIKĀ: deva, aham amunā bhavat|saṃbandhena carit'|ârthaṃ Mādhavasenaṃ sabhājayitum icchāmi, yadi me tava prasādaḥ.

DEVĪ: ⌜bhaavadi, ṇa juttaṃ amhe pariccattuṃ.⌟

RĀJĀ: bhagavati, madīyeṣu lekheṣu tatra|bhavatas tvām uddiśya sabhājan'|âkṣarāṇi pātayiṣyāmi.

PARIVRĀJIKĀ: yuvayoḥ snehena paravān ayaṃ janaḥ.

DEVĪ: ⌜āṇavedu ajja|utto, kiṃ bhūo vi piaṃ aṇuciṭṭhāmi?⌟

5.205 RĀJĀ: kim ataḥ param api priyam asti? tath" âp' îdam astu:

tvaṃ me prasāda|sumukhī bhava, caṇḍi, nityam—
etāvad eva mṛgaye pratipakṣa|hetoḥ.† [20*ab*]

BHARATA|VĀKYAM:

āśāsyam īti|vigama|prabhṛti prajānāṃ
saṃpatsyate na khalu goptari n' Âgnimitre. [20*cd*]

iti niṣkrāntāḥ sarve.

5.210 *iti pañcamo 'ṅkaḥ.*

iti mahā|kavi|Kālidāsa|viracitaṃ Mālavik"|Âgnimitraṃ nāma nāṭakaṃ samāptam.

KÁUSHIKI: Majesty, if you'll allow me, I wish to felicitate Mádhava·sena now that he's achieved his purpose, this alliance with you. 5.200

QUEEN: You ought not to leave us, reverend lady.

KING: Reverend lady, I'll drop some congratulatory words on your behalf in my letter to him.

KÁUSHIKI: Your kindness leaves me no choice.

QUEEN: Command me, my noble husband: what else shall I do to make you happy?

KING: Could anything make me happier? But anyway, this is what I'd like: 5.205

> Show me always your pleasant face, my fierce lady—
> this is all I seek for the sake of your co-wife.*

ACTORS' BENEDICTION: *

> As for my desires concerning my subjects,
> such as that calamities* avoid them—
> there's no way they won't come true so long as
> Agni·mitra is their protector.

Exeunt all.

End of Act Five. 5.210

End of the play "Málavika and Agni·mitra," composed by the great poet Kali·dasa.

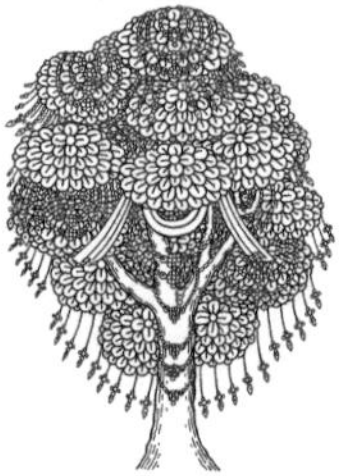

CHĀYĀ

The following is a Sanskrit paraphrase (chāyā) *of the Prakrit passages (marked with* ⌜corner brackets⌟ *in the play). References are to act and paragraph.*

1.16 ājñapt" âsmi devyā Dhāriṇyā «a|cira|pravṛtt'|ôpadeśaṃ chalitaṃ nāma nāṭyam antareṇa kīdṛśī Mālavik"?» êti nāṭy'|ācāryam ārya|Gaṇadāsaṃ praṣṭum. tad yāvat saṃgīta|śālāṃ gacchāmi.

1.19 halā Kaumudike, kutas ta iyaṃ dhīratā, yat samīpen' âpy atikrāmantī ito dṛṣṭiṃ na dadāsi?

1.20 amho, Bakulāvalikā! sakhi, idaṃ devyāḥ śilpi|sakāśād ānītaṃ nāga|mudrā|sanātham aṅgulīyakaṃ snigdhaṃ nidhyāyantī tav' ôpālambhe patit" âsmi.

1.21 sthāne khalu sajjati dṛṣṭiḥ! anen' âṅgulīyaken' ôdbhinna|kiraṇa|kesareṇa kusumita iva te 'gra|hastaḥ pratibhāti.

1.22 halā, kutra prasthit" âsi?

1.23 devyā vacanena nāṭy'|ācāryam ārya|Gaṇadāsaṃ praṣṭum, «upadeśa|grahaṇe kīdṛśī Mālavik"?» êti.

1.24 sakhi, īdṛśena vyāpāreṇ' â|saṃnihit" âpi dṛṣṭā kila sā bhartrā.

1.25 ām. sa jano devyāḥ pārśva|gataś citre dṛṣṭaḥ.

1.26 katham iva?

1.27 śṛṇu. citra|śālāṃ gatā devī pratyagra|varṇa|rāgāṃ citra|lekhām ācāryasy' âvalokayantī tiṣṭhati. tasminn antare bhart" ôpasthitaḥ.

1.28 tatas tataḥ?

1.29 upacār'|ân|antaram ek'|āsan'|ôpaviṣṭena bhartrā citra|gatāyā devyā parijana|madhya|gatām āsanna|dārikāṃ dṛṣṭvā devī pṛṣṭā—

1.30 kim iti?

1.31 «a|pūrv" êyaṃ dārikā tav' āsannā ālikhitā kiṃ|nāma|dhey"?» êti.

1.32 nanv ākṛti|viśeṣe ādaraḥ padaṃ karoti. tatas tataḥ?

1.33 tato 'vadhīrita|vacano bhartā śaṅkito devīṃ punar apy anubandhuṃ pravṛttaḥ. yāvad devī na kathayati, tāvat kumāryā Vasulakṣmy" ākhyātam: «āvutta, eṣā Mālavikā» iti.

1.34 sadṛśaṃ khalu bāla|bhāvasya! tataḥ paraṃ kathaya.

1.35 kim anyat? sāmprataṃ Mālavikā sa|viśeṣaṃ bhartur darśana|pathād rakṣyate.

1.36 halā, anutiṣṭha ātmano niyogam. aham apy etad aṅgulīyakaṃ devyā upaneṣyāmi.

1.38 eṣa nāṭy'|ācārya ārya|Gaṇadāsaḥ saṃgīta|śālāto niṣkrāmati. yāvad asy' ātmānaṃ darśayāmi.

1.43 ārya, vande.

1.45 ārya, devī pṛcchati: «apy upadeśa|grahaṇe n' âtikleśayati vaḥ śiṣyā Mālavikā?» iti.

1.48 atikrāmantīm iva Irāvatīṃ paśyāmi.

1.48 kṛt'|ârth" êdānīṃ vaḥ śiṣyā, yasyāṃ guru|jana evaṃ tuṣyati.

1.50 asti devyā varṇ'|âvaro bhrātā Vīraseno nāma. sa bhartrā Narmadā|tīre 'nta|pāla|durge sthāpitaḥ. tena «śilp'|âdhikāre yogy" êyaṃ dārik"» êti bhaginyai upāyanaṃ preṣitā.

1.53 atha kutra vaḥ śiṣyā?

1.55 tena hy anujānātu mām āryaḥ. yāvad asyā āryasya paritoṣa|nivedanen' ôtsāhaṃ vardhayāmi.

1.74 ājñapto 'smi tatra|bhavatā rājñā, «Gautama, cintaya tāvad upāyaṃ, yathā me yadṛcchā|dṛṣṭa|pratikṛtir Mālavikā pratyakṣa|darśanā bhavati» iti. may" âpi tat tathā kṛtam. yāvad asmai nivedayāmi.

1.77 vardhatāṃ bhavān!

1.81 prayoga|siddhiṃ pṛccha.

1.83 evam iva.

1.88 phalam apy a|cireṇa drakṣyasi.

1.107 samartham pratijñātam.

1.110 suṣṭhu bhavān bhaṇati.

1.114 bhagavati, Haradattasya Gaṇadāsasya ca samrambhe katham paśyasi?

1.116 yady apy evam, tath" âpi rāja|parigraho 'sya pradhānatvam upaharati.

1.119 avihā, avihā! upasthitā pīṭha|mardikāṃ paṇḍita|Kauśikīṃ puras|kṛtya devī.

1.125 jayatv ārya|putraḥ!

1.134 yadi māṃ pṛcchasi, etayor vivāda eva na me rocate.

1.136 bhavati, paśyāma urabhra|saṃpātam. kiṃ mudhā vetana|dānena?

1.137 nanu kalaha|priyo 'si.

1.138 m" âivam! anyonya|kalaha|priyayor matta|hastinor ekatarasminn a|nirjite kuta upaśamaḥ?

1.144 śrutam āryābhyāṃ bhagavatyā vacanam. eṣa piṇḍit'|ârtha: upadeśa|darśanān nirṇaya iti.

1.147 yadā punar manda|medhā śiṣyā upadeśaṃ malinayati, tadā ācāryasya doṣo nu?

1.150 katham idānīm?

1.150 alam ārya|putrasy' ôtsāha|kāraṇaṃ mano|rathaṃ pūrayitvā!

1.150 virama nir|arthakād ārambhāt.

1.151 suṣṭhu bhavatī bhaṇati. bho Gaṇadāsa, saṃgītak'|âpadeśena Sarasvaty|upāyana|modakāni khādataḥ kiṃ te su|labha|nigraheṇa vivādena?

1.154 a|cir'|ôpanītā vaḥ śiṣyā—tad a|pariniṣṭhitasy' ôpadeśasy' â|nyāyyaṃ prakāśanam.

1.156 tena hi dvāv api bhagavatyai upadeśaṃ darśayatam.

1.158 mūḍhe parivrājike! māṃ jāgratīm api suptām iva karoṣi?

1.162 nanu sa|kāraṇaṃ eva? ātmanaḥ pakṣo raksitavya, iti.

1.162 diṣṭyā kopa|vyājena devyā paritrāto bhavān. su|śikṣito 'pi sarva upadeśa|darśane na nipuṇo bhavati.

1.166 kā gatiḥ?

1.166 prabhavaty ācāryaḥ śiṣya|janasya.

1.170 bhaṇa viśrabdham. nanu prabhaviṣyāmy ātmanaḥ parijanasya?

1.172 bhagavati, bhaṇ' êdānīm.

1.175 tena hi dvāv api vargau prekṣā|gṛhe saṃgīta|racanāṃ kṛitvā atra|bhavato dūtaṃ preṣayatam. atha vā mṛdaṅga|śabda eva na utthāpayiṣyati.

1.178 vijayī bhava. na khalu vijaya|pratyarthiny aham āryasya.

1.185 yadi rāja|kāryeṣv īdṛśy upāya|nipuṇat" ārya|putrasya, tataḥ śobhanaṃ bhavet.

1.192 aho, a|vinaya ārya|putrasya!

1.194 bho, dhīraṃ gaccha! mā tatra|bhavatī Dhāriṇī visaṃvādayiṣyati.

2.13 upasthitaṃ nayana|madhu, saṃnihita|makṣikaṃ ca... tad a|pramatta idānīṃ prekṣasva.

2.15 prekṣatāṃ bhavān! na khalv asyāḥ praticchandāt parihīyate madhuratā.

2.22 dur|labhaḥ priyas; tasmin bhava, hṛdaya, nir|āśam. / aho, apāṅgako me prasphurati kim api vāmakaḥ! / eṣa sa cira|dṛṣṭaḥ katham upanetavyaḥ? / nātha, māṃ par'|âdhīnāṃ tvayi gaṇaya sa|tṛṣṇām.

2.24 bho, catuṣ|pada|vastukaṃ dvārī|kṛtya tvayy upakṣipta iv' ātmā tatra|bhavatyā...

2.28 bhavati, tiṣṭha! kim api vo vismṛtaḥ krama|bhedaḥ. taṃ tāvat prakṣyāmi.

2.33 nanu Gautama|vacanam apy āryo hṛdaye karoti?

2.37 sākṣiṇīṃ tāvat pṛccha. paścād yo mayā krama|bhedo lakṣitas, taṃ bhaṇiṣyāmi.

2.45 diṣṭyā parīkṣak'|ārādhanen' âryo vardhate.

2.47 pratham'|ôpadeśa|darśane prathamaṃ brāhmaṇasya pūjā kartavyā. sā punar vo vismṛitā?

2.53 mayā nāma mugdha|cātaken' êva śuṣka|ghana|garjite 'ntarikṣe jala|pānam iṣṭam.

2.55 tena hi paṇḍita|paritoṣa|pratyayā nanu mūḍha|jātiḥ. yady atra|bhavatyā śobhanaṃ bhaṇitaṃ, tata idam asyai pāritoṣikaṃ prayacchāmi.

2.57 tiṣṭha tāvat! guṇ'|ântaram a|jānan kim iti tvam ābharaṇaṃ dadāsi?

2.58 parakīyam, iti kṛtvā.

2.59 ārya|Gaṇadāsa, nanu darśit'|ôpadeśā vaḥ śiṣyā?

2.62 etāvān me mati|vibhavo bhavantaṃ sevitum.

2.65 sādhu, tvaṃ daridra ātura iva vaidyen' ôpanīyamānam auṣadhaṃ icchasi.

2.72 avidhā, avidhā, asmākaṃ bhojana|velā saṃvṛttā! atra|bhavato 'pi. ucita|vel"|âtikrame cikitsakā doṣam udāharanti. Haradatta, kim idānīṃ bhaṇasi?

2.77 nirvartayatv ārya|putro majjana|vidhim.

2.78 bhavati, viśeṣeṇa pāna|bhojanaṃ tvaraya.

2.81 bho, na kevalaṃ rūpe, śilpe 'py a|dvitīyā Mālavikā!

2.85 bhavat" âpy aham! dṛḍhaṃ vipaṇi|kandur iva ma udar'|âbhyantaraṃ dahyate.

2.87 gṛhīta|kṣaṇo 'smi. kim|tu megh'|āvalī|niruddhā jyotsn" êva parādhīna|darśanā tatra|bhavatī Mālavikā. bhavān api sūnā|paricara iva gṛdhra āmiṣa|lolupo bhīrukaś ca. tad an|āturo bhūtvā kārya|siddhiṃ prārthayamāno me rocase.

3.2 ājñapt" âsmi bhagavatyā, «upāyan'|ârthaṃ bīja|pūrakaṃ gṛhītv" āgacch'» êti. tad yāvat pramada|vana|pālikāṃ Madhukarikām anviṣyāmi.

3.2 eṣā tapanīy'|âśokam avalokayantī tiṣṭhati. yāvad enāṃ saṃbhāvayāmi.

3.4 Madhukarike, api sukhas ta udyāna|vyāpāraḥ?

3.5 aho, Samāhitikā! sakhi, svāgataṃ te.

3.6 halā, bhagavaty ājñāpayati: «a|rikta|pāṇin" âsmādṛśa|janena tatra|bhavatī devī draṣṭavyā. tad bīja|pūrakeṇa śuśrūṣitum icchām'» îti.

3.7 nanu saṃnihitaṃ bīja|pūrakam. kathay', ânyonya|saṃgharṣitayor nāṭy'|ācāryayor upadeśaṃ dṛṣṭvā kataro bhagavatyā praśaṃsita iti?

3.8 dvāv api kil' āgaminau prayoga|nipuṇau ca. kiṃ tu śiṣyā|guṇa|viśeseṇ' ônnamito Gaṇadāsaḥ.

3.9 atha Mālavikā|gataṃ kaulīnaṃ kiṃ śrūyate?

3.10 balavat khalu s'|âbhilāṣas tasyāṃ bhartā. kevalaṃ devyā Dhāriṇyāś cittaṃ rakṣann ātmanaḥ prabhutvaṃ na darśayati. Mālavik" âpy eṣu divaseṣu anubhūta|mukt" êva mālatī|mālā mlāyamānā lakṣyate. ataḥ paraṃ na jāne. visarjaya mām.

3.11 etac chākh"|âvalambitaṃ bīja|pūrakaṃ gṛhāṇa.

3.12 halā, tvam ap' îtaḥ peśalataraṃ sādhu|jana|śuśrūṣāyāḥ phalaṃ prāpnuhi.

3.14 sakhi, samaṃ eva gacchāvaḥ. aham apy asya cirāyamāṇa|kusum'|ôdgamasya tapanīy'|âśokasya dohada|nimittaṃ devyai vijñāpayāmi.

3.15 yujyate, adhikāraḥ khalu tava.

3.21 alaṃ bhavato dhīratām ujjhitvā paridevitena! dṛṣṭā mayā tatra|bhavatyā Mālavikāyāḥ priya|sakhī Bakulāvalikā. śrāvitā ca mayā yad bhavatā saṃdiṣṭaṃ.

3.23 «vijñāpaya bhartāram: anugṛhīt" âsmy anena niyogena. kiṃ tu sā tapasvinī devyā adhikataraṃ rakṣyamāṇā nāga|rakṣita iva nidhir na sukhaṃ samāsādayitavyā. tath" âpi ghaṭayiṣyām'» îti.

3.26 nanu bhaṇāmi, «tasmin sādhanīye kṛta upāy'|ôpakṣepa» iti? tat paryavasthāpayatu bhavān ātmānam.

3.28 nanu bhavān adya prathamaṃ vasant'|āvatāra|sūcakāni rakt'|âśoka|korakāṇy upāyanaṃ preṣya nava|vasant'|âvatār'|âpadeśen' Êrāvatyā Nipuṇikā|mukhena prārthitaḥ: «icchāmy ārya|putreṇa saha ḍol"|âdhirohaṇam anubhavitum» iti. bhavat" âpy asyai pratijñātam. tat pramada|vanam eva gacchāvaḥ.

3.30 katham iva?

3.33 n' ârhati bhavān antaḥ|pura|pratiṣṭhitaṃ dākṣiṇyam eka|pade pṛṣṭhataḥ kartum.

3.35 ita ito bhavān.

3.37 nanv etat pramada|vanaṃ pavana|bala|calābhiḥ pallav'|âṅgulibhis tvarayat' îva bhavantaṃ praveṣṭum.

3.40 praviśa nirvṛtti|lābhāya.

3.42 bho vayasya, avadhānena dṛṣṭiṃ dehi. etat khalu bhavantaṃ vilobhayitu|kāmayā pramada|vana|lakṣmyā yuvati|veṣa|lajjāpayitṛkaṃ vasanta|kusuma|nepathyaṃ gṛhītam.

3.46 a|vijñāta|hṛdayaṃ bhartāram abhilaṣanty ātmano 'pi tāval lajje. kuto vibhavaḥ snigdhasya sakhī|janasy' êmaṃ vṛttāntaṃ ākhyātum? na jāne, '|pratīkāra|gurukāṃ vedanāṃ kiyantaṃ kālaṃ madano māṃ neṣyat' îti.

3.46 kutra khalu prasthit" âsmi?

3.47 āḥ, saṃdiṣṭ" âsmi devyā, «Gautama|cāpalād ḍolā|paribhraṣṭāyāḥ sa|rujau mama caraṇau. tvaṃ tāvat tapanīy'|âśokasya dohadaṃ nirvartaya. yadi sa pañca|rātr'|âbhyantare kusumaṃ darśayati, tato 'haṃ tava...

3.47 abhilāṣa|pūrayitṛkaṃ prasādaṃ dāsyām'» îti. tad yāvan niyoga|bhūmiṃ prathamaṃ gatā bhavāmi. yāvad anupadaṃ mama caraṇ'|âlaṅkāra|hastayā Bakulāvalikay" āgantavyaṃ, paridevayiṣye tāvad visrabdhaṃ muhūrtakam.

3.49 hī hī! iyaṃ khalu sīdhu|pān'|ôdvejitasya matsyaṇḍik" ôpanatā!

3.51 eṣā khalu n" âti|paryāpta|veṣā paryutsuk" êv' âikākinī Mālavik" â|dūre vartate.

3.53 atha kim?

3.57 eṣā nanu taru|rāji|madhyān niṣkrāntā ita ev' āgacchati.

3.62 eṣ" âpi bhavān iva madana|vyādhinā parāmṛṣṭā bhaviṣyati.

3.64 ayaṃ sa lalita|dohad'|âpekṣī a|gṛhīta|kusuma|nepathya utkaṇṭhitāyā mam' ânukaroty aśokaḥ. yāvad asya pracchāya|śītale śilā|paṭṭake niṣaṇṇ" ātmānaṃ vinodayāmi.

3.65 śrutaṃ bhavatā? «utkaṇṭhit" âsm'» îti tatra|bhavatyā mantritam.

3.70 Irāvatīm iv' â|dūre prekṣe.

3.73 hṛdaya, nir|avalambān mano|rathād virama! kiṃ mām āyāsayasi?

3.77 sāṃpratam bhavato niḥ|saṃśayaṃ bhaviṣyati. eṣā arpita|madana|saṃdeśā vivikta enāṃ Bakulāvalikā upasthitā.

3.79 kim idānīm eṣā dāsyāḥ duhitā tava gurukaṃ saṃdeśaṃ vismarati? aham api tāvan na vismarāmi!

3.81 api sukhaṃ sakhyāḥ?

3.82 aho, Bakulāvalikā! sakhi, svāgataṃ te! upaviśa.

3.83 halā, tvaṃ tāvad idānīṃ devyā yogyatayā niyuktā. tad ekaṃ te caraṇam upanaya, yāvat s'|âlaktakaṃ, sa|nūpuraṃ karomi.

3.84 hṛdaya, alaṃ sukhitatay", «âyaṃ vibhava upasthita» iti! katham idānīm ātmānaṃ mocayeyam? atha v" âitad eva mama mṛtyu|maṇḍanaṃ bhaviṣyati?

3.85 kiṃ vicārayasi? utsukā khalv asya tapanīy'|âśokasya kusum'|ôdgame devī.

3.87 kiṃ khalu na jānāsi, a|kāraṇād devī imām antaḥ|pura|nepathyena na saṃyojayiṣyat' îti?

3.88 marṣaya tāvad enam!

3.90 ayi, śarīram asi me.

3.93 caraṇ'|ânurūpaḥ khalu tatra|bhavatyā adhikāra upakṣiptaḥ.

3.96 prahariṣyati tatra|bhavatī tvām aparāddham.

3.99 hañje Nipuṇike, śṛṇomi bahuśo, madaḥ kila strī|janasya viśeṣa|maṇḍanam iti. api satyo loka|vādo 'yam?

3.100 prathamaṃ loka|vāda eva. adya punaḥ satyaḥ saṃvṛttaḥ.

3.101 alaṃ mayi snehena. kuta idānīm avagataṃ, dolā|gṛhaṃ prathamaṃ gato bhart" êti?

3.102 bhaṭṭinyā a|khaṇḍitāt praṇayāt.

3.103 alaṃ sevayā! madhyasthatāṃ gṛhītvā bhaṇa.

3.104 vasant'|ôpāyana|lolupen' ārya|Gautamena kathitam. tvaratāṃ bhaṭṭinī.

3.105 hañje, madena klāmyamānam ātmānam ārya|putra|darśane hṛdayaṃ tvarayati. caraṇau punar na mārge prasarantaḥ.

3.106 nanu samprāpte svo dolā|gṛhaṃ.

3.107 Nipuṇike, n' âtr' ārya|putro dṛśyate!

3.108 avalokayatu bhaṭṭinī. parihāsa|nimittaṃ kutr'|âpi gūḍhena bhartrā bhavitavyam. āvām ap' îmaṃ priyaṅgu|latā|parikṣiptam aśoka|śilā|paṭṭakaṃ praviśāvaḥ.

3.110 avalokayatu bhaṭṭinī! cūt'|âṅkuraṃ vicinvatyor āvayoḥ pipīlikābhir daṣṭam.

3.111 kim iv' âitat?

3.112 eṣā Bakulāvalikā aśoka|pādapa|cchāyāyāṃ Mālavikāyāś caraṇ'|âlaṅ|kāraṃ nirvartayati.

3.113 a|bhūmir iyaṃ Mālavikāyāḥ. katham atra tarkayasi?

3.114 tarkayāmi, dolā|paribhraṣṭayā sa|ruja|caraṇayā devy" âśoka|dohad'|âdhikāre Mālavikā niyukt" êti. anyathā kathaṃ devī svayaṃ dhāritaṃ nūpura|yugalaṃ parijanasy' âbhyanujñāsyati?

3.115 mahatī khalv asyāḥ sambhāvanā.

3.116 kiṃ n' ânviṣyate bhartā?

3.117 hañje, na me caraṇāv anyataḥ pravartete, mano 'pi kim api vikārayati. āśaṅkitasya tāvad antaṃ gamiṣyāmi.

3.117 sthāne khalu kātaraṃ me hṛdayam.

3.118 api rocate te 'yaṃ rāga|rekhā|vinyāsaḥ?

3.119 ātmanaś caraṇa|gata iti lajje enaṃ praśaṃsitum. kathaya, kena prasādhana|kalāyām abhivinīt" âsi?

3.120 atra khalu bhartuḥ śisy" âsmi.

3.121 tvarasv' êdānīṃ guru|dakṣiṇāyai.

3.122 diṣṭyā na garvit" âsi.

3.123 upadeś'|ânurūpe caraṇe labdhv" âdya garvitā bhaviṣyāmi.

3.123 hanta, siddhaṃ me dautyam.

3.123 sakhi, ekasya te caraṇasy' âvasito rāga|vikṣepaḥ. kevalaṃ mukha|māruto lambhayitavyaḥ. atha vā... pravātam ev' âitat sthānam.

3.126 kutas te 'nuśayaḥ? ciraṃ bhavat" âitat krameṇ' ânubhavitavyam.

3.127 sakhi, aruṇa|śata|patram iva śobhate te caraṇam. sarvathā bhartur aṅka|parivartinī bhava.

3.130 halā, a|vacanīyaṃ mantrayase!

3.131 mantrayitavyam eva mayā mantritam.

3.132 priyā khalv ahaṃ tava.

3.133 na kevalaṃ mama...

3.134 kasya v" ânyasya?

3.135 guṇeṣv abhiniveṣino bhartur api.

3.136 alīkaṃ mantrayase. etad eva mayi n" âsti.

3.137 satyaṃ tvayi n" âsti? bhartuḥ kṛśeṣu dara|pāṇḍureṣv aṅgeṣu dṛśyate!

3.138 prathama|gaṇitam iva hat'|āśāyā uttaram.

3.139 anurāgo 'nurāgeṇa parīkṣitavya iti su|jana|vacanaṃ pramāṇī|kuru.

3.140 kim ātmanaś chandena mantrayase?

3.141 na hi! bhartur etāni praṇaya|mṛdukāny akṣarāṇi bimb'|ântaritāni.

3.142 halā, devīṃ vicintya na me hṛdayaṃ viśvasiti.

3.143 mugdhe, bhramara|saṃbādha iti vasant'|âvatāra|sarvasvaṃ kiṃ na cūta|prasavo 'vataṃsayitavyaḥ?

3.144 tvaṃ tāvad dur|jāte mam' âtyanta|sahāyinī bhava.

3.145 vimarda|surabhir Bakulāvalikā khalv aham.

3.148 hañje, paśya! kārit" âiv' âitasmin Bakulāvalikayā padaṃ Mālavikā!

3.149 bhaṭṭini, nir|vikārasy' âpy utsukatva|janaka upadeśaḥ.

3.150 sthāne khalu śaṅkitaṃ me hṛdayam. gṛhīt'|ârth" ân|antaraṃ cintayiṣyāmi.

3.151 eṣa dvitīyo 'pi te nirvṛtta|parikarmā caraṇaḥ. yāvad dvāv api sa|nūpurau karomi.

3.151 halā, uttiṣṭha. anutiṣṭha devyā aśoka|vikāsayitṛkaṃ niyogam.

3.153 śrutaṃ, devyā niyoga iti. bhavatv idānīm.

3.154 eṣa upārūḍha|rāga upabhoga|kṣamaḥ puratas te vartate—

3.155 kiṃ bhartā?

3.156 na tāvad bhartā. eṣo 'śoka|śākh"|âvalambī pallava|gucchaḥ. avataṃsaya tāvad enam.

3.157 api śrutaṃ bhavatā?

3.163 api nām' âvayoḥ saṃbhāvanā sa|phalā bhavet?

3.164 halā, n' âsti te doṣaḥ. nir|guṇo 'yam aśoko, yadi kusum'|ôdbheda|mantharo bhaved, ya īdṛśaṃ caraṇa|sat|kāraṃ labhate.

3.167 ehy enāṃ parihāsayiṣyāmi!

3.169 bhaṭṭini, bhart" âtr' âiva praviśati!

3.170 evaṃ prathamaṃ mama cintitaṃ hṛdayena.

3.171 bhavati, yuktaṃ nām' âtra|bhavataḥ priya|vayasyo 'śoko vāma|pādena tāḍayitum?

3.172 aho, bhartā!

3.173 Bakulāvalike, gṛhīt'|ârthayā tvay" âtra|bhavat" īdṛśam a|vinayaṃ kurvantī kasmān na nivāritā?

3.175 bhaṭṭini, paśya, kiṃ pravṛttam ārya|Gautamena!

3.176 kathaṃ brahma|bandhur anyathā jīviṣyati?

3.177 ārya, eṣā devyā niyogam anutiṣṭhati. etasminn atikrame paravat" îyam. prasīdatu bhartā.

3.181 yujyate. devy atra mānayitavyā.

3.185 aho, navanīta|kalpa|hṛdaya ārya|putraḥ!

3.186 Bakulāvalike, ehi. anuṣṭhitam ātmano niyogaṃ devyai nivedayāvaḥ.

3.187 tena hi vijñāpaya bhartāraṃ, visarjay' êti.

3.189 avahitā śṛṇu! ājñāpayatu bhartā.

3.191 pūraya, pūraya! aśokaḥ kusumaṃ na darśayati: ayaṃ punaḥ puṣpyati phalati ca!

3.194 kim anyat? jaṅghā|balaṃ eva!

3.195 Bakulāvalike, sādhu tvay" ôpakrāntaṃ! Mālavike, tvaṃ tāvad ārya|putraṃ sa|phala|prārthanaṃ kuru!

3.196 praviśatu bhaṭṭinī! ke āvāṃ bhartuḥ pranaya|parigrahasya?

3.198 aho, a|viśvasanīyāḥ puruṣāḥ! mayā khalv ātmano vañcanā|vacanaṃ pramāṇī|kṛtya vyādha|gīta|raktayā hariṇy" êv' â|saṅkitayā idaṃ na vijñātaṃ.

3.199 bho, pratipadyasva kim api! karma|gṛhītena kumbhīlakena «saṃdhi|cchedane śikṣito 'sm'» îti vaktavyaṃ bhavati.

3.201 viśvasanīyo 'si! mayā na vijñātam, «īdṛśaṃ vinoda|vastukam ārya|putreṇ' ôpalabdham» iti. anyathā manda|bhāginyā evaṃ na kriyate.

3.202 mā tāvad atra|bhavatī atra|bhavato dākṣiṇyasy' ôparodhaṃ bhaṇatu. samāpatti|dṛṣṭena devyāḥ parijanena saṃkath" âpi yady aparādhaḥ sthāpyate... atra tvaṃ eva pramāṇam.

3.203 nanu saṃkathā nāma bhavatu! kim ity ātmānam āyāsayiṣyāmi?

3.208 śaṭha, a|viśvasanīya|hṛdayo 'si!

3.210 iyam api hat'|āśā tvām ev' ânusarati!

3.214 kiṃ mām eva bhūyo 'py aparāddhāṃ karoṣi?

3.219 na khalv imau Mālavikā|caraṇau, yau te sparśa|dohadaṃ pūrayiṣyataḥ!

3.221 bho, uttiṣṭha. kṛta|prasādo 'si.

3.223 vayasya, diṣṭyā anen' â|vinayen' â|prasannā gatā. tad āvāṃ śīghram apakramāvo, yāvad Aṅgārako rāśim iv' ânuvakraṃ na karoti.

4.5 jayatu, jayatu bhartā! a|saṃnihito Gautamaḥ.

4.7 jayatu bhavān!

4.9 yad deva ājñāpayati.

4.12 yo biḍāla|gṛhītāyāḥ parabhṛtikāyāḥ.

4.14 sā khalu tapasvinī tayā piṅgal'|âkṣyā sāra|bhāṇḍa|bhū|gṛhe mṛtyu|mukha iva nikṣiptā.

4.16 atha kim?

4.18 śṛṇotu bhavān. parivrājikā me kathayati: hyaḥ kila tatra|bhavat" Īrāvatī ruj"|ākrānta|caraṇāṃ devīṃ sukha|pṛcchik" āgatā.

4.20 tataḥ sā devyā pṛṣṭā: «kiṃ nu n' ālokito vallabha|jana?» iti. tatas tay" ôktam: «mando vā ta upacāraḥ, yat te parijanasya vallabhatvaṃ jānaty api pṛcchas'» îti.

4.22 tatas tay" ânubadhyamānayā bhavato '|vinayam antareṇa parigṛhīt'|ârthā kṛtā devī.

4.24 ataḥ paraṃ kiṃ? Mālavikā Bakulāvalikā ca nigala|padyāv a|dṛṣṭa| sūrya|pādaṃ pātāla|vāsaṃ nāga|kanyake iv' ânubhavataḥ.

4.28 kathaṃ bhaviṣyati? yat sāra|bhāṇḍa|vyāpṛtā Mādhavikā devyā saṃdiṣṭā: «mam' âṅgulīyaka|mudrām a|dṛṣṭvā na moktavyā tvayā hat'|āśā Mālavikā Bakulāvalikā c'» êti.

4.30 asty atr' ôpāyaḥ...

4.32 ko 'py a|dṛṣṭaḥ śṛṇoti. karṇe te kathayāmi.

4.32 evam iva!

4.35 deva, pravāta|śayane devī niṣaṇṇā rakta|candana|dhāriṇā parijana| hasta|gatena caraṇena bhagavatyā kathābhir vinodyamānā tiṣṭhati.

4.37 tad gacchatu bhavān. aham api devīṃ draṣṭum a|rikta|pāṇir bhaviṣyāmi.

4.39 tathā.

4.39 bhavati, evam iva.

4.42 ita, ito devaḥ.

4.44 bhagavati, ramaṇīyaṃ kathā|vastu. tatas tataḥ?

4.46 aho, bhartā!

4.50 jayatv ārya|putraḥ!

4.53 asti me viśeṣaḥ.

4.55 paritrāyatāṃ! sarpeṇa daṣṭo 'smi!

4.58 devīṃ drakṣyām' îty ācāra|puṣpa|grahaṇa|kāraṇāt pramada| vanaṃ gato 'smi—

4.59 hā dhik, hā dhik! aham eva brāhmaṇasya jīvita|saṃśaya|nimittaṃ jātā.

4.60 tasminn aśoka|stabaka|kāraṇāt prasārite dakṣiṇa|haste koṭara| nirgatena sarpa|rūpiṇā kālena daṣṭo 'smi. nanv ete dve daṃsa| pade.

4.65 yad deva ājñāpayati.

4.67 aho, pāpena mṛtyunā gṛhīto 'smi!

4.69 katham na bheṣyāmi? simasimāyanti me 'ṅgāni!

4.71 hā, darśitam a|śubham vikāreṇa. halā, avalambadhvam enam!

4.73 bho, bhavato bālyāt priya|vayasyo 'smi. tad vicāry' â|putrāyā me jananyā yoga|kṣemaṃ vaha.

4.75 deva, ājñāpito Dhruvasiddhir vijñāpayati, «ih' âiv' ānīyatāṃ Gautama» iti.

4.77 tathā.

4.78 bhavati, jīveyaṃ vā, na vā: yan may" âtra|bhavantaṃ sevamānena te 'parāddhaṃ, tan mṛṣyasva.

4.79 dīrgh'|āyur bhava.

4.83 jayatu bhartā! Dhruvasiddhir vijñāpayati: «uda|kumbha|vidhāne sarpa|mudritaṃ kim api kalpayitavyam. tad anviṣyatām» iti.

4.84 idaṃ sarpa|mudritam aṅgulīyakam. paścān mama haste dehy etat.

4.87 yad deva ājñāpayati.

4.92 jayatu bhartā! nivṛtta|viṣa|vego Gautamo muhūrtakena prakṛti|sthaḥ saṃvṛttaḥ.

4.93 diṣṭyā vacanīyān mukt" âsmi.

4.94 eṣa punar amātyo Vāhatavo vijñāpayati: «rāja|kāryaṃ bahu mantrayitavyam. darśanen" ânugraham icchām'» îti.

4.95 gacchatv ārya|putraḥ kārya|siddhyai.

4.97 bālikāḥ, ārya|putra|vacanam anutiṣṭhata.

4.98 tathā.

4.101 ita, ito devaḥ.

4.103 atha kim?

4.106 jayatu bhavān! siddhāni me maṅgala|karmāṇi.

4.108 yad deva ājñāpayati.

4.111 devyā aṅgulīyaka|mudrikāṃ dṛṣṭvā kathaṃ vicārayati?

4.113 nanu pṛṣṭo 'smi. punar manden' âpi pratyutpanna|buddhinā mayā kathitam...

4.115 «daiva|cintakair vijñāpito rājā, ‹s'|ôpasargaṃ vo nakṣatram. sarva|bandhana|mokṣaḥ kriyatām› iti. tac chrutvā devy" Êravatyāś cittaṃ rakṣantyā ‹rājā kila mocayat'› îti ahaṃ saṃdiṣṭo 'sm'» îti. tato «yujyata» iti tayā saṃpādito 'rthaḥ.

4.118 tvaratāṃ bhavān! samudra|gṛhe sakhī|sahitāṃ Mālavikāṃ sthāpayitvā bhavantaṃ pratyudgato 'smi.

4.120 etu bhavān.

4.120 idaṃ samudra|gṛhakam.

4.122 aho, kumbhīlakaiḥ kāmukaiś ca pariharaṇīyā candrikā!

4.125 tathā.

4.128 halā, praṇama bhartāram!

4.130 namas te!

4.130 halā, vipralambhayasi māṃ!

4.133 nanv eṣa citra|gato bhartā.

4.134 jayatu bhartā!

4.135 halā, tadā saṃmukha|sthitā bhartū rūpa|darśanena na tathā vitṛṣṇ" âsmi, yath" âdya mayā vibhāvitaś citra|gata|darśano bhartā.

4.136 śrutaṃ bhavatā? atra|bhavatyā yathā dṛṣṭaś citre, na tathā dṛṣṭo bhavān iti mantritam. mudh" êdānīṃ mañjūṣ" êva ratna|bhāṇḍaṃ yauvana|garvaṃ vahasi.

4.139 halā, k" âiṣā īṣat|parivṛtta|vadanena bhartrā snigdhayā dṛṣṭyā nidhyāyate?

4.140 nanv iyaṃ bhartuḥ pārśva|gatā Irāvatī.

4.141 sakhi, a|dakṣiṇa iva bhartā me pratibhāti, yaḥ sarvaṃ devī|janam ujjhitvā ekasyā mukhe baddha|lakṣaḥ.

4.142 citra|gataṃ bhartāraṃ param'|ârthataḥ saṃkalpy' âsūyati. bhavatu, krīḍayiṣyāmi tāvad etayā.

4.142 halā, bhartur vallabhā eṣā.

4.143 tataḥ kim idānīm ātmānam āyāsayāmi?

4.147 anunaya|sajja idānīṃ bhava.

4.148 ārya|Gautamo 'py atr' âiva sevata enam!

4.150 na khalu kupit" êdānīṃ tvam?

4.151 yadi ciraṃ kupitām eva māṃ manyase, eṣa pratyānīyate kopaḥ!

4.154 jayatu bhartā!

4.155 kathaṃ? citra|gato bhartā may" âsūyitaḥ?

4.157 kiṃ bhavān udāsīna iva?

4.159 mā tāvad, atra|bhavatyāṃ tav' â|viśvāsaḥ?

4.162 sakhi, bahuśaḥ kila bhartā vipralabdhaḥ. tat tāvad ātmā viśvasanīyaḥ kriyatām!

4.163 sakhi, mama punar manda|bhāgyāyāḥ svapna|samāgamo 'pi bhartur dur|labha āsīt!

4.164 bhartaḥ, dehy asyā uttaram.

4.166 anugṛhīte svaḥ.

4.167 Bakulāvalike, eṣa bāl'|âśoka|vṛkṣasya pallavāni hariṇo laṅghitum āgacchati! ehi, nivārayāva enam.

4.168 tathā.

4.171 evam api Gautamo nanu saṃdiśyate?

4.172 ārya Gautama, aham a|prakāśe tiṣṭhāmi. tvaṃ dvāra|rakṣako bhava.

4.173 yujyate.

4.175 idaṃ tāvat sphaṭika|sthalam āśrito bhavāmi.

4.175 aho sukha|sparśatā śīlā|viśeṣasya!

4.178 devyā bhayen' ātmano 'pi priyaṃ kartuṃ na pārayāmi.

4.180 yo na bibheti, sa mayā bhaṭṭinī|darśane dṛṣṭa|sāmarthyo bhartā!

4.187 hañje Nipuṇike, satyaṃ tvaṃ parigat'|ârthā, Candrikayā samudra|gṛh'|âlindake ārya|Gautama ekākī dṛṣṭa iti?

4.188 anyathā kathaṃ bhaṭṭinī vijñāpyate?

4.189 tena hi tatr' âiva gacchāvaḥ. saṃśayān muktam ārya|putrasya priya|vayasyaṃ praṣṭuṃ ca...

4.190 s'|âvaśeṣam iva bhaṭṭinyā vacanam.

4.191 anyac ca... citra|gataṃ bhartāraṃ prasādayitum.

4.192 ath' êdānīṃ bhart" âiva kiṃ na pratyanunīyate?

4.193 mugdhe, yādṛśaś citra|gato, na tādṛśa ev' ânya|saṃkrānta|hṛdaya ārya|putraḥ. kevalam upacār'|âtikramaṃ pramārṣṭum ayam ārambhaḥ.

4.194 ito, ito bhaṭṭinī.

4.197 jayatu bhaṭṭinī. devī bhaṇati: «na me eṣa matsarasya kālaḥ. tava khalu bahu|mānaṃ vardhayituṃ vayasyayā saha nigala|bandhane kṛtā Mālavikā. yady anumanyase, ārya|putram api tava kṛte vijñāpayiṣyāmi. yat tav' êṣṭaṃ, tad bhaṇa» iti.

4.198 Nāgarike, vijñāpaya devīm: «kā vayaṃ bhaṭṭinīṃ niyojayitum? parijana|nigraheṇa mayi darśito 'nugrahaḥ. kasya v" ânyasya prasāden' âyaṃ jano vardhata?» iti.

4.199 tathā.

4.201 eṣa dvār'|ôddeśe samudra|gṛhasya vipaṇi|gata iva vṛṣabha ārya|Gautama āsīna eva nidrāyate.

4.202 atyāhitam! na khalu s'|âvaśeṣa|viṣa|vikāro bhavet?

4.203 prasanna|mukha|varṇo dṛśyate. api ca Dhruvasiddhinā cikitsitaḥ. tad asy' â|śaṅkanīyaṃ pāpam.

4.204 bhavati Mālavike!

4.205 śrutaṃ bhaṭṭinyā? kasy' âiṣa ātmanīno hat'|āśaḥ kitavaḥ? sarva|kālam ita eva svasti|vācana|modakaiḥ kukṣiṃ pūrayitvā, sāṃprataṃ Mālavikām utsvapnāyate!

4.206 Irāvatīm atikrāmantī bhava!

4.207 etad atyāhitam! bhujaṅga|bhīruṃ brahma|bandhum anena bhujaṅga|kuṭilena daṇḍa|kāṣṭhena stambh'|ântaritā bhīṣayiṣyāmi.

4.208 arhati kṛta|ghna upadravasya.

4.210 avihā! avihā! bho, darvīkaro ma upari patitaḥ!

4.212 bhartaḥ, mā tāvat sahasā niṣkrāma! sarpa iti bhaṇati.

4.213 hā dhik, hā dhik! bhartā ita eva dhāvati.

4.214 kathaṃ? daṇḍa|kāṣṭham idam! ahaṃ punar jāne, yan mayā ketakī|kaṇṭakābhyāṃ daṃśaṃ kṛtvā sarpasy' êva daṃśaḥ kṛtaḥ, tat|phalitam iti.

4.216 mā tāvad bhartā praviśatu! iha kuṭila|gatiḥ sarpa iva dṛśyate.

4.217 api nir|vighna|mano|ratho divā|saṃketo mithunasya?

4.220 Bakulāvalike, diṣṭyā dauty'|âdhikāra|viṣayā saṃpūrṇā te pratijñā.

4.221 prasīdatu bhaṭṭinī! kiṃ nu khalu dardurā vyāharant' îti devaḥ pṛthivyāṃ varṣituṃ smarati?

4.222 mā tāvat! bhavatyā darśana|mātreṇ' âtra|bhavān praṇipāta|laṅghanaṃ vismṛtaḥ. bhavatī punar ady' âpi prasādaṃ na gṛhṇāti?

4.223 kupit" âp' îdānīṃ kiṃ kariṣyāmi?

4.226 «a|sthāna» iti suṣṭhu vyāhṛtam ārya|putreṇa. anya|saṃkrāntesv asmākaṃ bhāgya|dheyeṣu yadi punaḥ kupyeyaṃ, tato hāsyā bhaveyam.

4.229 Nipuṇike, gaccha, devīṃ vijñāpaya: «dṛṣṭaṃ devyāḥ pakṣa|pātitvam ady'» êti.

4.230 tathā.

4.232 aho, an|arthaḥ saṃpatitaḥ! bandhana|bhraṣṭo gṛha|kapoto biḍālik"|āloke patitaḥ.

4.234 bhaṭṭini, yadṛcchā|dṛṣṭayā Mādhavikay" ākhyātam: «evaṃ khalv etan nirvṛttam» iti.

4.236 upapannam eva. satyam ayam atra brahma|bandhuna udbhinno duṣ|prayogaḥ.

4.236 iyam asya kāma|tantra|sacivasya nītiḥ!

4.237 bhavati, yadi nītyā ekam apy akṣaraṃ paṭheyaṃ, tato Gāyatrīm api vismareyam.

4.240 deva, kumārī Vasulakṣmī kandukaṃ anudhāvantī piṅgala|vānareṇa balavad uttrāsitā, aṅka|niṣaṇṇā devyāḥ pravāta|kisalayam iva vepamānā na kim api prakṛtiṃ pratipadyate.

4.242 tvaratām ārya|putra enām samāśvāsayitum! mā asyāḥ saṃtrāsa|janito vikāro vardhatām.

4.245 sādhu, re piṅgala|vānara, sādhu! paritrātas tvayā sva|pakṣaḥ.

4.247 halā, devīṃ cintayitvā vepate me hṛdayam. na jāne 'taḥ paraṃ kim anubhavitavyaṃ bhaviṣyati.

4.248 āścaryam, āścaryam! a|pūrṇa eva pañca|rātre dohadasya, mukulaiḥ saṃnaddhas tapanīy'|âśokaḥ! yāvad devyai nivedayāmi.

4.250 āśvasitu sakhī. satya|pratijñā devī.

4.251 tena hi pramada|vana|pālikāyāḥ pṛṣṭhato bhavāvaḥ.

4.252 tathā.

5.2 upakṣipto mayā kṛta|satkāra|vidhes tapanīy'|âśokasya vedikā|bandhaḥ. yāvad anuṣṭhita|niyogam ātmānaṃ devyai nivedayāmi.

5.2 aho, daivasy' ânukampanīyā Mālavikā! tasyāṃ tathā caṇḍikā devī anen' âśoka|kusuma|vṛttāntena prasāda|sumukhī bhaviṣyati. kutra nu khalu devī bhavet?

5.2 aho, eṣa devyāḥ parijan'|âbhyantaraḥ kim api jatu|mudrā|lāñchitāṃ mañjūṣikāṃ gṛhītvā catuḥ|śālāt kubjaḥ Sārasako niṣkrāmati. prakṣyāmi tāvad enam.

5.4 Sārasaka, kutra prasthito 'si?

5.5 Madhukarike, vidyā|pāra|gāṇāṃ brāhmaṇānāṃ nitya|dakṣiṇā dātavyā. tad ārya|purohitasya hastaṃ prāpayiṣyāmi.

5.6 kiṃ|nimittam?

5.7 yadā prabhṛti śrutaṃ, «senā|patinā yajña|turaga|rakṣaṇe niyukto bhartṛ|dārako Vasumitra» iti, tadā prabhṛti tasy' āyuṣo nimittam aṣṭādaśa|suvarṇa|parimāṇāṃ dakṣiṇāṃ devī dakṣiṇīyaiḥ pratigrāhayati.

5.8 yujyate. atha kutra devī? kiṃ v" ânutiṣṭhati?

5.9 maṅgala|gṛhe āsana|sthā bhūtvā Vidarbha|viṣayād bhrātrā Vīrasenena preṣitaṃ lipi|karair vācyamānaṃ lekhaṃ śṛṇoti.

5.10 kaḥ punar Vidarbha|rāja|vṛttāntaḥ?

5.11 vaśī|kṛtaḥ kila Vīrasena|pramukhair bhartur vijaya|daṇḍair Vidarbha|nāthaḥ. mocito 'sya dāyādo Mādhavasenaḥ. dūtaś ca tena mahā|sārāṇi ratnāni, vāhanāni, śilpa|kārikā|bhūyiṣṭhaṃ parijanaṃ c' ôpāyānī|kṛtya bhartuḥ sakāśaṃ preṣitaḥ, śvaḥ kila bhartāraṃ drakṣyati.

5.12 gaccha, anutiṣṭh' ātmano niyogam. aham api devīṃ drakṣyāmi.

5.16 ājñapt" âsmy aśoka|satkāra|vyāpṛtayā devyā: «vijñāpay' ārya|putram, ‹icchāmy ārya|putreṇa sah' âśoka|vṛkṣasya prasūna|lakṣmīṃ pratyakṣī|kartum› iti.» yāvad dharm'|āsana|gataṃ devaṃ pratipālayāmi.

5.21 eṣa jaya|śabda|sūcita|prasthāno bhart" êta ev' āgacchati. aham api tāvad asya pramukhāt kim apy apasṛtya etan mukh'|âlinda|toraṇaṃ samāśritā bhavāmi.

5.25 yath" âhaṃ paśyāmi, tath" âik'|ânta|sukhito bhavān bhaviṣyati.

5.27 adya kila devyā Dhāriṇyā paṇḍita|Kauśikī bhaṇitā: «yadi tvaṃ prasādhana|garvaṃ vahasi, tad darśaya Mālavikāyāḥ śarīre Vaidarbhaṃ vivāha|nepathyam» iti. tay" âpi sa|viśeṣ'|âlaṃkṛtā Mālavikā. tatra|bhavatī kad" âpi pūrayed bhavato mano|ratham.

5.29 jayatu bhartā! devī vijñāpayati: «tapanīy'|âśokasya kusuma|saubhāgya|darśanena mam' ārambhaḥ sa|phalī|kriyatām» iti.

5.31 atha kim. yath"|ârha|saṃmāna|sukhitam antaḥ|puraṃ visṛjya Mālavikā|puro|geṇ' ātmanaḥ parijanena saha devaṃ pratipālayati.

5.33 ita, ito devaḥ.

5.35 bho vayasya, kiṃ cit parivṛtta|yauvana iva vasantaḥ pramada|vane lakṣyate.

5.38 bho, ayaṃ sa datta|nepathya iva kusuma|stabakais tapanīy'|âśokaḥ. avalokayatu bhavān!

5.41 bho, viśrabdho bhava! asmāsu saṃnihiteṣv api Dhāriṇī pārśva|parivartinīṃ Mālavikām anumanyate.

5.45 jānāmi nimittaṃ kautuk'|âlaṃkārasya. tath" âpi bisinī|patra|gataṃ salilam iva vepate me hṛdayam. api ca dakṣiṇ'|êtarad api me nayanaṃ bahuśaḥ sphurati.

5.46 bho vayasya, vivāha|nepathyena sa|viśeṣaṃ khalu śobhate 'tra|bhavatī Mālavikā!

5.49 jayatv ārya|putraḥ!

5.50 vardhatāṃ bhavatī.

5.54 eṣa te 'smābhis taruṇī|jana|sahāyasy' âśokaḥ saṃketa|gṛhaṃ saṃkalpitaḥ.

5.55 bho, ārādhito 'si!

5.58 bho, visrabdho bhūtvā tvaṃ yauvanavatīm imāṃ paśya.

5.59 kām?

5.60 tapanīy'|âśokasya kusuma|śobhām.

5.69 halā Rajanike, a|pūrvam apy etad rāja|kulaṃ praviśantyāḥ prasīdati mam' âbhyantara|gata ātmā.

5.70 Jyotsnike, mam' âpy evam. asti khalu loka|vādaḥ: «āgāmi sukhaṃ vā duḥkhaṃ vā hṛdaya|samavasthā kathayat'» îti.

5.71 sa idānīṃ satyo bhavatu!

5.74 jayatu bhartā! jayatu bhaṭṭinī!

5.78 bhartaḥ, saṃgīte 'bhyantare svaḥ.

5.80 Mālavike, itaḥ paśya! katarā te saṃgīta|sahacāriṇī rocate?

5.81 aho, bhartṛ|dārikā!

5.81 jayatu, jayatu bhartṛ|dārikā!

5.84 deva, iyam asmākaṃ bhartṛ|dārikā!

5.86 śṛṇotu bhartā. yaḥ sa bhartur vijaya|daṇḍair Vidarbha|nāthaṃ vaśī|kṛtya bandhanān mocitaḥ kumāro Mādhavaseno nāma, tasy' êyaṃ kanīyasī bhaginī, Mālavikā nāma.

5.87 katham? rāja|dārik" êyam? candanaṃ khalu mayā pāduk"|ôpayogena dūṣitam!

5.89 vidher niyogena.

5.90 śṛṇotu bhartā. dāyāda|vaśaṃ gate 'smākaṃ bhartṛ|dārake Mādhavasene, tasy' âmātyen' ārya|Sumatin" âsmādṛśaṃ parijanaṃ ujjhitvā gūḍham apanīt" âiṣā.

5.92 ataḥ paraṃ na jānīvaḥ.

5.94 ārya|Kauśikyā iva svara|saṃyogaḥ!

5.95 nanu sā eva.

5.96 yati|veṣa|dhāriṇī ārya|Kauśikī duḥkhena vibhāvyate. bhagavati, vandāvahe.

5.100 tena hi kathayatu bhagavatī atra|bhavatyā vṛttānta|śeṣam.

5.110 mā bibhehi! atikrāntaṃ khalu tatra|bhavatī kathayati.

5.116 hā, hataḥ Sumatiḥ!

5.117 ataḥ khalu bhartṛ|dārikāyā iyaṃ samavasthā saṃvṛttā.

5.125 kiṃ nu khalu sāmprataṃ bhartā bhaṇati?

5.128 bhagavati, tvay" âbhijanavatīṃ Mālavikām an|ācakṣāṇay" â|sāṃpratam kṛtam.

5.130 kim iva tat kāraṇam?

5.140 bhartṛ|dārike, diṣṭyā bhartṛ|dārako 'rdha|rājye pratiṣṭhāṃ gamiṣyati!

5.141 etāvat tāvad bahu mantavyam, yaj jīvita|saṃśayān muktaḥ.

5.148 aho, tato|mukham eva no hṛdayam! śroṣyāmi tāvad guru|jana|kuśal'|ânantaraṃ putrasya Vasumitrasya vṛttāntam. ati|bhāre khalu me putrakaḥ senā|patinā niyuktaḥ.

5.153 anen' āśvastaṃ me hṛdayam.

5.158 bhavati, parituṣṭo 'smi yat pitaram anujāto vatsa iti.

5.164 Jayasene, gaccha, Irāvatī|pramukhānām antaḥ|purāṇāṃ putrasya vijaya|vṛttāntaṃ nivedaya.

5.165 tathā.

5.167 ehi tāvat!

5.168 iyam asmi.

5.169 yan may" âśoka|dohada|niyoge Mālavikāyai pratijñātaṃ, tad asyā abhijanaṃ ca nivedya, mama vacanen' Êrāvatīm anunaya, «tvay" âhaṃ satyān na paribhraṃśayitavy"» êti.

5.170 yad devy ājñāpayati.

5.170 bhaṭṭini, putra|vijaya|nimittena paritoṣeṇ' ântaḥ|purāṇām ābharaṇānāṃ mañjūṣ" âsmi saṃvṛttā!

5.171 kim atr' āścaryam? sādhāraṇaḥ khalu tāsāṃ mama c' âyaṃ abhyudayaḥ.

5.172 bhaṭṭini, Irāvatī vijñāpayati: «sadṛśaṃ khalu devyāḥ prabhavantyāḥ. tava vacanaṃ prathama|saṃkalpitaṃ na yujyate 'nyathā kartum» iti.

5.173 bhagavati, tvay" ânumatā icchāmi ārya|Sumatinā prathama|saṃkalpitām Mālavikāṃ ārya|putrasya pratipādayitum.

5.175 ārya|putra idaṃ priya|nivedan'|ânurūpaṃ pāritoṣikaṃ pratīcchatu.

5.177 kim avadhīrayati mām ārya|putraḥ?

5.178 bhavati, eṣa loka|vyavahāraḥ: sarvo 'pi nava|varo lajj"|āturo bhavat' îti.

5.180 atha vā, devy" âiva kṛta|praṇaya|viśeṣāṃ datta|devī|śabdāṃ Mālavikām atra|bhavān pratigrahītum icchati.

5.181 etasyā rāja|dārikāyā abhijanen' âiva datto devī|śabdaḥ. kiṃ punar|uktena?

5.184 marṣayatu bhagavatī, abhyudaya|kathayā mayā na lakṣitam. Jayasene, gaccha tāvat! kauśeya|patr'|ōrṇam upanaya.

5.185 yad devy ājñāpayati.

5.185 devi, etat.

5.186 idānīm ārya|putraḥ pratīcchatu.

5.189 aho devyā anukūlatā!

5.191 jayatu bhaṭṭinī!

5.196 jayatu bhartā! Irāvatī vijñāpayati: «yad upacār'|âtikrameṇa tadā bhartre aparāddhaṃ, tat svayaṃ bhartur anukūlaṃ may" ācaritam. sāṃpratam pūrṇa|maṇorathena bhartrā prasāda|mātreṇa saṃbhāvayitavy"» êti.

5.197 Nipuṇike, avaśyaṃ tasyāḥ saṃdeśaṃ sevitum ārya|putro jñāsyati.

5.198 yad devy ājñāpayati.

5.201 bhagavati, na yuktam asmān parityaktum.

5.204 ājñāpayatv ārya|putraḥ, kiṃ bhūyo 'pi priyaṃ anutiṣṭhāmi?

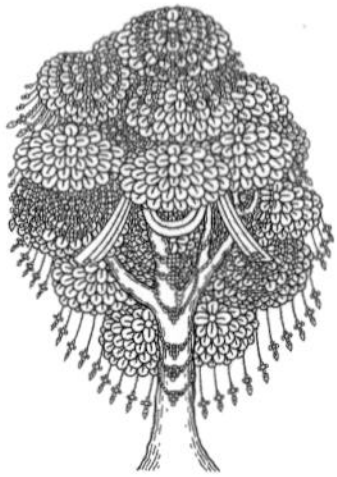

NOTES

Bold *references are to the English text;* ***bold italic*** *references are to the Sanskrit text. An asterisk (*) in the body of the text marks the word or passage being annotated.*

1.1 **Wearing but a raw hide**: an untanned hide is the traditional garb of ascetics. Shiva is the foremost of ascetics and is often depicted clad in a tiger or leopard skin. He is also said to have defeated an elephant demon and danced his wild dance wearing the raw hide cut from its body.

1.1 **Body merged with his beloved**: Shiva is not only sexually united with his partner the universal Goddess (*devī*), but actually shares a body with her in the form known as *ardha|nār"|īśvara*, the half-woman Lord.

1.1 The **eight bodies** of Shiva are said to be the five elements (earth, water, fire, air and ether), the sun, the moon, and the personified deity Pashu·pati, the latter often equated with the individual soul or the sacrificer. His eight forms are also referred to in the benedictory verse of the *Abhijñānaśākuntala*, where VASUDEVA (2006) interprets them as earth, fire, air, space, the sun, the moon, the offering and the sacrificer.

1.1 **Lord**: the word *īśa* means "lord" in the sense of one with mastery and control. It is most frequently used to denote Shiva. The benedictory verse plays on the contrary nature of Shiva.

1.2 The **director** (*sūtradhāra*) is the leader of the troop of actors. Sanskrit plays traditionally begin with an appearance of the director with an actor or actress. Their dialogue introduces the play to the audience, and at the end of the introductory scene the director connects to the beginning of the fiction in a sort of verbal cross-fade.

1.3 The back-stage (*nepathya*) is the actors' dressing room behind the stage. It is from here that characters enter the stage, and where sounds heard "offstage" or "in the air" originate. The back-stage is separated from the visible stage by a wall with two doorways obstructed by a curtain (*paṭa* or *paṭī*). See e.g. GITOMER (1999) for a description of the stage.

1.7 **Contemporary poet**: this statement in the prologue of the play has led to the general opinion that "Málavika and Agni·mitra" must be the first play of Kali·dasa; see p. xv.

1.7 **Bhasa** (*Bhāsa*; in some versions of "Málavika and Agni·mitra" called *Bhāsaka* or *Bhāskara*; elsewhere *Bhāvaka* or *Dhāvaka* is named in his place) is an illustrious dramatist tentatively dated to the fourth century CE, whose work was thought for a long time to have been lost. In the early twentieth century a manuscript of thirteen plays attributed to him was discovered in Kerala, though their authenticity remains debated.

1.7 **Saumílla** (*Saumilla*; in other versions also called *Saumillaka* and *Sominda*) is probably identical to Sómila (*Somila*), who is recorded as having co-authored with a poet named Rámila (*Rāmila*; possibly his brother or son) a certain *Śūdrakakathā*, ("The Story of Shúdraka"). No record of his dramatic work is preserved, unless he is identifiable as Shyámilaka (*Śyāmilaka* or *Śyāmala*), author of the comedy *Pādatāḍitaka*, ("The Kick")—but this Shyámilaka was in all probability a contemporary of (and possibly junior to) Kali·dasa, not a revered predecessor.

1.7 **Kavi·putra** (*Kaviputra*; in other versions also called *Kavimiśra* and *Kavimitra*) is the most obscure of the three; nothing is known of his work except a verse attributed to him (or rather to a pair of Kavi·putras) in a fifteenth-century anthology.

1.16 The **chálita dance** (Sanskrit *chalita*; variants *calita* and *chalika*) is a very obscure type of performance. Many commentators cite a verse about it (without attribution; with variations in the spelling of the name of the dance and some corruption in some versions): *tad etac chalitaṃ nāma sākṣād yad abhinīyate / vyapadiśya* *purāvṛttaṃ svābhiprāyaprakāśakam*, "The one called *chálita* is that which is acted out openly (?), showing one's own desires under the pretext of an old story." This definition tallies so well with what happens later (2.22 [4] onward) and sounds so unlikely that it was very likely written on the basis of this very play. Acceptance of this definition may be the reason why the Prakrit name ⌜*chalia*⌟ is usually translated to Sanskrit as *chalita*, "tricky." The other explanation cited by many commentators says it is a genre that involves fourfold acting (cf. note to 1.54), is accompanied by *jātisvara* (rhythmic singing without lyrics), is predominantly of the erotic mood, and is rhythmical (*caturvidhābhinayavad yaj jātisvarasaṃbhṛtam / śṛṅgārarasabhūyiṣṭhaṃ salayaṃ calitaṃ viduḥ*). From the use of the term in other texts (though rare and vague), it seems that *chalika* is the older name of the genre, and that it may have meant a particular kind of music before being applied to a certain type of dance. See RAGHAVAN (1978: 538ff.) for a more detailed discussion.

1.20 The **snake seal** on the ring is probably just a general symbol of fertility and/or good luck. Although both Kā and Nī say such a ring is intended for neutralizing snake poison, we believe they are influenced by what happens later. See also p. xxiii.

1.33 **Papa** translates ⌜*āutta,*⌟ a Prakrit word possibly related to Sanskrit *āryaputra* or even *rājaputra*. Available commentators do not explain the word satisfactorily. For the *chāyā* (*āvutta*) Kā quotes the *Amarakośa* (1.8.12, *bhaginīpatir āvuttaḥ*) to the effect that this term is used in drama for (addressing) one's sister's husband, without any further comment. However, it is unlikely that Vasu·lakshmi is Queen Dhárini's sister. Her title "Princess" intimates that she is the daughter of Agni·mitra (presumably by Dhárini), and the similarity of her name to that of Prince Vasu·mitra corroborates this. We have therefore assumed that ⌜*āutta*⌟ is a vernacular word used to address one's father.

1.42 **Rudra divided it into two parts**: the two basic aspects of dance are *tāṇḍava* and *lāsya*. The former is the masculine type of dancing, relying mainly on technical skill and strength; the latter is the feminine type of movement that includes acting by body language and facial expressions.

1.42 **Body ... mingled with Uma**: see note to 1.1.

1.42 **Various sentiments**: *rasa*, literally "flavor, essence," is a central concept of Indian aesthetics, meaning the sensation experienced by the reader, listener or spectator of a literary work. The various *rasas* are induced by the sentiments (*bhāva* or *sthāyibhāva*, "durable sentiment") said to be so called because they induce or bring into existence (*bhāvayanti*) the aesthetic experience (*rasa*) in the spectator. The *rasas* are eight in number (NŚ 6.15), corresponding to eight *bhāvas* (NŚ 6.17): *śṛṅgāra* (erotic) to *rati* (passion), *hāsya* (comic) to *hāsa* (laughter), *karuṇa* (pathetic) to *śoka* (sadness), *raudra* (furious) to *krodha* (anger), *vīra* (heroic) to *utsāha* (ardor), *bhayānaka* (terrible) to *bhaya* (fear), *bībhatsa* (odious) to *jugupsā* (disgust), and *adbhuta* (marvelous) to *vismaya* (amazement).

1.42 The **three qualities** (*guṇas*) are the fundamental qualities or constituent principles of the world elaborated in Sankhya philosophy. They are *sattva*, *rajas* and *tamas*, often (loosely) translated as goodness, passion and darkness.

1.48 Iyer says in his explanatory notes that **Irávati** studies dance with Hara·datta and that Málavika surpasses her in aptitude too—but we see no convincing reason for this assumption.

1.50 The **baseborn brother** (*varṇ'|âvaraḥ*, literally "of a lower class") would have been born from a lower-caste concubine of Dhárini's father rather than from his primary wife. The *Manusmṛti* (3.12) enjoins twice-born men (members of the three upper *varṇas* or classes, i.e. brahmins, kshatriyas and vaishyas) to marry women of the same class as theirs, but allows love-marriages with women of a lower class.

1.50 The **Nármada** is a major sacred river of central India, flowing immediately south of the Vindhya range and forming a natural border between the territories of Vídisha and Vidárbha. The variant reading ⌜*Mandāiṇī*⌟ (Sanskrit *Mandākinī*) appears instead of ⌜*Ṇammadā*⌟ (*Narmadā*) in a number of manuscripts. This name is most often used for the Ganges or for a particular Himalayan tributary of the Ganges, but may be applied to any significant river, and it is probably safe to assume that the Nármada is meant by *Mandākinī* in the variant.

1.52 **Water ... becomes a pearl when dropped in an oyster**: a common topos in Indian poetry.

1.54 The **art of fivefold acting** (*pañc'|âṅg'|âbhinaya*) might also be "acting by the five limbs." Commentators and editors seem as uncertain as we are. Kā says it means fivefold acting (i.e. acting that involves five techniques), and equates it to a type of performance called *preraṇa*, for which he quotes a rather obscure definition from a text he calls *Nṛttaratnākara* (or *Saṃgītaratnākara*, according to an edition of Kā's commentary quoted by Iyer). Nī is a "five limbs" proponent, quoting a verse without attribution that says it means acting with the two hands, two legs and the head (*karābhyāṃ caranābhyāṃ ca śirasā cābhinīyate / yatra vastv iti vijñeyaḥ pañcāṅgābhinayo hi saḥ*; repeated with slight variations in the *Sārārthadīpikā*). The *Sārārthadīpikā* and Tarkavachaspati quote another (also unattributed) definition by which the five limbs would be the mind, the eyes, the eyebrows, the hands and the feet (*cittākṣibhrūhastapādair aṅgaiḥ*). According to the NŚ, the limbs involved in acting are six in number: the head, the hands, the hips, the chest, the flanks and the legs (8.12: *śirohastakaṭīvakṣaḥ-pārśvapādasamanvitaḥ / aṅgapratyaṅgasaṃyuktaḥ ṣaḍaṅgo nāṭya-saṃgrahaḥ*), while acting is normally said to be fourfold, involving gestures, speech and voice, costumes, and the physiological signs of emotions (8.9: *āṅgiko vācikaś caiva hy āhāryaḥ sāttvikas tathā*). According to Kā, Gana·dasa is implying that Málavika has finished learning the *chálita* dance and has moved on to a new subject.

1.60 We follow Iyer's edition in spelling the minister's name Váhatava (*Vāhatava*), but in other sources his name varies. Our intuition is that the original Sanskrit name might have been *Bārhataka* or *Vārhataka*, Prakritized to ⌜*Vāhatao*⌟. In orthography this might easily have been changed to ⌜*Vāhatavo*⌟ (and re-Sanskritized to *Vāhatava*), while the variation *Vāhanava* is probably the result of a copyist mistaking a *ta akṣara* for *na*. Proving this theory would require more attention to actual manuscript evidence.

1.60 **Vaidárbha** is Yajña·sena, the king of the Vidárbha country.

1.64 The identity of the **Maurya minister** is not discussed elsewhere in the play. Agni·mitra's father, Pushpa·mitra, founded the Shunga dynasty after supplanting the Maurya kings (see p. xvi and Introduction, note 22), so it is not impossible that a former Maurya minister is held captive by Agni·mitra. Kā, however, interprets *Mauryasaciva* to be the name of Yajña·sena's brother-in-law, a solution we consider less likely. In other versions of the text he is also referred to as *Āryasaciva* and *Maudgalasaciva* (interestingly, it is this latter form that appears as a *pratīka* in the commentary of Nī, but it is glossed by *Mauryasaciva*).

1.65 The king of Vidárbha (called Yajña·sena) is Agni·mitra's **natural enemy** because their countries are adjacent. On this matter, the *Manusmṛti* (7.158) states: *anantaram ariṃ vidyād arisevinam eva ca / arer anantaraṃ mitram udāsīnaṃ tayoḥ param*, "He should recognize that his immediate neighbor is his enemy, as also anyone rendering assistance to the enemy; that his enemy's immediate neighbor is an ally; and that the one beyond these two is neutral." The *Arthaśāstra* elaborates this idea further, and calls the immediate neighbor a natural enemy: *bhūmyanantaraḥ prakṛtyamitraḥ* (6.2.19). He **provokes** Agni·mitra (more literally: "acts disagreeably") by asking him to remain neutral even though Agni·mitra had already accepted Mádhava·sena's offer of alliance and agreed to marry the latter's sister.

1.65 **He is ripe for an attack** (literally "in the class of those to be marched against," *yātavya/pakṣe*), probably because there is internal discord in his kingdom: his rivalry with his cousin Mádhava·

sena. The *Arthaśāstra* (6.2.16) says *arisampadyuktaḥ sāmantaḥ śatruḥ, vyasanī yātavyaḥ, anapāśrayo durbalāśrayo vocchedanīyaḥ*, "A neighbouring prince possessed of the excellences of an enemy is the foe; one in calamity is vulnerable [*yātavyaḥ*]; one without support or with a weak support is fit to be exterminated." See BOESCHE (2003) for a discussion of the concept of war in the *Arthaśāstra*. See also the next note.

1.69 The minister's verse elaborates the message of *Arthaśāstra* 8.2.18: *prakṛtiṣv arūḍhaḥ sukham ucchettuṃ bhavatīti*, "not being rooted among his subjects, he becomes easy to uproot."

1.91 **Dramatic sentiments** (*bhāva*): see note to 1.42. In this case the two dance masters possibly embody the *bhāva* of *krodha*, anger. The word *bhāva* is also used as a form of address to learned men, particularly the stage director (see 1.5, there translated "sir," and see note to 1.2 on the stage director).

1.109 The queen might **suspect prejudice** because Gana·dasa is her protégé, while Hara·datta is the king's.

1.116 The **king's favor**: the Sanskrit word *parigraha* also means "association, company" and "wife," and Káushiki alludes to these meanings in her answer.

1.118 **The sun's favor ... strengthens the brilliance of fire**: the idea is that the sun confers its power on fire when it sets, thus making fires at night more brilliant than they are in the daytime. For corroboration Kā quotes the *Aitareya Brāhmaṇa* (8.5.28): *ādityo vā astaṃ yann agnim anupraviśati*, "Setting, the sun enters fire." (Misquoted or misprinted in KALE's edition as *ādityo vā astaṃ yanna praviśati*.) An alternative interpretation of the statement (more in line with the secondary meaning of "company," q.v. the previous note) would be that in the midday heat a fire burns hotter than in the cool night.

1.118 **Lady Night**: the Sanskrit word *niśā*, "night," is grammatically feminine and is thus an apt metaphor for the queen whose favor can enhance the luster of her pet dance master.

1.119 **Her crony**: *pīṭha/mardikā*, literally "[female] back-rubber," is a very unusual word to describe a venerable nun. In the *Kāmasūtra*, a *pīṭhamarda* (masculine) is something like a professional go-between, a man without wealth who ekes out a living performing favors for the sophisticated bon vivant and serving him as a messenger of love. The *pīṭhamarda* is also a stock character in drama performing much the same function, that is, aiding the hero in various matters, especially conciliating women and winning their favors for the hero. It is possible that the jester calls Káushiki so because he knows that she too wants to marry Málavika to Agni·mitra; in this case "our crony" would be the right translation. Yet we are inclined to believe that at this point Gáutama does not know he has an ally in the nun (see p. xxix), and he simply uses this word for her in mockery. See also note to 1.136 about the possibility that the jester might repeatedly be alluding to the *Kāmasūtra*.

1.124 Queen **Dhárini**'s name means "Earth," (literally: "supporting") and an Indian king is conventionally said to be married to the earth. The other metaphysical wife of the king is *śrī* or *lakṣmī*, "royal glory" or "plenty," to whom Málavika is compared in 5.43 [6]. A further punning interpretation besides "whose crop is lushly verdant" is possible if we analyze the Sanskrit as *mah"/āsāra/prasava*: "who produces crop as a result of great showers."

1.133 **Or what does the queen think?** Some sources (the main text of AIYANGAR's edition, also noted as a variant in KALE, IYER and SASTRI) put this sentence in the king's mouth. The connective *vā*, "or," is a point against this, though its use by a new speaker would be less jarring in Sanskrit than it is in English.

1.136 The **clash** of the rams is ⌜*saṃvāda*⌟ in Prakrit, corresponding to the Sanskrit *saṃpāta*. However, the Prakrit word corresponding to Sanskrit *saṃvāda*, "dispute," would be homophonous, and indeed some *chāyā* versions have *saṃvāda* as the Sanskrit translation of this word. We assume that Kali·dasa used this ambiguous word intentionally. For the **rams** (⌜*urabbha*⌟, Sanskrit *urabhra*) there is a variant, ⌜*uaraṃbhari*⌟ (Sanskrit *udaraṃbhari*), "belly-fillers" (i.e. in this context drones or parasites), a rather unusual but legitimate compound. We speculate—but cannot be anywhere near certain—that the Prakrit word ⌜*urabbha*⌟ may have been another homophone that meant both "ram" and "belly-filler," turning the entire compound into a Prakrit double entendre: "let's see the dispute of the drones" or "let's see the clash of the rams." It would not have been possible to translate such a pun directly into Sanskrit, so *urabhra* and *udaraṃbhari* may originally have been parallel glosses of one Prakrit word. Of our commentators, Nī seems to have known only of the ram-clash version (*urabhrasaṃpātaṃ meṣayuddham*), while Kā treats the ram-clash as the primary reading and the drone-dispute as a *pāṭhāntara* (*urabhrasaṃpātaṃ meṣayuddham iti narmoktiḥ. ... udaraṃbhari-saṃvādam iti pāṭhe udaraṃbharyoḥ svodarabharaṇaparayoḥ saṃvādam*). Ram fights do not seem incongruous with ancient Indian palace life. For example one of the stories in the *Pañcatantra* (*Candrabhūpatikathā*, tale 9 in *Aparīkṣitakāraka*, the fifth book) is about rams kept as pets (play mounts for the young princes) in a palace, who become spoiled and cheekily raid the kitchens. The *Kāmasūtra* (1.4.8), while describing the pastimes of the bon vivant, says *bhojanānantaraṃ śukasārikāpralāpanavyāpārāḥ, lāvaka-kukkuṭameṣayuddhāni, tās tāś ca kalākrīḍāḥ, pīṭhamardaviṭavidū-ṣakāyattā vyāpārāḥ, divāśayyā ca*: "After eating, he passes the time teaching his parrots and mynah birds to speak; goes to quail-fights, cock-fights, and ram-fights; engages in various arts and games; and passes his time with his libertine, pander and clown." Interestingly, the word *pīṭhamarda* (here translated "pander;" see note to 1.119) is used in this *Kāmasūtra* passage. Given that *vidūṣaka* ("jester" in our translation) also appears in the passage, added to the generic correspondence of "various arts" to the ensuing dance (and possibly the tenuous similarity of exercising [grammatically feminine] mynah birds to Málavika's performance or to eventual conversation with her), we wonder if the jester (described as the king's *kāma/tantra/saciva*, "Minister of Amorous Affairs" by Irávati [4.236] and as *kāry'/ântara/saciva*, "my other minister, in charge of some quite different affairs" by the king [1.76]) is actually hinting at the *Kāmasūtra* with his rather unexpected use of the words *pīṭhamarda* and *urabhrasaṃpāta*.

1.150 The stage directions in this paragraph are rather confused in the various manuscript sources, and the apparatuses of available editions do not give a completely clear picture. The exact arrangement we have chosen to follow as being the most logical to our mind is apparently not found anywhere except in AIYANGAR's edition. We agree with IYER that the sentence "stop playing into my husband's hands" could not possibly be spoken openly (and disagree with KALE who says that this must have been spoken to herself, else Gana·dasa would have obeyed her), but we prefer to read "What now?" as meant only for the audience's ears, not for any of the characters on the stage.

1.151 **Sarásvati** is the goddess of learning and the arts.

1.167 **I shouldn't have doubted that** is a liberal translation of a rather vague statement: *ciram a/pade śaṅkito 'smi*, literally perhaps "for long I have been doubtful in the wrong place." We follow Kā in our interpretation that he has worried the queen might not let him order his pupil as he likes after all, and now feels assured in his rights. An alternative suggested by IYER is that *saṅkitaḥ* can be understood as a proper passive participle: "I have been wrongly suspected [to be incompetent by the queen]." There is also a variant *apadeśaśaṅkito* for *apade śaṅkito*, which might mean "I have been suspecting some pretext," but we do not feel this makes the line more intelligible.

1.173 See note to 1.16 on the **chálita dance**.

1.173 A **chatush·pada song** (literally: "four-footed") might consist of four lines (as almost all classical poetry does, and the lines are normally called *pāda*, not *pada*), or of four parts. Most commentators either fail to explain the meaning and stick to a grammatical analysis of the compound, or offer confusing (and probably confused) explanations. Given that in 2.8 the "fourth movement" of the song is mentioned (but see also note to 2.8), we are inclined to believe that this is a genre of song with four parts or four verses. However, the fact that of the single four-line poem that is actually sung, each line apparently represents a different mood (see 2.23 and note thereof), may also suggest that "fourth movement" is a corruption (or our misunderstanding), and the *catuṣpada* is a song whose four lines are independent mini-compositions in various moods.

1.190 **Rumble of the membrane**: the verse abounds in technical terms, and we have sacrificed the accuracy of the translation in an attempt to render the onomatopoeia of the Sanskrit. *Mārjanā*, literally "rubbing," refers to the tuning of a drum by applying a soft paste to the center of the membrane. The *māyūrī*, literally "associated with or favored by peacocks," is a particular way of tuning the faces of the *mṛdaṅga* drum, based on the middle note or *madhyama/svara* (corresponding to Fa in the western solfège scale, or F in a C major scale). See MARASINGHE (1989: 148) for more details. Peacocks are said to be fond of thunder because they perform their courtship dance at the beginning of the rainy season.

1.191 **We shouldn't be late for the rendezvous**: our translation is based on a reading (*sāmayikā bhavāmaḥ*) that is rather poorly attested in sources (but mentioned by Kā as a *pāṭhāntara* extant in his time). The king may have said this in complete innocence (in this case more accurately translated "let us be on time"), but he might have meant (or the queen might have understood) *sāmayika* as one who attends a tête-à-tête with a lover. In the other, better attested readings (*sāmavāyikā bhavāma* and *sāmājikā bhavāma*, both essentially meaning "let us join the company") we do not perceive a double meaning that would warrant the queen's remark about her "husband's tactlessness." It is, however, possible that one of these was indeed the original reading, and the tactlessness was not the choice of this word, but the use of *tasyāḥ*, "her/its (company)" before it (omitted in IYER's edition but attested in numerous sources). In this case the king might have referred to the subject of Káushiki's verse, the sound of the drum (*mārjanā*, feminine in Sanskrit), while the queen might have understood *tasyāḥ* to refer to Málavika. Finally, it is also possible that the king's tactlessness is nothing more than his unseemly haste.

2.1 **Enter the king seated**: Sanskrit drama was performed on a practically blank stage with a minimal set and few props. A mobile curtain, called *yavanikā* or *javanikā*, would be held in the required spot and raised or lowered as needed by a pair of stage hands, as can be seen in present-day Keralan *kūṭiyāṭṭam* performances (MEHTA 1995; BHAT 1975). According to TARLEKAR (1991) the *yavanikā* may have been a curtain hung on fixtures that could be drawn aside at need. When a character is entered "seated," he probably comes on stage earlier and takes up position hidden by this curtain, to be revealed when required. Alternatively, he might—without any curtain wizardry—use a special gesture to show that he is sitting, and/or mime sitting down after entering.

2.8 **Sharmíshtha** was the daughter of a demon king named Vrisha·parvan. According to the *Mahābhārata* (Book 1 'The Beginning,' *Ādiparvan*, canto 73) she quarreled with Devayáni, daughter of the high priest of the demons, but by a quirk of fate ended up as the latter's serving maid. Devayáni's husband, King Yayáti, fell in love with Sharmíshtha and had three sons by her, including Puru, the mythical ancestor of many of India's ruling dynasties. Her situation—in love with a king but in service to the king's wedded wife—parallels that of Málavika, but elsewhere we find no reference to her having composed songs. **Tempo moderato**: there are three kinds of tempo (*laya*) in classical Indian music: fast (*druta*), moderate (*madhya*) and slow (*vilambita*). According to the NŚ (17.131: *hāsyaśṛṅgārayor madhyalayaḥ*), the moderate tempo may be used for an erotic or a humorous piece.

2.8 **Fourth movement**: the meaning of *caturtha/vastu* is somewhat uncertain, as *vastu* normally means "subject" or "plot" in a literary context. In accordance with our concept of the *chatush·pada* as a song consisting of four parts (q.v. note to 1.173) we assume only the last part of the song is sung and danced here. Kā and Nī corroborate this by glossing this instance of *vastu* as *prabandha*, "composition," and *rūpaka* "play," respectively.

2.12 **Standing in the back-stage**: Málavika may at this moment be standing behind one of the curtained entryways to the stage (see note to 1.3), or she might be in a cloth-walled cubicle allowing glimpses of her feet and hair, then gradually revealing her body as the attendants lower the cloth (see note to 2.1 on mobile curtains). Note also the variant *nepathyaparigatāyāḥ*, in which case *nepathya* could mean "(heavy) costume" or "drapery;" this, however, would contradict Káushiki's explicit request in 1.182.

2.14 **Grace**, *sauṣṭhava* seems to be used in the play in a fairly general sense (cf. 1.139 and 1.182), but also has a technical meaning which may be intended here. *Sauṣṭhava* in this strict sense means the ease and balance of a pose assumed before dancing, and according to the NŚ, it comprises "a still, straight pose, all limbs at ease, feet in motion but not raised up, the waist, elbows, shoulders and head even and unmoving like the ears, and the chest raised" (10.91–92: *acañcalam akubjaṃ ca sannagātram athāpi ca / nātyuccaṃ calapādañ ca sauṣṭhavāṅgaṃ prayojayet / kaṭī karṇasamā yatra kūrparāṃsaśiras tathā / samunnatam uraś caiva sauṣṭhavaṃ nāma tad bhavet*; translation following Bhat, 1975).

2.20 **Autumn** in India means the period following the rainy season, when clouds disperse and haze disappears from the sky. The moon is particularly clear and limpid at this time.

2.21 **Verse**: we take *vastu* to mean "part" or "movement" (see note to 2.8), and apparently one part of this song consists of one verse.

2.22 Throbbing in a woman's **left eye** is believed to be a good omen, particularly one indicating union with her lover.

2.23 **Enacts ... in the respective moods** (*yathā/rasam abhinayati*): it seems that in Kali·dasa's usage *rasa* and *bhāva* are vaguely synonymous (see also *tanmayatvaṃ raseṣu* in 2.40 [8], where *bhāveṣu* would be expected in the light of traditional aesthetics). In this case the durable sentiment (*sthāyibhāva*, q.v. note to 1.42) of the song would be passion. The erotic *rasa* evoked is categorized as *vipralambhaśṛṅgāra* or love where union is not achieved, and within this as *ayoga*, where the reason union is not achieved is that the lovers are separated by external factors (loosely following Kā). Apart from *sthāyibhāva*, aesthetic theory enumerates a set of *vyabhicāribhāva*s or transitory sentiments, which are not matched one to one with *sthāyibhāva*s: each may accompany various durable sentiments, and the durable sentiment in a given composition may be expressed through a succession of several transitory sentiments. In the case of this verse the transitory sentiment changes from line to line. At first it is *nirveda*, despondency; followed by *harṣa*, joy accompanied by *vismaya*, surprise; then *cintā*, anxious thought; and finally *dainya*, melancholy. Each of these would be acted out whilst singing the corresponding line.

2.26 **Seeing no path for love**, i.e. thinking she cannot express her love directly because the king's senior wife is present. Alternatively: not seeing the course of love, i.e. its effects, in the king, who was controlling his expressions because of the presence of his queen.

2.32 **A tassel of millet**: the plant to which her right hand is compared is simply called *śyāmā*, "dark" in Sanskrit, which is not quite definite. Kā glosses it as *phalinī*, "fruiting," still rather vague. The most likely candidate is foxtail millet (*Setaria italica*, formerly *Panicum italicum*), which is more often called *priyaṅgu* in Sanskrit, a word for which both *śyāmā* and *phalinī* may be used as synonyms (though *priyaṅgu* may also mean various other plants; cf. note to 3.108). The ripening ears of millet may well be compared to a hand held in a relaxed position, though the word *viṭapa* more commonly means a branch or a shoot. The finger millet (*Eleusine coracana*) is a positively hand-like relative that has a long history of cultivation in India, but we find no evidence that *śyāmā* can mean this plant. Other plants that may be called *śyāmā* include the lesser bulrush (*Typha angustifolia*), which does not evoke an image of a hand drooping freely, and two medicinal vines (*Hemidesmus indicus* and *Ichnocarpus frutescens*, both also called Indian sarsaparilla), which may be droopy, but look rather nondescript. In the *Meghadūta* of Kali·dasa (verse 2.101 in MALLINSON 2006) the plant *śyāmā* is compared to the body or limbs of a beloved woman. BANERJI (1968) tentatively identifies *śyāmā* as *Echnocarpus frutescens* (sic).

2.35 The **mud-cutter fruit,** *paṅka/cchid*, is identified by both Kā and Nī as *kataka/bīja*. The fruits of this plant, *Strychnos potatorum* (a relative of the deadly *Strychnos nux-vomica* but containing no strychnine; also called cleaning nut), are to this day used in rural India for rubbing the inside of water-storage jars. Its juices act as a natural coagulant and disinfectant, making contaminated water more suitable for drinking.

2.40 The verse is highly technical and obscure; our translation is correspondingly liberal. **Hand gestures** translates *śākhā*, literally "branch," a little-used term that the NŚ defines as one of the six subcategories of acting with the body, involving the successive movement of the head, face, buttocks, thighs, hands and feet (22.43: *ṣaḍātmakas tu śārīro vākyaṃ sūcāṅkuras tathā / śākhā nāṭyāyitaṃ caiva nivṛttyaṅkura eva ca* and 22.47: *yattu śiromukha-jaṅghorupāṇipādair yathākramaṃ kriyate / śākhādarśanamārgaḥ śākhābhinayaḥ sa vijñeyaḥ*). Apparently this definition was either not well understood or not liked by later authorities on dance; according to BHAT (1975), the *Saṅgītaratnākara* (VII.37–38) "defines *śākhā* as the flourish of the gesticulating hand (*kara-vartanā*) which precedes the dramatic speech; and *aṅkura* means such a flourish which follows the speech." Kā seems to interpret the word as a (rhythmic?) measure of hand signs (*śākhā nāma nṛttahastānāṃ mānapracāraḥ. yathoktam—śākhā tu nṛttahastānāṃ yā mātrā citranartane iti*). Nī goes for an even simpler explanation, taking *śākhā* to mean fingers (*śākhāyoniḥ: śākhāḥ aṅgulayaḥ. aṅgulībhyaḥ samudbhavaḥ śākhāyoniḥ*). IYER cites a few more authorities and comes to the conclusion that "*śākhā* means primarily hand gestures"—which we are happy to accept.

2.50 **The best of our domain**: the Sanskrit expression *sva/viṣayaḥ*, "own domain," could be understood both as the king's and as the eye's domain. The eye's domain is form, called *rūpa* in Sanskrit, which also means beauty.

2.52 **Inaugural performance**: the reading *savana* (literally: "pressing [of soma juice]" or "sacrifice") is somewhat uncertain. We feel that its obscurity might confirm its originality, and it could also explain the less meaningful variants *sadana* and *sevana*. The main alternative, *nepathyasaṃgītaka* (glossed by Nī as *yavanikāntaḥsaṅgītam*, "singing behind the curtain;" also known to but not commented on by Kā), seems irrelevant. Kā treats *savana* as the main reading and comments *tatra savanaṃ nāṭyamaṇḍape vighnopaśāntaye ādau kriyamāṇo yajñaḥ bharatena nāṭyaśāstrārambhe proktaḥ*, "in this context *savana* means a sacrifice performed at the beginning in the dance hall to ward off obstacles, as prescribed by Bharata at the beginning of the *Nāṭyaśāstra*." However, we find no mention of *nepathyasavana* (or anything similar) in the NŚ, though the end of the first chapter does prescribe that a proper sacrifice (referred to as *yajana* and *bali*) involving foodstuffs (*bhojyair bhakṣaiś ca pānaiś ca*) be made on the stage. We speculate that in the present context *prathamaṃ nepathyasavanam* would mean an inaugural performance, which would involve at least presents given to brahmins, and probably a proper sacrifice as well.

2.53 The **chátaka bird** (a species of cuckoo, most likely *Clamator jacobinus*, the pied crested cuckoo) is said in poetic fancy to subsist on nothing but raindrops. The local migrations of the pied cuckoo are largely controlled by the south-west monsoon (Ali 2002), and presumably its calls are more frequently heard (thus their presence is more conspicuous) during or just before the monsoon rains.

2.55 **Dimwits must rely...**: this line recalls "the thoughts of dimwits go with the herd" from 1.9 [2] in the prologue.

2.55 **I'll offer this reward to her**: clearly to Málavika, but it is probably intentional that he does not name her, expecting a moment's confusion in which to bestow the bracelet. After all he could have meant Káushiki.

2.65 We are not entirely sure why a **poor patient** in particular would **want the doctor to bring him medicine.** KALE says he wants the doctor to come to him instead of going to the doctor's house, but this seems beside the point. The purport of the sentence is clearly that the king wants the jester to do everything for him. (Kā agrees: *ayaṃ bhāvaḥ: tvaṃ svayaṃ kim api na karoṣi. mayā tvatsaṃnidhāv ānīyamānāṃ mālavikām icchasi.* Nī only comments on some of the words, but not on the simile.) We believe that a doctor would normally only prescribe the medicine and expect the patient to buy it from a herbalist, and the point about the poor patient is that he wants the doctor to buy the medicine and give it to him for free.

2.71 **Hovers about the water-wheel**: it is not quite clear exactly what the *vāri|yantra* (literally: "water-mechanism") is, and whether *bhrāntimat*, "revolving," should be construed as an adverb pertaining to the action of the peacock or as an adjective qualifying the *vāri|yantra*. Given the caesura in the line and the opinion of both our commentators, the latter is more likely, i.e. we are dealing with a revolving water-mechanism here rather than a circling peacock. Kā glosses *vāriyantram* by *jalodgāriyantraṃ*, "water-spouting device." KALE uses both "fountain" and "water-wheel" in his translation. It might be possible that Kali·dasa had a sort of revolving fountain in mind, possibly similar to a modern-day lawn sprinkler. This would give better sense to the prefix in *parisarati*, "runs around" (softened in our translation to "hovers about"). But we are more inclined, based on Nī (*vāriyantraṃ udghāṭanaṃ ghaṭīyantram*) to picture the kind of device usually called a Persian wheel and to this very day often seen in the arid regions of northwestern India. This serves for lifting water out of a well or waterhole and consists of a wheel similar to that of a watermill, but rather than being propelled by the water, it is driven by oxen and a chain of buckets hangs down from the wheel. As the wheel revolves, each bucket in turn is submerged, filled with water, and is then lifted back again, pouring its contents into a trough at the highest point of the wheel.

2.71 **The seven-horsed sun**: Surya, the Vedic god of the sun, rides a radiant chariot drawn by seven horses.

2.85 We are not sure why a **cauldron in the marketplace** (*vipaṇikandu*, alternatively perhaps "the cauldron [or frying pan] of a merchant") would burn in particular. Nī remains silent on the matter, while Kā simply glosses *paṇyavīthikāyāṃ vrīhipacanapātram*, "a rice-cooking vessel in a market alley." It may be that such a pot burns (or cooks) very intensely because it serves a large number of shoppers; or that it is emptied quickly and, left on the fire, it burns; or that, not attended as carefully as one at home, it boils over or the frying oil in it catches flame; or that it is not being used for cooking at all, but being seasoned by burning a film of oil into its surface.

2.87 **I shall grab the first opportunity for it**: the Sanskrit text *gṛhīta/kṣaṇo 'smi* literally means "I am one by whom the moment is grabbed." The commentators interpret *kṣaṇa*, "moment," as a moment of leisure and say this means the jester will dedicate his free time to the king's cause. KALE adds that according to a text called the *Śaunakasmṛti* the polite way of asking a brahmin to officiate at a ceremony involves the phrase *karaṇīyaḥ kṣaṇas tvayā*, literally "a moment should be made by you," i.e. "will you please devote a little bit of your precious time to this affair." We, however, prefer to understand "moment" as a moment of opportunity, which we feel fits the context better.

3.2 A **citron** (*Citrus medica*) is a fruit similar to a lemon in appearance, but larger and far bitterer in taste. It is considered an auspicious fruit suitable for presentation to a high-ranking person. Káushiki wants an audience with the queen and wishes to offer a citron as a token of courtesy.

3.2 **Golden** *ashóka* **tree**: *ashóka*, the "tree without sorrow" (*Saraca asoca*, syn. *Saraca indica, Jonesia asoka*) is a small evergreen tree that flowers occasionally throughout the year, but in great profusion at the end of winter. Its tiny flowers bloom in large clusters, orange-yellow when they burst, maturing to dark red. The tree is traditionally associated with fertility and love (see note to 3.14). Sir William Jones, one of the first philologists to note and systematically study the relationship of Sanskrit to Latin and Greek, wrote that "The vegetable world scarce exhibits a richer sight than the Ashoka tree in full bloom" (quoted by NAIRNE 1894) and he made a plea that the botanical name of the species preserve the Indian name *aśoka*. Honoring his request, taxonomists went further and actually named the genus after Sir William, so the tree's binomial name came to be *Jonesia asoka*. KALE quotes Malli·natha's commentary on the *Meghadūta* to the effect that a white *ashóka* brings success in many things, while a red one enhances love. KALE speculates that the "golden" (*tapanīya*, literally "to be heated," used for gold purified by melting, or gold in general) *ashóka* mentioned here would have been a rare variety with yellow flowers, thus all the anxiety about its flowering. Variants and related species do indeed exist with yellow or whitish flowers. Kā says the word indicates a yellow-red (orange) color: *tena pītaraktatvaṃ lakṣyate*.

3.9 **The grapevine**: the Sanskrit word *kaulīna* means gossip, particularly of a malicious kind. The word is clearly derived from *kula*, "group, tribe, family," and no negative flavor seems to be implied in the present context. Commentators only mention the derogatory meaning, glossing as *lokāpavādaḥ*, "the reproach of the people." Kā adds a fanciful derivation of *kaulīna* from *kau līna*, "merged into the earth" because of being contemptible (*kau pṛthivyāṃ līnaṃ kutsitatvāt*). We prefer to interpret the word in a neutral sense as "[talk] of the house."

3.10 **Jasmine**: the word *mālatī* may mean the classical jasmine flower (*Jasminum grandiflorum*) or an unrelated but similarly white and scented flower (*Aganosma dichotoma*).

3.14 **It's got the cravings**: Indian folklore says the *ashóka* tree will burst into flower when struck by the foot of a woman (Kā: *pādāhataḥ* *pramadayā vikasaty aśokaḥ*). It is assumed that the tree craves this touch as a pregnant woman craves particular foods.

3.24 **My lord born in the womb of desire**: Love.

3.25 The **hope-inspiring weapons** of the god of love are arrows fashioned of flowers, which one would expect to bring pleasure rather than pain.

3.25 "**The soft is harsher than the harsh**" is apparently a proverb (Kā: *loke mṛdu sukumāraṃ vastu tīkṣṇataram atiprakharam iti yad ucyate*).

3.28 **Red ashóka**: see note to 3.2.

3.31 **Your lady friend**: when a man mentions his wife or lover to another man, it is a polite way of expression to refer to her as the other man's friend.

3.39 The male of the black Indian **cuckoo** or koel (*kokila*, *Eudynamys scolopacea*) has a penetrating call (not "cuck-koo" but an unbroken "kuoo") that is traditionally associated with love and longing. The bird is largely silent in the winter, and its calls are heard with increasing frequency as the weather turns hot in the spring (Ali 2002).

3.39 **Mango blossoms** (growing in large sprays of sweetly scented but rather plain-looking tiny greenish-white flowers) are also associated with spring and love.

3.44 **Lac** (*alaktaka*) is a red dye obtained from the juice of various plants or from the cochineal insect.

3.44 The **bimba** is a small, oblong gourd (of the genus *Momordica*, *Coccinia* or *Bryonia*), which turns bright red on ripening and to which the lips of women are frequently compared.

3.44 The **kúrabaka** is a plant whose identification appears quite uncertain. It is often translated "red amaranth" and some *Amaranthus* species native to India are good candidates to the name. These sport tiny red flowers in tassels, and some have dark-green leaves splotched in red or purple on the underside. Plants of the genus *Barleria* (e.g. *Barleria cristata*, the crested Philippine violet, a shrub of the *Acanthus* family) are also mentioned (sometimes equated to red amaranth), but the common variety of this plant apparently has no red coloring, an essential feature of the *kurabaka*.

3.44 **Red poised against dark,** *śyām'|âvadāt'|âruṇa*, literally "dark-opposite-ruddy" is slightly unclear. It seems to be interpreted mostly as "dark plus the opposite of dark plus ruddy," e.g. Kā: *śyāmāvadātāruṇaṃ śyāmaṃ ca tadavadātaṃ sitam aruṇaṃ ca tathoktam*; KALE: "darkish and white-red." But given the awkwardness of such an interpretation and the variegated colors of the likelier *kurabaka* candidate, contrasting black(ish) and red(dish) colors are more likely to be meant here, evoking the image of a colored design drawn on dark skin. In "How Úrvashi was Won" (*Vikramorvaśīya*, translated by VELCHERU NARAYANA RAO & DAVID SHULMAN, CSL, 2009, Act II, verse 7) Kali·dasa describes the *kurabaka* as *agre strī|nakha|pāṭalaṃ kurabakaṃ śyāmaṃ dvayor bhāgayor*, "dark on both sides but light red on top, like the fingernails of a woman."

3.44 **Face marks,** *viśeṣaka*, are ornamental designs drawn on the forehead or cheeks with scented and/or colored substances, often in the shape of leaves or other floral motifs.

3.44 **Tílaka flowers** are again uncertain; MW (s. v. *tilaka*) identifies them as *Clerodendrum phlomoides* (*Symplocos racemosa*), but these are the names of two quite unlike and unrelated plants. Clerodendrum are shrubs and small trees of the Verbena family, usually with highly decorative flowers in a variety of colors and striking patterns, while Symplocos are distant relatives of rhododendrons, tea and heather, and usually have rather inconspicuous white flowers. The more common Sanskrit name of *Symplocos racemosa* is *lodhra*.

3.44 **Forehead designs**, also *tilaka* in Sanskrit (and *tilak* in modern Hindi), are marks drawn on the forehead for decoration or to show caste and sect affiliation, in a variety of substances such as white clay, yellow sandalwood paste or red paint. The ornamental designs mentioned here would probably involve a light color fill accentuated with black dots or designs drawn in lampblack (*añjana*), similar to bees clinging to the flower.

3.46 **And where do I find the strength to tell...**: The source text is rather vague and may also mean "What right do my intimate friends have to tell (pass on) this story?" Since her friends already know her feelings and do talk about it, we might assume that this is what she meant. But it is slightly preferable to have her talk about her own feelings and inner conflict right now, assuming that her friends have only speculated about her and that she has not told them anything outright. Kā also prefers to understand the genitive *sakhījanasya* in a dative sense: *sakhījanasya caturthyarthe ṣaṣṭhī*. She hopes to lighten her heart by sharing her feelings, but cannot find the strength to do so. Compare *Abhijñānaśākuntala*, after verse 3.30, where Shakúntala's friends urge her to talk of her feelings, saying *saṃvibhaktaṃ khalu duḥkhaṃ sahyavedanaṃ bhavati*, "grief, shared, becomes sorrow that can be borne."

3.47 **Foot jewelry** is needed for fulfilling the *ashóka* tree's craving; see note to 3.14. Jewelry enhances the beauty of the foot and thus its effectiveness in making the tree flower; it also gives the act a ritual context. As a humble handmaiden, Málavika probably has no precious jewelry of her own, and is to wear the queen's ornaments on this occasion (see 3.114).

3.49 **Brown sugar** translates ⌜*macchaṇḍiā*⌟ (Sanskrit *matsyaṇḍikā*), which according to Dutt (1877) is "sugar-cane juice boiled down to a solid consistence but which still exudes a little fluid on drawing," probably similar to muscovado sugar. Its name literally means fish-roe, indicating its granular but moist consistency. We have found no mention of its use as an antidote to drunkenness or hangovers, except one quoted here by Kā, according to which crystalline sugar (not *matsyaṇḍikā*) mixed with ghee is supposed to prevent inebriation if consumed right after drinking. **Rum** translates *sīdhu*, an alcoholic drink derived from cane sugar. The king is reeling drunk with longing for Málavika, for which her actual presence is the antidote.

3.51 **Wearing scant jewelry**: or "scantily dressed" (⌜*ṇ' ādi/pajjatta/vesā*⌟), but given that foot ornaments are to be brought to her shortly (see note to 3.47) and jewelry is expressly mentioned in 3.61 [8] below, the former translation is more likely. For the earlier dance presentation she would have been bedecked in heavy jewelry. Her present lack of ornamentation may also serve to imply that she feels her love is hopeless.

3.55 **Crane**: most likely a sarus crane (*Grus antigone*), whose English name is derived (via Indian vernaculars) from the Sanskrit word *sārasa*, "associated with water." It is a very tall wading bird with light grayish plumage and a strikingly red, featherless head. The sarus crane mates for life and performs spectacular courtship dances in the breeding season; it is thus a symbol of marital bliss and fidelity. Its call is a far-reaching trumpeting sound (ALI 2002).

3.59 **Melon buttocks ... eyes very long**: the classical sketch of feminine beauty by Indian standards, as illustrated for example in the sculptures of Khajuraho. The "melon" is *bimba* in the Sanskrit text, for which see note to 3.44; the word may also mean anything round. An interesting feature of this verse in the original is that all the adjectives are in the neuter gender agreeing with "life" (*jīvitam*), the subject of the metaphor, while their intended subject is so very clearly feminine. In traditional aesthetics such gender mismatch in a metaphor is frowned upon, but apparently it did not bother Kali·dasa very much. Compare note to 4.136 and note to 4.232.

3.60 **Quite different**: this statement, *avasth"/ântaram upārūḍhā*, literally "grown into a different condition," is usually interpreted as "even more beautiful," but the words themselves do not imply this, and both the next verse and the following dialogue indicate that the main issue is her change of mien.

3.61 **Sallow like the stalk of a reed**: Sanskrit *śara* may mean any reed in general (as well as an arrow, usually made of a reed stalk), or a relative of the sugarcane (*Saccharum sara*) in particular. The stalk (*kāṇḍa*, literally a section between two nodes) is probably shiny and yellowish light brown in color, evoking cheeks that are still beautiful, but paler than Málavika's usual complexion or than her flush while she was dancing.

3.61 **Jasmine creeper**: the word *kunda* designates the star jasmine (*Jasminum multiflorum*) or the downy jasmine (*Jasminum pubescens*), and is associated in literature with brilliant whiteness, which suggests that her jewels, though few, are bright. There is probably also an implication that her jewelry is made of silver, not gold as the queen's ornaments, shortly to be brought to her, must be.

3.61 **Late in the spring**: the original term, *mādhava* simply means "sweet" or "honeylike," and has been used earlier in the play in the general sense of "spring." It is also the name of a particular month of the Indian lunar calendar more commonly known as *Vaiśākha*, corresponding to late April and early May, when in most of India the weather is dry and exceedingly hot—this is the meaning preferable in the present context.

3.61 **Leaves aged**: in Sanskrit, *pariṇata* means "transformed" or "ripened;" probably used here to imply that the leaves have taken on a yellowish color, but are not actually wilted.

3.67 The **wind from the south** is wind from the Málaya region in the original. The mountain range of the Western Ghats along the west coast of southern India is famous for its sandalwood production, and the wind blowing from its direction in spring, laden with the scent of sandalwood, is topically said to be particularly scented and passion-inducing.

3.71 **The elephant ... when he sees a lotus plant**: the elephant's attraction to the lotus plant is of course rather more prosaic than Agni·mitra's to Málavika: elephants tear up lotus plants to eat their succulent rhizomes.

3.76 **Lovely-legged girl**: in the original, *rambh"|ōru*, meaning one whose thighs are like the plantain tree. The plantain is not a true tree but a large herbaceous plant, and its stem, particularly the inner core, is round and glossily smooth.

3.77 *enāṃ* in the *chāyā* for ⌜*ṇaṃ*⌟ is an emendation, supported only by SASTRI's edition (where it may be the editor's emendation as well). All other editions translate ⌜*ṇaṃ*⌟ with *nanu*, which we feel is not suited to the present context (leaving ⌜*uvaṭṭhidā*⌟ without an object, and implying that the king should be aware of Bakulávalika's coming).

3.83 **The queen gives you a fitting task**: literally, "you've been appointed by the queen according to your capability." She means that Málavika's beauty deserves a special task like making the *aśoka* bloom, and she shouldn't be just one of the many maids. An alternative interpretation—but probably not an explicit punning insinuation—would be: "you've been appointed [to such a task] as befits a queen."

3.87 **Harem finery**, i.e. jewels normally worn by the queens of the harem, not by maids. See also note to 3.47.

3.88 **Sorry about this**: the foot is traditionally an unclean part of the body, and Málavika is excusing herself for offering her foot to Bakulávalika.

3.92 Kama, the love god, was **scorched by Shiva** with the fire from the third eye on his forehead when Kama fired a flower-arrow at him in an attempt to arouse his desire for Párvati. The **tree of Love** is not an actual tree but a metaphor in which the god is likened to a tree. The red lac evokes the coppery color of a new shoot, and he sees in it a sign that his love is not hopeless.

3.95 **Fresh misdeed**: games between lovers, as depicted in Sanskrit poetry, traditionally include the man being inconsiderate or faithless, then returning to his lover and trying to propitiate her by bowing his head at her feet and begging. She would initially (while his misdeed is fresh) reject his advances, e.g. by administering a gentle kick, but let herself be won over gradually. The focus of this scenario is not on self-debasement and aggression but on relishing the entire gamut of feelings associated with love.

3.102 **Mistress**: the *Amarakośa* (1.8.13: *devī kṛtābhiṣekāyām itarāsu tu bhaṭṭinī*; quoted here by Kā) suggests that *bhaṭṭinī* is the address used for unanointed wives of the king.

3.104 **Spring gifts** are presents (probably sweets) given to brahmins on the occasion of the arrival of the spring. Most commentators and translators gloss over the fact that the jester cannot have told Nípunika that the king is already at the swing gazebo, since he has been continuously on stage ever since persuading the king to go there. KALE opines that either this is a white lie, or Nípunika may have inferred from Gáutama's eagerness for spring gifts that the king will be at the gazebo. We find the former unlikely and the latter unconvincing (seeing little connection between a general penchant for sweets and the fact that the king is at a particular place at a given moment). See p. xxix for our speculation on the matter.

3.105 **In a way befitting her state**: the NŚ (7.38–46) says that inebriation should be represented on stage in different ways for characters of different natures. As a middling (neither noble nor ignoble) character, Irávati would stumble, roll her eyes, move her arms in an uncoordinated way, and walk crookedly and haltingly (*skhalitāghūrṇitanayanaḥ srastavyākulitabāhuvikṣepaḥ / kuṭilavyāviddhagatir madhyamado madhyamaprakṛtiḥ*). Since she does not drink on stage, her intoxication should lighten gradually as the scene proceeds (*kāryo madakṣayo vai yaḥ khalu pītvā praviṣṭaḥ syāt*).

3.108 **Priyángu plants** might be a variety of mustard or millet (see also note to 2.32), but most often they are identified as the Indian beautyberry (*Callicarpa macrophylla*), a large shrub that bears purple berries in conspicuous clusters.

3.110 **Mango sprouts** are coppery red, often compared to the lac-painted fingers of beautiful ladies. The young sprouts are used for festive decoration and worn as ornaments. It is also possible that mango buds are meant; compare note to 3.143. KALE quotes an acquaintance relating that certain red ants habitually live in mango trees. The point of Nípunika's metaphor would then be that they should have expected this annoyance.

3.143 **Mango flowers** (see note to 3.110) are traditionally used as **ear ornaments** by women.

3.145 The **bákula** (*Mimusops elengi*), also known as the Spanish cherry or Indian medlar, is an ornamental tree with small, fragrant, white blossoms. The flowers are well suited for twining into garlands, and they retain their fragrance when dry. It is likely that the petals themselves contain an aromatic oil that would account for this, and also for the scent growing stronger when bruised.

3.151 **Do the queen's command and make the ashóka bloom**: again, not an explicit pun, but an implied second meaning would be "Perform the queenly task of promoting sorrowlessness."

3.165 The *aśoka*'s craving is **like a playful lover's** because it's expected to bloom in joy (comparable to blushing or ecstatic horripilation) once it's been lovingly struck by a girl's foot. See note to 3.95.

3.168 The king and the jester **enter** the center of the stage or the range of vision of the girls; previously they would have stood off to one side of the stage, assumed by theatrical conventions to be invisible to the others present.

3.171 The **left foot** is perceived as particularly unclean (see also note to 3.88).

3.173 **You know how things stand**: at face value the jester simply says that Bakulávalika knew Málavika was going to kick the tree and ought to have prevented her. But he also insinuates that Bakulávalika should not take the reprimand seriously as it's just a ruse for the king to join the maids.

3.176 Gáutama is only a **son-of-a-brahmin** because by right of descent he is entitled to call himself a brahmin, but lacks proper qualifications for a priest.

3.180 The Sanskrit does not specify the object of **takes ... by the hand and pulls ... to her feet**; it is possible that he does this to both girls simultaneously.

3.181 The statement **"got to respect the queen here"** at face value means that the king should not hold the girls at fault because they were carrying out Dhárini's command. But there may be an allusion in it to "the queen here," i.e. Málavika, the latest candidate for queenship. This interpretation is possibly supported by the king's laugh in the next line.

3.199 **Practicing conjugation** is an attempt at transcreating the grammatical pun in *saṃdhi/cchedana*. The original text has a burglar, not an adulterer. The most common technique of burglary in India, if we can believe literature, was to open holes in the sides of buildings by cutting out the mortar from the joins (*saṃdhi/cchedana*) and removing building blocks. Commentators and translators seem to understand this riposte mostly as "I'm just practicing my robbery skills, not actually trying to steal anything," but we feel this would be rather weak, and prefer to see a pun here. The term *saṃdhi/cchedana* also means splitting, i.e. resolving sandhi, the fusion of the final and initial sounds of words in a Sanskrit sentence. This can be a serious hurdle in learning Sanskrit, made easy for CSL readers. Sanskrit was not a vernacular language in the times of Kali·dasa, but a man of culture would be expected at least to understand it, and thus to be able to split sandhi—effectively quite similar to how a gentleman in early twentieth-century Europe would be expected to know Latin conjugation.

3.206 The **girdle** (*raśanā*) referred to here is an ornamental jewel belt worn low on the waist by women. It has presumably slipped down her legs and is now hindering her movement, but because of her anger or tipsiness she does not notice or care. Thus the king has time to catch up.

3.209 **Contempt bred by our familiarity**: because of sandhi, the Sanskrit word *paricayavaty* may be construed as *paricayavatī*, agreeing with *avadhīraṇā* ("your contempt connected to [your] familiarity [with me]" or "your contempt, which is familiar [to me]"), or as *paricayavati*, agreeing with *mayi* ("your contempt for me, who am familiar [to you]").

3.223 Disregarding the king's falling at her feet was **impolite** of Irávati, and thus the king has scored a point against her.

3.223 A planet's **retrograde** motion is when (due to the difference in the orbit of the Earth and that planet) it appears to reverse its usual course in the sky. In Indian as well as western astrology, retrograde motion is believed to augment a planet's negative influences. Mars is a risky planet to begin with, and its great destructive potential is further enhanced by retrograde motion—like Irávati, already a fly in their soup and able to cause much damage if she were now to reappear suddenly.

3.226 The stage direction ***iti parikramya niṣkrāntāḥ sarve*** (literally: "all walk about and leave") is somewhat strange given that only the king and the jester are on stage. KALE prints *iti niṣkrāntaḥ saha vayasyena* ("exit the king with his companion"), which sounds more logical, but is not attested in any of our other sources, which unanimously go with the *sarve* version. BHAT (1975: xlvii) observes that *niṣkrāntāḥ* sarve is sometimes used at the end of an act even if only one or two characters are left on the stage.

4.20 The text of this passage is both corrupt and ambiguous. The commentaries available to us neglect it altogether except for a brief gloss on one tiny fragment by Kā. We have preserved the readings of IYER's edition with a slight conjectural emendation. In the translation "**Hasn't he met you, his favorite?**" all the pronouns have been supplied by us; a more literal translation would be "Hasn't the favorite person been seen?" (and the word *jaṇa* may even refer to plural "people" rather than "person"). "Have you met our beloved [the king]?" or even "Why aren't you meeting your beloved [the king, rather than me]?" would be equally possible, and the variant readings allow yet more interpretations. A wide gamut of variants is available for "**Not too polite, are you**"—a rather liberal rendering of our chosen source text, literally "Your politeness is weak indeed." "**You know full well that his favorite is your maidservant**" is also ambiguous; a more literal translation might be "You are aware of the belovedness of your servant." Besides referring to Málavika's newfound place in the king's heart, it is also possible that Irávati uses "your servant" to refer to herself (with a touch of mock humility) and says the queen should know how loved Irávati is by the king: not at all any more.

4.24 **naga girls**: serpent spirits thought to inhabit the underworld.

4.35 **Red sandal paste** may be a preparation of sandalwood (from the true sandalwood tree, *Santalum album*), but is more likely to come from an unrelated tree, possibly *Pterocarpus santalinus*. Trees in the genus *Pterocarpus* yield the wood known as padauk or red sandalwood, prized in furniture-making for its toughness and decorativeness. Red sandal paste is used as a perfume and applied in Ayurvedic medicine to disinfect and heal wounds.

4.43 **Enter the queen reclining on a bed**: see note to 2.1.

4.54 The **sacrificial thread** is a triple strand worn across the chest by the members of the three upper echelons of society (vaishyas and kshatriyas, and most especially brahmins). The thread is conferred at the rite of passage called *upanayana*, "leading to [a master]," performed at the commencement of Vedic studies.

4.60 **Emerged from a hollow**: incidentally, the king had used the same word (*koṭara*, the hollow of a tree) in 4.26 [2] immediately before the jester had the idea of faking an encounter with a snake.

4.63 **Cutting the bite...**: making incisions in the bitten area and pressing to bleed it out is intended to expel venom from the system; cauterization is meant to neutralize venom before it spreads. Note that none of these procedures (including the application of a tourniquet) are recommended as first aid by modern snakebite experts. We are not sure what the difference is between cutting the bite (*chedo daṃśasya*) and bleeding the wound out (*kṣate raktamokṣaṇaṃ*). We believe (after Kā's *daṣṭasthānasya cchedaḥ*) that the former means excising the bitten area; alternatively it might even mean amputating the bitten limb.

4.70 On the **effects of poisoning** in mimetic art, Kā quotes the *Vasantarājīya* (untraced): *vaivarṇyaṃ vepathur dāhaḥ phenaḥ skandhasya bhañjanam / duḥkhaṃ jāḍyaṃ mṛtiś ceti viṣavegāḥ syur aṣṭadhā* (Kā's text as reproduced in AIYANGAR's edition substitutes *hikkā jṛmbhā* for *duḥkhaṃ jāḍyaṃ*): "The eightfold effects of poisoning are pallor, shivering, burning, frothing, jerking (breaking?) of the shoulder, dejection, torpor (or with the AIYANGAR version, hiccoughing and yawning) and death."

4.81 **Dhruva·siddhi**: the name means "certain success."

4.83 The **waterpot rite**, *uda/kumbha/vidhāna*, is a ritual for curing snakebites. Kā quotes a detailed description from a text he calls *Bhairavatantra*, but this rite does not involve the image of a snake. He cites another procedure, called *nāga/mudrā/vidhi*, "the rite of the snake seal," from the *Rasaratnāvalī* (probably a text on alchemy), which does involve both a snake image and a waterpot.

4.86 The **task** that the king refers to publicly is the curing of the snakebite, but as Jaya·sena is part of the sham, she ought to understand the allusion to the release of Málavika and Bakulávalika.

4.89 Káushiki's expression of her hope that **Gáutama should be free of poison** again carries a double meaning. On the surface, she is just reassuring everyone that the jester will be all right, but actually she is trying to feel out if the whole snake scene had been a ruse.

4.118 The **water pavilion** is probably a building cooled by water, used as a retiring place in hot weather. The Sanskrit term *samudra/gṛha* literally means "ocean house" and is interpreted as a bath house or bathroom by MONIER-WILLIAMS. Kā quotes the *Hārāvalī* of Puruṣasiṃhadeva to prove that it means "a house with fountains," (*samudragṛham ity uktaṃ jalayantraniketanam*) but also notes that "some" (*ke cit*) analyze it as *sa/mudra/gṛha*, "a house with seals" (or possibly coins, imprints, etc.), so apparently the word was already a source of difficulty for the fourteenth-century commentator. "Some" may refer to a predecessor of Nī, who writes *samudragṛhe mudrāyukte gṛhe mudritagṛhadvāra ity arthaḥ* (we are not sure what he means by this, but probably a building with sealed doors). Other possibilities include a pavilion in the middle of a body of water, or perhaps the type of building known in modern India as a *bāvalī* or step-well, a building of several subterranean stories constructed around a well.

4.122 ... **must avoid moonlight**: the name Chándrika means "moonlight."

4.129 Presumably a **picture** painted on the wall.

4.136 **You looked different in life than you do in the picture**: more literally: "she did not see you as she saw you in the picture." This is generally understood as a teasing paraphrase of Málavika's statement, implying that the king looks much better in the picture than he does in life. The king ignores the gibe and reacts as if the jester had simply repeated what Málavika had said, that she could not get a good look at the king when she was performing in front of him. There are a number of variants for this sentence; a flippant but probably secondary one (reported by IYER) says "She had not looked at you as much as you had at her" (⌜*atthabhodī tue jaha diṭṭhā tahā ṇa diṭṭho bhavaṃ*⌟).

4.136 The **casket** (*mañjūṣā*) is feminine in gender; compare note to 3.59.

4.136 **Youthfulness**, *yauvana*, would be more accurately translated as adulthood or "prime of life." The word, just like the Latin cognate *iuventus*, refers to an age of full maturity before old age.

4.148 **Helping him with that**: i.e. winning the favors of Irávati.

4.153 **Lotus-eyed lady**, *kuvalaya|nayane*: *kuvalaya* is not actually a lotus, but a blue waterlily said to bloom at night. In southern India, the word *kuvalaya* is also used for the water hyacinth (*Eichhornia sp.*), which has a prominent eye-like (though yellow) spot on the upper petal of its blue flowers.

4.163 **Even in my dreams**: by this Málavika implies that the king could at least get some sleep, while she's been so tormented she could not.

4.165 **Fire as my witness**: Hindu marriage vows are traditionally made in the presence of fire. The *Kāmasūtra* (3.5.14) says *agnisākṣikā hi vivāhā na nivartanta ity ācāryasamayaḥ*, "the scholars' rule says, 'weddings witnessed by the consecrated fire cannot be revoked.'"

4.170 **It's me you should guard**: apparently Agni·mitra does not realize this is precisely what the jester is doing, and the deer is just a pretext.

4.177 The **atimúkta** (literally, "surpassing pearls;" also called *mādhavī*, "vernal" or "honeyed") is a creeper with scented white flowers. The way it enfolds trees—particularly mango trees in literary fancy—is a common metaphor for a woman embracing a man. The plant is most likely *Hiptage benghalensis* (syn. *Gaertnera racemosa*), a vigorous creeper that may also be trained into a small tree if grown without support. Its asymmetrical flowers, brilliant white with one strikingly yellow petal, appear throughout the year but most profusely in the late winter and early spring. Imported as a garden ornamental, it has now become an invasive species in many tropical and subtropical areas of the world.

4.181 The name or word **Báimbika** (*Baimbika*) is a perplexing one. In form it appears to be a patronymic, "a descendent of Bimba (or Bímbika)." We assume, but are by no means certain, that this refers to Agni·mitra's family, and Kali·dasa uses it here for the sake of euphony with **bimba-lipped girl** (q.v. note to 3.44). See p. xix for a discussion of whether this is indeed a historic name of Agni·mitra's dynasty. According to VSA (s. v.), *baimbika* means "a man who is assiduous in his attentions to ladies, a gallant, lover"—this is apparently an educated guess based on the context of this single occurrence of the word, and "family tradition" (*kula/vrata*, literally, "family vow") would not really be applicable to such a meaning (though it might also mean "group vow," i.e. an obligation common to all chevaliers). Kā only says, *baimbikās tadvaśyā rājānaḥ*, "Báimbikas are kings subject to him [or it]," without telling us who or what they would be subject to. Nī, apparently trying to go for both explanations at once, comments: *baimbikānām agnimitravaṃśajānāṃ saralasukhaprasādaśīlānām ity arthaḥ*, "of Báimbikas, i.e. of those born in Agni·mitra's dynasty, which means [people who are] characterized by being easily gratified by pleasure" (plenty of other interpretations of the vague compound are possible). Pandit is of the opinion that *baimbikas* are lovers, and justifies this by remarking that *bimba* is often used as a metaphor for "loins" (compare note to 3.59 on "melon buttocks"), so presumably a *baimbika* would be one devoted to this part of the female anatomy. Of the variants for this word, we believe *vaidikānāṃ* is a corruption of *baimbikānāṃ*, while *nāyakānāṃ* is in our opinion an inferior easy way out of the problem (and *nāyikānāṃ* is utter nonsense).

4.214 The **kétaki** (*Pandanus fascicularis, syn. Pandanus odoratissimus*) is a species of screw-pine, a large shrub with a branching trunk, many prop roots and long, spiky, strap-shaped leaves. The thorns mentioned by the jester refer to the spikes on the leaves. The *ketakī* bears inflorescences resembling a thorny corncob, with an overpoweringly intense, sweet and aromatic scent. The flowers are used for decorating and perfuming buildings, and the fragrance known as kewra or kewda is distilled from them. Other Pandanus species are common houseplants in the western world, while the leaves of yet others are used in southeast Asian cooking.

4.215 Entering with a **toss of the curtain** is a theatrical convention that indicates hurry and agitation. While this meaning is certain, the exact action involved is ambiguous. Actors would normally enter the stage folding aside the curtain on the entryways (see note to 1.3 about the setup of the stage). This sort of abrupt entry may be interpreted as "with a toss of the curtain" (*paṭ'/ākṣepeṇa*, often also *apaṭī/kṣepeṇa*, where *apaṭī* is understood as an alternative form of *paṭī*), but may also be read as "without a toss of the curtain" (*paṭ'/â/kṣepeṇa* and *a/paṭī/kṣepeṇa*), i.e. simply rushing through the curtain without pausing to fold it out of the way. See MARASINGHE (1989: 103ff.) for a discussion.

4.221 **The god**: Indra, the god of rain and storms (following Kā).

4.221 What Bakulávalika probably means by "**Does the god need the frogs' croaking...**" is that Agni·mitra's falling in love with Málavika was by the king's own will (or nature), and Bakulávalika's insignificant "croaking" had nothing to do with it. Frogs are of course associated with the rainy season, whose arrival they welcome with a chorus (described as early as the *Ṛgveda*, 7.103), but their sound was probably not believed actually to bring rain, except in some forms of rain magic. The problem with this reading is that Málavika is equated to the earth in the metaphor (compare note to 1.124), and KALE rejects it on the grounds that a maid like Bakulávalika could never have the nerve to do this in the face of Irávati. We nevertheless prefer this variant to the widespread alternative that reads *visumaredi* for *sumaredi*, turning the sentence into its opposite: "Does the god forget to shower rain on the earth because frogs croak?" In this case the earth would be understood as Irávati, and the line as an assurance that the king will continue to love her—but even as a rhetorical question, we see no reason why anyone would suppose the frogs' croaking might make the deity of rain forget his job.

4.232 **On her**: the source text uses a masculine word, ⌜*kavodao*⌟ (*kapotaḥ*), for the dove. Compare note to 3.59.

4.237 The **Gayátri** is a Vedic mantra (found e.g. in *Ṛgveda* 3.62.10) that is said to be the mystical essence of all Vedic knowledge. The nuance of this sentence is not certain. We prefer our translation, assuming that the jester is implying in his (mock) humility that he is too stupid to remember two things at a time. Another interpretation (following KALE) would be that he is swearing a sort of oath: "May I forget the Gayátri if I ever studied a syllable of polity." A third (following Kā) would be: "I'd as soon study polity as forget the Gayátri," i.e. both of these are impossible. GEROW points out (in STOLER MILLER 1999) that a learned Indian audience would probably have savored a humorous touch in Gáutama's aversion to even **a single syllable of polity**, as his name implies that he belongs to the clan of the sage Gótama, who was the author of the *Nyāyasūtra*, the classical treatise on logic.

4.240 **Ginger monkey**: or, as KALE and SASTRI suggest, the monkey called Píngala (*piṅgala*, a reddish or yellowish color).

4.245 The jester probably calls himself the monkey's **kin** (*sva/pakṣa*, literally its "own side") in his usual self-deprecatory way, referring to his ungainliness (or, according to Kā's primary explanation, to his mischievousness). KALE's explanation—that the monkey is a captive one and the property of the king, which puts it on the same side with the king and the jester—is in our opinion weak and forced, while Kā's alternative explanation, that they are on the same side because the monkey has just saved them, is a circular argument.

5.2 The **platform** is a circular dais built of bricks or stone around the roots of a tree. Such platforms are to this day found throughout India, both under religiously significant trees for ritual purposes and under good shade trees where they serve as a socialization area. In the present case it is probably needed for the queen's official visit to the tree; see also 5.54.

5.2 The *ashóka* has been **worshipped** (*kida/sakkāra*) by Málavika, who satisfied its craving; Kā notes that it may instead have been decorated, e.g. by plastering the ground around it with smooth mud and drawing designs there.

5.7 **The General**: Pushpa·mitra, Agni·mitra's father. See also p. xvi.

5.7 The Vedic horse sacrifice (*aśvamedha*) is performed as a confirmation of dominion over the known world. The **sacrificial horse**, a stallion, must be allowed to wander free for a year, guarded by a company of young men. During this time any neighboring rulers who attempt to capture the horse must be subjugated. When the year is up, the actual sacrifice takes place in the form of an exceedingly elaborate ritual.

5.9 The **house shrine**, *maṅgala/gṛha*, would be a part of the palace dedicated to worship and pious activities (UPADHYAYA 1947). Presumably the queen has gone there to offer thanks for the good news, or perhaps she had wanted the news revealed to her in that place in an attempt to ensure that they would be good news.

5.19 Love is **disembodied** because Shiva had burned away his body. See note to 3.92. Besought by **Rati**, "Passion"—the wife of the love god—to resurrect her husband, the ascetic deity allowed Kama to live on in a disembodied form.

5.19 **The Vídisha** is a minor river that joins the Betwa (historically called Vétravati) near the modern town of Vidisha (which may have been the site of the ancient capital), while the **Várada** is a river in the Vidárbha heartland.

5.20 In the Sanskrit text, **arms** (*dorbhiḥ*) is in the plural instead of the expected dual. We believe this is because the author had Krishna's four-armed divine form in mind, though in the course of his earthly acts he normally appears in his two-armed human form. An alternative explanation of the plural may be that the word is to be taken with both Krishna and Agni·mitra (referring to their four arms in total). Our commentators offer no explanation, though

Nī glosses "with many arms" (*bahubbhiḥ dorbhiḥ*), perhaps taking this as a reference to the arms of the king's troops.

5.20 The **Kratha·káishikas** are the people of Vidárbha. The word is a combination of the clan names Kratha and Káishika, explained as two sons of a legendary olden king of Vidárbha. **Krishna** was the eighth incarnation of the preserver deity Vishnu. **Rúkmini** was the daughter of a Vidárbhan king named Bhíshmaka, and is considered to have been an incarnation of Vishnu's wife Lakshmi. She and Krishna had fallen in love, but Bhíshmaka promised Rúkmini to a king named Shishu·pala. Krishna abducted her, defeated Shishu·pala and Rúkmini's brother who tried to stop him, and married Rúkmini.

5.27 In his synopsis of the drama, TIEKEN (2001) says the **Vidárbhan wedding costume** was part of the booty sent by Vira·sena (see 5.11). The suggestion sounds interesting, but we see nothing in the text to support it. Note also that ⌜*Vedabbhaṃ*⌟ is omitted in many versions of the play.

5.43 The king is said to have two metaphysical wives: the **Earth** and **Glory** (see also note to 1.124). Glory, personified as the goddess Lakshmi, carries a **lotus** in her hand as one of her attributes. We prefer to read *vismṛta*, "forgotten," implying that all Málavika would need to become a perfect image of Lakshmi is a lotus in her hand. The alternative reading, *vistṛta*, "extended," would require two different interpretations of *hasta/kamalayā*: for the goddess the compound would mean "who extends a lotus in her hand," while for Málavika it would have to be construed as "who extends her lotus-like hand" (following Kā's interpretation of what he records as a *pāṭhāntara*).

5.45 **I know the simple reason**, i.e. that the queen simply wanted to see Káushiki's skill in dressing. Nevertheless her **heart quivers** in anticipation, as though expecting her hope of being married to the king to be fulfilled, and her **left eye twitches**, which is by poetic convention an auspicious omen for women (and an ill one for men).

5.48 **Spring night** translates *Caitra*, the name of the first month of spring in the Indian lunar calendar (also the first month of the year by the most widespread reckoning), corresponding to mid-March to mid-April in the Gregorian calendar.

5.57 Although the verse is not a fully fledged pun, the ***aśoka*** tree is certainly meant to be a metaphor for the king (who is *a/śoka*, without sorrow, now that the queen appears to have consented to his love for Málavika). But Dhárini should be well aware that he, unlike the tree that did not flower at the proper time but only when the queen arranged for a ceremony, has not entirely ignored the command of the vernal goddess. INGALLS (1976: 21) sees a complete double entendre in this quatrain, in which Agni·mitra "refers to his own restraint ... and implicitly subjects ... himself to [the queen's] kindly rule."

5.63 The **chakra gander** (*cakravāka*, here referred to as *rath'/âṅga/nāman*, "that which is named after a part of the chariot," i.e. the wheel, *cakra*) is the ruddy shelduck or Brahminy duck (*Tadorna ferruginea*). By poetic convention it is supposed to be separated from its mate every night.

5.122 **Donned the russets**: an expression for putting on monastic robes. See also p. xxviii.

5.132 It is quite possible that Málavika too had known of this **prophecy**, which may have helped her to bear her fate with patience.

5.136 The concept of the **double kingship** (*dvairājya*) is mentioned briefly in the *Arthaśāstra* (8.2.5–8). Anonymous "teachers" are said to view it as a danger to the kingdom, but Kauṭilya disagrees and says that double kingship is not harmful if practiced by a father and his son or by two brothers. Interestingly, this remark is omitted from some texts of the *Arthaśāstra* (apparently due to eyeskip), so certain versions simply mention double kingship as a danger to the kingdom. Whether or not such division is beneficial for Vidárbha, it will certainly be advantageous to Agni·mitra, as expressed in 5.144 [14].

5.149 **Greek**: the Sanskrit word *Yavana* (etymologically cognate to "Ionian") originally means Greek, but may refer to any (western) foreign people, and could thus also be rendered as "barbarian." Nī says they could be Greeks or (anachronistically) Turks: *yavanānāṃ yavanadeśarājñāṃ tuluṣkāṇāṃ* (sic) *vā*. We believe that the clash was with the people of one of the Hellenized kingdoms of the northwest of the Indian subcontinent.

5.149 We take the **royal sacrifice** (*rāja/yajña*) to refer to the horse sacrifice. Dwivedī remarks that this interpretation is sound because the horse sacrifice can only be performed by kshatriyas, and the word *rājan* ("king") can mean "kshatriya" (*rājapadam atra rājanyaparam, tena rājayajño 'tra rājanyaikānuṣṭheyo 'śvamedhaḥ*). Kā quotes the *Trikāṇḍaśeṣa* (untraced) to show that *rāja/yajña* can mean either the horse sacrifice or the sacrifice performed at the inauguration of a king (*rājayajño nāmāśvamedhaḥ. rājayajño rājasūyākhyaḥ. rājasūyo nṛpādhvaraḥ*). Indeed, the variant *rāja/sūya/yajña* seems fairly widespread, but we see no way in which that sacrifice could be relevant to the context. See note to 5.7 for the horse sacrifice and p. xvi for its performance by Pushpa·mitra.

5.149 The **Indus** (*Sindhu*) might also be interpreted as a common noun, "a river," but again we feel that the actual Indus river fits the context best. Nī mentions both options and expresses no preference (*sindhoḥ saritaḥ. sindhur nāma sarit*), while Kā is for the great river named Indus (*sindhor nāma nadasya*). The expression *dakṣiṇe rodhasi* could also mean "right bank" rather than **southern bank.**

5.154 As described in the *Rāmāyaṇa* (Book 1, 'Boyhood,' *Bālakāṇḍa*, 36–40), **Ságara**, an ancestor of Rama, wished to perform a horse sacrifice (q.v. note to 5.7). The sacrificial horse was kidnapped by Indra in the guise of a monster. The sixty thousand sons of Ságara, sent to retrieve the horse, were subsequently burnt to ashes by the sage Kápila (also identified with Vishnu). It was **Ánshumat**, the grandson of Ságara, who finally retrieved the horse, making the completion of the sacrifice possible.

5.154 **Emptying your mind of anger**: our sources seem as clueless as we are about why Agni·mitra should have been angry in the first place. The simplest explanation would be that this is a mere phrase: he should attend the sacrifice with a tranquil mind. Nī explains *vigata/roṣaḥ* (literally, "[being] one whose anger has departed") as *nivṛttakoṣaḥ*, which we can only interpret as "one whose treasury has vanished," unless *koṣaḥ* in the gloss is a typographical error in AIYANGAR's edition for *krodhaḥ*, "wrath." Kā only analyses the compound and offers no explanation. The *Sārārthadīpikā* opines that Agni·mitra may be angry with Pushpa·mitra because the latter had appointed the young prince to guard the sacrificial horse without the former's consent (*vigataḥ roṣaḥ madviṣayakaḥ krodhaḥ yasya tat ceto yasya tena. agnimitrānumatiṃ vinā tatputrasya yajñīyaturagarakṣādhikāritve niyogo 'tra saṃbhāvito roṣahetuḥ bodhyaḥ*). Pandit is of the same persuasion. KALE counters this with the note that "no true Kṣatriya would shrink from … such a mission;" we in turn are not so sure about this, or about Agni·mitra being a true kshatriya (either in attitudes or technically; see p. xix). Tawney proposes in the introduction to his translation that there might have been a tension between father and son because of their different attitudes to Buddhism (see p. xxi).

5.158 There is considerable confusion in our sources as to the speaker of this line and the next. There are also a number of variant readings that do not significantly alter the meaning, and others that suit the identity of the speaker (e.g. *parituṭṭha* for *parituṭṭho* if this line is spoken by the king; omission of *Maudgalya* if that line is spoken by the chamberlain, and in some sources an introductory line by the chamberlain before the verse). **"I'm pleased that the son takes after his father"** is said by the queen in a variant noted by KALE and SASTRI, and in three manuscripts consulted in DWIVEDĪ's edition. **"It appears the elephant calf is imitating the prime bull"** is spoken by Káushiki in the main text of KALE and in a variant mentioned by IYER. Interestingly, DWIVEDĪ puts this latter line in the mouth of the chamberlain (who then goes on to say the verse "It is no surprise…"), though this appears to be based on a single manuscript, while he does not mention Káushiki as the speaker at all. IYER opines that the probable reason why some sources designate Káushiki is that they do not want the king to flatter himself (by calling himself a prime elephant bull).

5.160 **The thigh-born sage** is Aurva, whose story as described in the *Mahābhārata* (*Ādiparvan*, cantos 169–171) goes as follows: the (kshatriya) sons of a king named Krita·virya wished to obtain the wealth of the (brahmana) descendants of Bhrigu, but when they realized that the latter had hidden their riches in the ground, they decided to slaughter the Bhrigu clan down to children still in the womb of their mothers. One of the Bhrigu ladies hid her fetus in her thigh (*ūru* in Sanskrit), and after its birth the child was named *aurva*, "of the thigh." He blinded the sons of Krita·virya by his brilliance, and though he forgave them and returned their eyesight when they begged his pardon, he then proceeded to burn up all the world with his ascetic power. At the behest of his own slaughtered ancestors he finally gave up the plan, but his promise to scorch the world could not be revoked. The ancestors suggested that he release his anger into the ocean, where it took the form of a fire in the shape of a horse's head. Known as *vaḍavāgni*, "the mare fire," it bides its time checked by water and constantly burning up the ocean's extra water supplies, until it is unleashed at the end of the world to burn everything up.

5.161 According to the *Arthaśāstra* (13.5), after a new conquest a king should, among other acts, release all his **prisoners**.

5.206 **This is all I seek for the sake of your co-wife**: we take *pratipakṣa/hetoḥ*, literally "for the sake of [your] rival," to refer to Málavika, who has now become one of the king's wives. Our feeling is that this would have been the original reading (corroborated by Nī, who glosses *pratipakṣahetoḥ sapatnījanam uddiśya*, "'for the sake of the rival' means 'with respect to the co-wives'"). It might have been changed to the widespread variant *hṛdaye pratipālanīyam*, "(this is all) that should be cherished in [your] heart" by redactors who felt, like KALE, that it would be impolite of Agni·mitra to ask a boon for the sake of Málavika, and on top of that, to refer to her as Dhárini's *pratipakṣa*. Dwivedī also follows the second, softer reading even though it is attested in only two of his manuscripts, but finds our preferred reading (supported by three of his manuscripts, and another that reads *varaye pratipakṣahetoḥ*) worthy of a comment. His opinion (which we find forced) appears to be that *pratipakṣa* does not mean co-wife, but refers to the traditional political enmity between the countries of Mágadha and Vidárbha, which comes to an end with the marriage of Agni·mitra and Málavika.

5.207 **Actors' benediction**: it is customary in Sanskrit drama that after the happy ending the hero is asked what else he would like, to which he replies something along the lines of "could anything make me happier?" and then recites a verse in which he asks for prosperity in general for the kingdom and its king. This verse in a way transports the audience back from fiction to reality, and is often styled *bharata/vākya*, literally the "actors' speech." The final benediction in "Málavika and Agni·mitra" is an unusual one, as the king is hardly ever named in the benedictions of other plays. Furthermore, here it is only the second half of the verse (and that only in some sources) that is styled *bharata/vākya*, while the first half is entirely about the king's private wishes. See also Introduction, note 24.

5.208 **Calamities** (*īti*) may be meant in a specialized sense. Kā quotes a verse (also cited in VSA s. v. *īti*) to show that they can be of six particular kinds: excessive rain, lack of rain, locusts, mice, parrots and neighboring kings (*ativṛṣṭir anāvṛṣṭiḥ śalabhā mūṣakāḥ śukāḥ / pratyāsannāś ca rājānaḥ ṣaḍ etā ītayaḥ smṛtāḥ*, untraced).

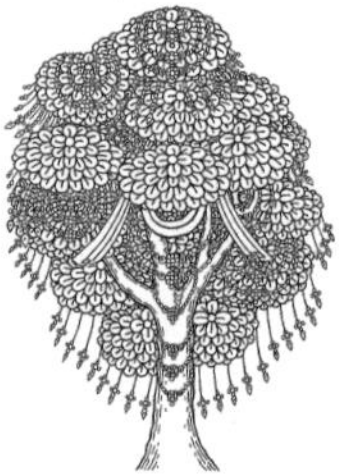

VARIANT READINGS

1.23 *devīe* DelV Kal Sri : *devīe evva* Del KalV Mad SriV.

1.51 °*vinaya*° Del Mad : °*viśeṣa*° Kal Sri : omit DelV KalV MadV SriV.

1.60 *vāhatava* Del KalV Mad : *vāhataka* DelV Kal Sri : *vārhataka* DelV : *vāhanava* DelV.

1.63 *tan na vo na viditaṃ* DelV Kal Mad Nī Sri : *tan na vo viditaṃ* Del KalV SriV : *tatra vo na viditaṃ* DelV KalV : *etan nanu vo viditaṃ* KalV MadV.

1.63 *bhūmihareṣu* Kal Kā Sri : *bhūmidhareṣu* Del KalV Mad : *bhūmer iva* DelV SriV : omits SriV.

1.63 *īdṛk* KalV MadV Sri : omit Del KalV Mad SriV : *īdṛśī* Kal.

1.86 *vikatthya* Kal Kā Mad Sri : *vikathya* Del.

1.94 *tathā hi* Kal DelV Sri : omit Del Mad.

1.129 *vidyamāne 'pi* DelV Kal Mad Sri : *sati* Del KalV MadV.

1.136 *urabbha*° Del Kal Mad Sri : *uaraṃbhari*° KalV SriV.

1.139 °*sauṣṭhavābhinayam* DelV Kal Kā MadV Sri : °*sauṣṭhavātiśayam* Del KalV Mad SriV : *sauṣṭhavam* KalV SriV.

1.149 *gaṇadāsaḥ* DelV KalV Mad Sri : omit Del Kal SriV.

1.150 *svagatam* Kal Mad Sri : *gaṇadāsaṃ vilokya janāntikam* Del.

1.150 *gaṇadāsaṃ vilokya janāntikam* KalV DelV Sri : *gaṇadāsaṃ vilokya prakāśam* Mad : omit Del Kal.

1.150 *prakāśam* Del Sri : *gaṇadāsaṃ vilokya prakāśam* Kal : omit DelV Mad.

1.182 *vigata*° Del KalV Mad Nī SriV : *virala*° DelV Kal MadV Sri : *vihita*° DelV : *virakta*° DelV.

1.191 *sāmayikā* KalV KāV : *sāmavāyikā* Del KalV KāV Mad Nī SriV : *sāmājikā* Kal Kā MadV Sri : *pratyanantarī*° DelV : *sāhyavādikā* KalV.

1.195 *°rāgo* DelV KalV Kā Mad Nī Sri : *°rāvo* Del MadV : *°nādo* DelV Kal SriV.

2.12 *gṛhagatāyāś* Del KalV Mad Sri : *parigatāyāś* DelV Kal Mad SriV : *pariṇatāyāś* KalV.

2.22 *vāmao* Del KalV Mad Sri : *vāmo* Kal MadV.

2.44 *vidvatsu* DelV Kal MadV SriV : *yuṣmāsu* Del KalV Mad Sri Nī.

2.52 *°savanam* Del KalV Kā MadV SriV : *°sadanam* DelV : *°sevanam* KāV : *°saṃgītakam* DelV Kal Nī Sri : *°pradarśanam* DelV KalV KāV Mad SriV.

2.71 *samagras* DelV KalV Mad Nī Sri : *samagrais* Del Kal Kā.

2.77 *majjaṇa* Del Kal Mad Sri : *madhyāhna* SriV MadV.

3.12 *ido* Del Mad Sri : *ado* Kal.

3.12 *pesaladaraṃ* DelV Kal : *varaṃ* Del : *varaṃ pesaladaraṃ* Mad Sri.

3.12 *pāehi* Del : *pāvehi* KalV : *pāvahi* Mad : *lahehri* (sic; em. lahehi?) DelV : *aṇubhavissasi* DelV Kal : *aṇuhohi* DelV Mad : *pāvidā hohi* MadV Sri : *pāvidā hodi* KalV.

3.21 *suṇāvidā a mae jaṃ bhavadā saṃdiṭṭhaṃ* DelV Kal Mad Sri : *suṇāvidā a mae taṃ atthaṃ jo bhavadā saṃdiṭṭho* Del : *suṇāvidā a mae taṃ atthaṃ bhavadā saṃdiṭṭhaṃ* KalV : *suṇāvido aaṃ attho jo bhavadā saṃdiṭṭho* KalV MadV.

3.26 *sāhaṇijje* DelV Kal MadV : *sāhaṇijje kajje* Del Kal Mad Sri.

3.76 *°raso* DelV Kal Kā MadV Nī Sri : *°phalo* Del Mad.

3.83 *upaviśya* Kal Mad Sri : omits Del.

3.83 *jāva* DelV Kal Mad Sri : *jāva ṇaṃ* Del KalV.

3.84 *mocaeaṃ* Kal Sri : *moceaṃ* Del Mad.

3.105 *hañje* Kal Mad Sri : *halā* Del : *ceṭi* KalV.

3.117 *maṇo vi kiṃ vi* DelV Mad Sri : *maṇo maha* DelV : *maṇo maha kiṃ vi* Kal : *mado maṃ* Del MadV : *maṇo vi mado maṃ* KalV.

3.123 *prakāśaṃ rāgaṃ vilokya* Mad Sri : *rāgaṃ vilokya prakāśam* Kal : *prakāśam* Del.

3.123 *ṇikkhevo* DelV Kal Mad Sri : *°vikkhevo* Del KalV.

3.137 *dara°* Del Kā Nī SriV : *daravara°* KalV : *vara* Mad : *sundara°* DelV KalV MadV Sri : *īsipari°* DelV Kal.

3.143 *°saṃbādho* DelV Kal Kā Sri : *°saṃpādo* Del Mad : *°saṃbandho* KalV : *°saṃpādo bhavissadi* KalV : *°bādho bhavissadi* SriV.

3.171 *juttaṃ* DelV Kal Kā Sri MadV : *ṇa juttaṃ* Del KalV Mad.

3.196 *vaaṃ* Del Mad Sri : *amhe* Kal.

4.3 *klāntaṃ* DelV Kal MadV Nī Sri : *kāntaṃ* Del KalV Mad.

4.20 *maṃdo* em : *kudo* Del.

4.21 *tatas tataḥ* Mad Sri : omit Del Kal.

4.26 *ravā* DelV KalV MadV Sri : *svarā* Del Kal Mad : *svanā* SriV : *girā* DelV.

4.26 *parabhṛtikā* DelV KalV MadV Sri : *parabhṛtā* Del Kal Mad SriV : *parabhṛtiḥ* KalV.

4.60 *edāiṃ* DelV Kal Sri : *ede* Del Mad.

4.121 *°avacaya°* DelV Kal Sri : *°apacaya°* Del Mad.

4.138 *samāgatānām* DelV KalV Nī Sri : *samāgamānām* Del Kal Kā Mad.

4.139 *pāsapariuttavaaṇeṇa* Kal Kā Mad : *pāsapariuttamuheṇa* KalV : *pāsaparivattidavaaṇeṇa* DelV : *īsipariuttavaaṇā* KalV : *īsappari-uttaraaṇā* (sic) Del : *īsapparivaṭṭidavadanā* MadV : *īsiparivatti-davaaṇā* Sri : *īsipāsavaṃ* (sic) DelV.

4.161 *abalā satī* DelV KalV KāV Nī MadV Sri : *sakhī tava* Del Kal Kā Mad.

4.166 *mha* Kal MadV : *mhi* Del Mad Sri.

4.177 *gate* Kal Kā Mad Nī Sri : *tate* Del.

4.181 *baimbikānāṃ* Del Kal Mad Sri : *nāyakānāṃ* DelV KalV MadV : *nāyikānāṃ* DelV : *vaidikānāṃ* DelV.

4.185 *°cakṣur* DelV Kal MadV Sri : *°netram* Del KalV MadV SriV.

4.208 *kidaggho* DelV Kal Mad SriV : *kidavo* Del KalV Sri.

4.236 *°bandhuṇo* em : *°bandhuṇā* Del Kal Mad Sri.

5.43 *vismṛta* Kal Kā MadV Sri : *vistṛta* Del KalV KāV Mad Nī.

5.64 *°viṣaya°* DelV Kal Kā MadV : *°rāja°* Del KalV Mad Sri.

5.127 *patrorṇevopayujyate* DelV KalV Mad Sri : *patrorṇaṃ vopayujyate* Del Kal Kā MadV : *patrorṇam upayujyate* KalV.

5.144 *°avagraha°* DelV Kal Kā Sri : *°anugraha°* Nī MadV SriV : *°upagraha°* Del KalV Mad.

5.149 *rāja°* DelV Kal Kā Mad : *rājasūya°* Del KalV Sri : *aśvamedha°* MadV.

5.169 *paribbhaṃsaïdavvetti* DelV Kal : *paribbhaṃsaïdavva tti* Sri : *vibhaṃsidavvetti* Mad : *bhasidaghetti* (sic) Del.

5.206 *mṛgaye pratipakṣahetoḥ* KalV MadV Nī Sri : *varaye pratipakṣahetoḥ* Del Mad : *hṛdaye pratipālanīyam* Kal Kā MadV.

GLOSSARY OF NAMES AND TERMS

Be warned: the Glossary contains spoilers about some of the characters in the play. Refer to the Cast of characters for a "safe" description of the key figures.

AGNI·MITRA (*Agnimitra*) The king of Vídisha and hero of the play. Past the prime of his youth, he is apparently quite effective as a ruler, but not quite the lord of his own home. His chief wife is Queen Dhárini (by whom he has an adolescent son, prince Vasu·mitra) and his second wife is Irávati. He is presently looking for a young and pretty new woman, and when he sets his eye on Málavika, the plot of the play begins. However, he must proceed with extreme care so as to spare the feelings of his two queens. He is aided by the jester Gáutama. His name means "friend of [the god] Fire."

ÁNSHUMAT (*Aṃśumat*) The grandson of Ságara in the *Rāmāyaṇa*, who retrieved the sacrificial horse of his grandfather. His name means "possessing rays," i.e. "sun." See also note to 5.154.

ASHÓKA (*aśoka*) The "tree without sorrow" (*Saraca asoca*), a small evergreen tree that flowers in great profusion at the end of winter. Indian folklore says the *ashóka* tree will burst into flower when struck by the foot of a woman. See also notes to 3.2 and 3.14.

ATIMÚKTA (*atimukta*) "Surpassing pearls," a creeper with scented, white flowers. The way it enfolds trees—particularly mango trees in literary fancy—is a common metaphor for a woman embracing a man. See also note to 4.177.

BÁIMBIKA (*Baimbika*) Probably an ancestral name of Agni·mitra, meaning "descendent of Bimba (or Bímbaka)." See note to 4.181 for a discussion of other possibilities and p. xix for the question of the historicity of the name.

BÁKULA (*bakula*) An ornamental tree with small, fragrant, white blossoms (*Mimusops elengi*). The flowers retain their fragrance when dry. See also note to 3.145.

BAKULÁVALIKA (*Bakulāvalikā*) Queen Dhárini's maid and Málavika's friend. Her name means "garland of *bákula* flowers."

BHASA (*Bhāsa*) An illustrious dramatist tentatively dated to the fourth century CE. See also note to 1.7.

BIMBA (*bimba*) A small, oblong gourd (of the genus *Momordica*, *Coccinia* or *Bryonia*), which turns bright red on ripening and to which the lips of women are frequently compared.

CHAKRA (*cakra*) The ruddy shelduck (*Tadorna ferruginea*), also known as *cakravāka*. By poetic convention it is supposed to be separated from its mate every night. See also note to 5.63.

CHÁNDRIKA (*Candrikā*) Irávati's handmaid. Her name means "moonlight."

CHÁTAKA (*cātaka*) A species of cuckoo which is said in poetic fancy to subsist on nothing but raindrops. See also note to 2.53.

DHÁRINI (*Dhāriṇī*) King Agni·mitra's primary wife. A proud and practical woman past the bloom of her youth, her chief interest is in preserving proprieties and maintaining harmony in the palace. She has an adolescent son, the heir apparent Vasu·mitra, and a young daughter, Vasu·lakshmi. She also has a half-caste brother, Vira·sena. Her name means "earth" and "supporter" (see also note to 1.124).

DHRUVA·SIDDHI (*Dhruvasiddhi*) The court physician of Agni·mitra. His name means "certain success."

GANA·DASA (*Gaṇadāsa*) A teacher of dance and acting patronized by Queen Dhárini, in rivalry with Hara·datta. His name means "servant of the hosts [of Shiva]."

GÁUTAMA (*Gautama*) The jester, a personal companion and friend of King Agni·mitra. He is a brahmin by birth but performs no priestly function and speaks Prakrit, unlike proper brahmins, who would speak Sanskrit. Timid and gluttonous, he has a ready wit, which he employs in the service of the king's amorous affairs. His name means "descendent of [the sage] Gótama." See also note to 4.237.

GAYÁTRI (*Gāyatrī*) A Vedic mantra that is said to be the mystical essence of all Vedic knowledge. See also note to 4.237.

HARA·DATTA (*Haradatta*) A teacher of dance and acting patronized by King Agni·mitra, in rivalry with Gana·dasa. His name means "[he who was] given by Shiva."

IRÁVATI (*Irāvatī*) King Agni·mitra's junior queen, subordinate to Queen Dhárini. She is young, beautiful and jealous of her position. Her name, literally "refreshing" or "watery," is the name of a North-Indian river (and goddess) whose modern name is Ravi (*Rāvī*, contracted from *Irāvatī*, not Sanskrit *Ravi*, one of the names of the Sun). The Burmese river Ayeyarwady (formerly spelt Irrawaddy in English) bears the same name.

JAYA·SENA (*Jayasenā*) The usheress: a female official of the harem subordinate to the chamberlain Maudgálya. She runs errands, announces visitors and ceremoniously leads royalty around the palace. Her name roughly means "army of victory."

JYÓTSNIKA (*Jyotsnikā*) One of a pair of slave girls skilled in music (the other is Rájanika), sent to King Agni·mitra by General Vira·sena in a consignment of war booty after defeating Yajña·sena. Her name means "daylight."

KÁUMUDIKA (*Kaumudikā*) One of the maids in the palace. Her name means "moonlight" or "white waterlily."

KÁUSHIKI (*Kauśikī*) A mendicant woman (*parivrājikā*; probably of the Buddhist persuasion, but this is never clearly stated) staying in the palace, respected by Queen Dhárini and sympathizing with Málavika and King Agni·mitra. In fact she is the younger sister of Súmati, the erstwhile minister of Mádhava·sena of Vidárbha. She is dedicated to aiding Málavika in getting noticed by and subsequently married to Agni·mitra. On the question of whether she is actually in league with the jester Gáutama, see p. xxix.

KAVI·PUTRA (*Kaviputra*) An ancient playwright whose identity is uncertain. See note to 1.7.

KÉTAKI (*ketakī*) A species of screw-pine (*Pandanus fascicularis*), a large shrub with a branching trunk, many prop roots, sweetly scented flowers and long, spiky, strap-shaped leaves. See also note to 4.214.

KRATHA·KÁISHIKA (*Krathakaiśika*) The people of Vidárbha, from two clan names, Kratha and Káishika. See also note to 5.20.

KRISHNA (*Kṛṣṇa*) The eighth incarnation of Vishnu, the preserver god of the Hindu pantheon. Krishna is one of the most popular deities in modern Hinduism: in his youth a mischievous cowherd known for his amorous pastimes, and in adulthood a cunning and unscrupulous chieftain and politician. His name means "black."

KÚRABAKA (*kurabaka*) A plant with reddish markings, probably a species of amaranth. See also note to 3.44.

MÁDHAVA·SENA (*Mādhavasena*) The prince of Vidárbha who hopes to ally himself to King Agni·mitra by marrying his sister Málavika to Agni·mitra. At the beginning of the play, he is held captive by his cousin and rival Yajña·sena. Subsequently he is freed by Agni·mitra's army and becomes his vassal ruling over half of Vidárbha. His name probably means "he whose army is Krishna;" several other interpretations are possible.

MÁDHAVIKA (*Mādhavikā*) A woman in charge of the palace strong-room or dungeon. Her name means "vernal" or the *atimúkta* creeper.

MADHU·KÁRIKA (*Madhukarikā*) A servant woman in charge of the palace gardens. Her name means "(little) bee."

MÁLAVIKA (*Mālavikā*) A maid in Queen Dhárini's retinue, recently sent as a present to the palace by general Vira·sena, commander of a borderland fort. She studies dance under Gana·dasa and is hopelessly in love with King Agni·mitra. Her cause is fostered by her friend Bakulávalika and by the mendicant woman Káushiki. She is actually the princess of Vidárbha, younger sister of Prince Mádhava·sena. She fled from Yajña·sena with minister Súmati, and was separated from him in an attack by outlaws. She was found by Vira·sena, who sent her to Agni·mitra's palace. Her name means "woman of Málava [country]" (see p. xxvii).

MAUDGÁLYA (*Maudgalya*) The chamberlain at King Agni·mitra's court, a high-ranking elderly servant in charge of the palace and the harem. His name means "descendent of [the sage] Múdgala."

MAURYA (*Maurya*) The ancient Indian dynasty founded in 322 BCE by Chandra·gupta Maurya and expanded in the third century BCE by his famous grandson Ashóka. It was Pushya·mitra Shunga (called Pushpa·mitra in this play), the father of Agni·mitra, who brought an end to the Maurya dynasty by staging a palace coup.

NAGA (*nāga*) Literally "snake" or "cobra," in Hindu mythology *naga*s are a class of supernatural beings with snake-like characteristics. They are associated with water and fertility, and are said to inhabit a particular level of the underworld. See also p. xxiii for Naga as a proper name.

NÁGARIKA (*Nāgarikā*) A maid in the service of Irávati. Her name means "sophisticated [woman]."

NÁRMADA (*Narmadā*) A major sacred river of central India, flowing immediately south of the Vindhya. Its name (formerly also spelt Narbada and Nerbudda in English) means "pleasure-giving." See also note to 1.50.

NÍPUNIKA (*Nipuṇikā*) Maid and companion of Irávati, a shrewd and meddlesome young woman. Her name means "shrewd woman."

PRIYÁNGU (*priyaṅgu*) A plant of uncertain identity. See note to 3.108.

PUSHPA·MITRA (*Puṣpamitra*) King Agni·mitra's father; his name means "friend of flowers." Known to historians as Pushya·mitra Shunga (*Puṣyamitra*, "friend of [the lunar mansion] Pushya"), he overthrew the Maurya dynasty and founded his own, but never actually proclaimed himself a king, preferring to stick to his old title of *senāpati*, "general."

RÁJANIKA (*Rajanikā*) One of a pair of slave girls skilled in music (the other is Jyótsnika), sent to King Agni·mitra by General Vira·sena in a consignment of war booty after defeating Yajña·sena. Her name means "night."

RATI (*Rati*) The wife of Kama, the god of love. Her name means "passion." See also note to 5.19.

RUDRA (*Rudra*) Originally the Vedic god of storms, in Hinduism identified with Shiva. His name probably means "howling," though other derivations are possible.

RÚKMINI (*Rukminī*) One of the most important of Krishna's sixteen thousand wives. Her name means "golden" or "adorned with gold." She was the daughter of Bhíshmaka, a legendary king of Vidárbha. See also note to 5.20.

SÁGARA (*Sagara*) An ancient mythical king who undertook to perform a horse sacrifice. The sacrificial animal was stolen by a monster and retrieved subsequently by his grandson Ánshumat. His name is said to mean "with poison," because his pregnant mother had been given poison by a rival wife to postpone the child's birth. See also note to 5.154.

SAMÁHITIKA (*Samāhitikā*) A maid serving Káushiki. Her name probably means "composed" or "concentrating woman." Her name is *Samābhṛtikā*, "brought together" (?) in some versions of the play, and *Parabhṛtikā*, "[little female] cuckoo" in others.

SÁRASAKA (*Sārasaka*) A hunchback footman in the service of Queen Dhárini. His name means "crane," probably referring to his crooked posture. (See note to 3.55 on the sarus crane.)

SARÁSVATI (*Sarasvatī*) The Hindu goddess of eloquence, music and learning. Originally a river goddess, her name means "watery" or "possessing marshes."

SAUMÍLLA (*Saumilla*) An ancient playwright whose identity is uncertain. See note to 1.7.

SHARMÍSHTHA (*Śarmiṣṭhā*) The daughter of a mythical demon king who became the foremother of many of India's ruling dynasties by conceiving three sons from King Yayáti. See also note to 2.8.

SHASTRA (*śāstra*) A treatise or textbook; the collective name for ancient Indian scientific literature.

SHIVA (*Śiva*) The god of destruction and re-creation in the Hindu pantheon. A deity of many aspects, he is the supreme self-restraining ascetic, but also the unrestrained god of procreation and virility. In the form of Nata·raja, "king of dancers" (commonly known as the dancing Shiva) he is also the divine patron of dancers and actors. His name means "auspicious" or "gracious"—generally believed to derive from a conciliatory epithet applied to the fierce god Rudra.

SHUNGA (*Śuṅga*) The dynasty founded ca. 185 BCE by Pushya·mitra (called Pushpa·mitra in this play), who dethroned the last of the Maurya rulers. See also p. xvi].

SÚMATI (*Sumati*) Minister or chief secretary of Mádhava·sena and elder brother of Káushiki. His name means "clever."

TÍLAKA (*tilaka*) A plant of uncertain identity, probably patterned in contrasting colors and reminiscent of forehead designs, also *tilaka* in Sanskrit. See also note to 3.44.

UMA (*Umā*) The wife of Shiva, also called Párvati. She is the female counterpart to Shiva, and inhabits the left half of the representation of these two deities in one body. As an independent goddess, she is the daughter of the mountain-god Himálaya. Her name is traditionally explained as "oh no!" shouted by her mother when Párvati became an ascetic to win the attention of Shiva.

VÁHATAVA (*Vāhatava*) Minister or chief secretary of King Agni·mitra. The meaning (and proper spelling) of his name is uncertain. See also note to 1.60.

VAIDÁRBHA (*Vaidarbha*) Literally "belonging to Vidárbha," this term is used in the play for the ruler of the Vidárbha country.

VÁRADA (*Varadā*) A river of the Vidárbha heartland. Formerly also spelt Wardha in English, its name means "boon-giving."

VASU·LAKSHMI (*Vasulakṣmī*) A child princess, daughter of King Agni·mitra and Queen Dhárini. See also note to 1.33.

VASU·MITRA (*Vasumitra*) The adolescent heir apparent, son of King Agni·mitra and Queen Dhárini. At the time of the events in the play he is undergoing what is probably the first test of his manliness: he has been appointed by Pushpa·mitra as the guardian of a sacrificial horse.

VIDÁRBHA (*Vidarbha*) A country in central India, south of the Nármada river. At the commencement of the play it is ruled by Yajña·sena, who has overthrown and captured his cousin and rival Mádhava·sena.

VÍDISHA (*Vidiśā*) A country in northern Central India, ruled by King Agni·mitra and extending as far as the Nármada river in the south. Also the name of a river (now usually called Bes, an Anglicization of its vernacular name) near the modern town of Vidisha, which may have been the site of the ancient capital.

VINDHYA (*Vindhya*) A mountain range in Central India, separating the northern Indo-Gangetic Plain from the Deccan Plateau in the south.

VIRA·SENA (*Vīrasena*) The commander of a borderland fort, serving King Agni·mitra. He is the half-brother of Queen Dhárini by a lower-caste woman. See also note to 1.50.

YAJÑA·SENA (*Yajñasena*) A contender to the throne of Vidárbha, enemy of King Agni·mitra. He imprisons his cousin and rival Mádhava·sena. He is subsequently defeated by Agni·mitra, but allowed to continue ruling half his country as Agni·mitra's vassal.

METERS USED

The following meters are used in this text:

āryā Act 1. [3], [5]–[9], [13], [18], [20], [22]; Act 2 [1], [2], [10]–[14]; Act 3 [7], [9], [13], [16], [18]–[20], [22], [23]; Act 4. [2], [3], [5], [7], [10], [17]; Act 5 [4]–[6], [19]

drutavilambita Act 3 [6]; Act 4 [13]; Act 5 [7]

hariṇī Act 4 [11]; Act 5 [1], [2]

indravajrā Act 5 [17]

mālabhāriṇī Act 3 [3], [11]

mālinī Act 2 [5]; Act 3 [12]

mandākrāntā Act 2 [6], [8]; Act 3 [4]; Act 4 [1]

mātrāsama Act 2 [4]

praharṣiṇī Act 1 [21]

pṛthvī Act 3 [17]

puṣpitāgrā Act 1 [11]

rucirā Act 4 [16]

śālinī Act 3 [14], [21]; Act 5 [8]

śārdūlavikrīḍita Act 1 [4]; Act 2 [3]; Act 3 [5]; Act 4 [15]

śloka Act 1 [10], [14], [15], [19]; Act 2 [7], [9]; Act 3 [8]; Act 4 [4], [6], [12], [14]; Act 5 [9], [11]–[13], [15], [16], [18]

sragdharā Act 1 [1]; Act 2 [12]

upajāti Act 1 [2], [16], [17]; Act 3 [10]; Act 4 [8]; Act 5 [14]

vaṃśasthavila Act 3 [15]

vasantatilakā Act 1 [12]; Act 3 [1]; Act 4 [9]; Act 5 [3], [10], [20]

viyoginī Act 3 [2]

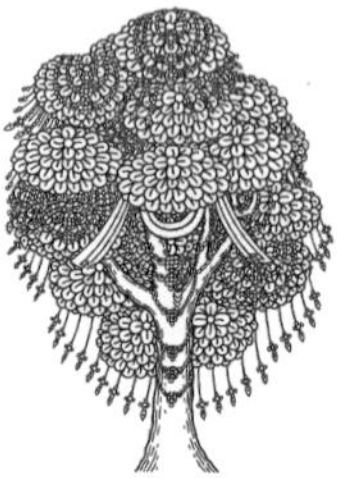

THE CLAY SANSKRIT LIBRARY

For further details please consult the CSL website.

1. The Emperor of the Sorcerers (*Bṛhatkathāślokasaṃgraha*) (vol. 1 of 2) by *Budhasvāmin*. Sir James Mallinson
2. Heavenly Exploits (*Divyāvadāna*). Joel Tatelman
3. Maha·bhárata III: The Forest (*Vanaparvan*) (vol. 4 of 4) William J. Johnson
4. Much Ado about Religion (*Āgamaḍambara*) by *Bhaṭṭa Jayanta*. Csaba Dezső
5. The Birth of Kumára (*Kumārasaṃbhava*) by *Kālidāsa*. David Smith
6. Ramáyana I: Boyhood (*Bālakāṇḍa*) by *Vālmīki*. Robert P. Goldman. Foreword by Amartya Sen
7. The Epitome of Queen Lilávati (*Līlāvatīsāra*) (vol. 1 of 2) by *Jinaratna*. R.C.C. Fynes
8. Ramáyana II: Ayódhya (*Ayodhyākāṇḍa*) by *Vālmīki*. Sheldon I. Pollock
9. Love Lyrics (*Amaruśataka, Śatakatraya & Caurapañcāśikā*) by *Amaru, Bhartṛhari & Bilhaṇa*. Greg Bailey & Richard Gombrich
10. What Ten Young Men Did (*Daśakumāracarita*) by *Daṇḍin*. Isabelle Onians
11. Three Satires (*Kaliviḍambana, Kalāvilāsa & Bhallaṭaśataka*) by *Nīlakaṇṭha, Kṣemendra & Bhallaṭa*. Somadeva Vasudeva
12. Ramáyana IV: Kishkíndha (*Kiṣkindhākāṇḍa*) by *Vālmīki*. Rosalind Lefeber
13. The Emperor of the Sorcerers (*Bṛhatkathāślokasaṃgraha*) (vol. 2 of 2) by *Budhasvāmin*. Sir James Mallinson
14. Maha·bhárata IX: Shalya (*Śalyaparvan*) (vol. 1 of 2) Justin Meiland
15. Rákshasa's Ring (*Mudrārākṣasa*) by *Viśākhadatta*. Michael Coulson

16. Messenger Poems (*Meghadūta, Pavanadūta & Haṃsadūta*)
by *Kālidāsa, Dhoyī & Rūpa Gosvāmin.* Sir James Mallinson
17. Ramáyana III: The Forest (*Araṇyakāṇḍa*)
by *Vālmīki.* Sheldon I. Pollock
18. The Epitome of Queen Lilávati (*Līlāvatīsāra*) (vol. 2 of 2)
by *Jinaratna.* R.C.C. Fynes
19. Five Discourses on Worldly Wisdom (*Pañcatantra*)
by *Viṣṇuśarman.* Patrick Olivelle
20. Ramáyana V: Súndara (*Sundarakāṇḍa*) by *Vālmīki.*
Robert P. Goldman & Sally J. Sutherland Goldman
21. Maha·bhárata II: The Great Hall (*Sabhāparvan*)
Paul Wilmot
22. The Recognition of Shakúntala (*Abhijñānaśākuntala*) (Kashmir Recension) by *Kālidāsa.* Somadeva Vasudeva
23. Maha·bhárata VII: Drona (*Droṇaparvan*) (vol. 1 of 4)
Vaughan Pilikian
24. Rama Beyond Price (*Anargharāghava*)
by *Murāri.* Judit Törzsök
25. Maha·bhárata IV: Viráta (*Virāṭaparvan*)
Kathleen Garbutt
26. Maha·bhárata VIII: Karna (*Karṇaparvan*) (vol. 1 of 2)
Adam Bowles
27. "The Lady of the Jewel Necklace" & "The Lady who Shows her Love" (*Ratnāvalī & Priyadarśikā*) by *Harṣa.*
Wendy Doniger
28. The Ocean of the Rivers of Story (*Kathāsaritsāgara*) (vol. 1 of 7)
by *Somadeva.* Sir James Mallinson
29. Handsome Nanda (*Saundarananda*)
by *Aśvaghoṣa.* Linda Covill
30. Maha·bhárata IX: Shalya (*Śalyaparvan*) (vol. 2 of 2)
Justin Meiland
31. Rama's Last Act (*Uttararāmacarita*) by *Bhavabhūti.*
Sheldon Pollock. Foreword by Girish Karnad

32. "Friendly Advice" (*Hitopadeśa*) by *Nārāyaṇa* &
"King Víkrama's Adventures" (*Vikramacarita*). JUDIT TÖRZSÖK
33. Life of the Buddha (*Buddhacarita*)
by *Aśvaghoṣa*. PATRICK OLIVELLE
34. Maha·bhárata V: Preparations for War (*Udyogaparvan*) (vol. 1 of 2)
KATHLEEN GARBUTT. Foreword by GURCHARAN DAS
35. Maha·bhárata VIII: Karna (*Karṇaparvan*) (vol. 2 of 2)
ADAM BOWLES
36. Maha·bhárata V: Preparations for War (*Udyogaparvan*) (vol. 2 of 2)
KATHLEEN GARBUTT
37. Maha·bhárata VI: Bhishma (*Bhīṣmaparvan*) (vol. 1 of 2)
Including the "Bhagavad Gita" in Context
ALEX CHERNIAK. Foreword by RANAJIT GUHA
38. The Ocean of the Rivers of Story (*Kathāsaritsāgara*) (vol. 2 of 7)
by *Somadeva*. SIR JAMES MALLINSON
39. "How the Nagas were Pleased" (*Nāgānanda*) by *Harṣa* &
"The Shattered Thighs" (*Ūrubhaṅga*) by *Bhāsa*.
ANDREW SKILTON
40. Gita·govínda: Love Songs of Radha and Krishna (*Gītagovinda*)
by *Jayadeva*. LEE SIEGEL. Foreword by SUDIPTA KAVIRAJ
41. "Bouquet of Rasa" & "River of Rasa" (*Rasamañjarī & Rasataraṅgiṇī*) by *Bhānudatta*. SHELDON POLLOCK
42. Garland of the Buddha's Past Lives (*Jātakamālā*) (vol. 1 of 2)
by *Āryaśūra*. JUSTIN MEILAND
43. Maha·bhárata XII: Peace (*Śāntiparvan*) (vol. 3 of 5)
"The Book of Liberation" (*Mokṣadharma*). ALEXANDER WYNNE
44. Little Clay Cart (*Mṛcchakaṭikā*) by *Śūdraka*.
DIWAKAR ACHARYA. Foreword by PARTHA CHATTERJEE
45. Bhatti's Poem: The Death of Rávana (*Bhaṭṭikāvya*)
by *Bhaṭṭi*. OLIVER FALLON
46. "Self-Surrender," "Peace," "Compassion," and "The Mission of the Goose": Poems and Prayers from South India
(*Ātmārpaṇastuti, Śāntivilāsa, Dayāśataka & Haṃsasaṃdeśa*)
by *Appayya Dīkṣita, Nīlakaṇṭha Dīkṣita & Vedānta Deśika*.

Yigal Bronner & David Shulman
Foreword by Gieve Patel

47. Maha·bhárata VI: Bhishma (*Bhīṣmaparvan*) (vol. 2 of 2)
Alex Cherniak

48. How Úrvashi Was Won (*Vikramorvaśīya*) by *Kālidāsa*
Velcheru Narayana Rao & David Shulman

49. The Quartet of Causeries (*Caturbhāṇī*)
by *Śūdraka, Śyāmilaka, Vararuci & Īśvaradatta.*
Csaba Dezső & Somadeva Vasudeva

50. Garland of the Buddha's Past Lives (*Jātakamālā*) (vol. 2 of 2)
by *Āryaśūra.* Justin Meiland

51. Princess Kadámbari (*Kādambarī*) (vol. 1 of 3)
by *Bāṇa.* David Smith

52. The Rise of Wisdom Moon (*Prabodhacandrodaya*)
by *Kṛṣṇamiśra.* Matthew T. Kapstein
Foreword by J.N. Mohanty

53. Maha·bhárata VII: Drona (*Droṇaparvan*) (vol. 2 of 4)
Vaughan Pilikian

54. Maha·bhárata X & XI: Dead of Night & The Women
(*Sauptikaparvan & Strīparvan*). Kate Crosby

55. Seven Hundred Elegant Verses (*Āryāsaptaśatī*)
by *Govardhana.* Friedhelm Hardy

56. Málavika and Agni·mitra (*Mālavikāgnimitram*) by *Kālidāsa.*
Dániel Balogh & Eszter Somogyi